Experiential Spirituality

The Mystic Answer to Everything

David McMurdo

To my mother, to John, and to Iona, for their support.
And to Jay and to Jax, for a future yet unknown.

Table of Contents

Preface

Yeshua said, "Take heed of the Living One while you are alive, lest you die and seek to see Him, and find yourself unable do so."

- The Gospel of Thomas, Saying 59

You will die one day, and on that day you will be faced with spiritual realities that you know nothing about. I often find myself having to remind souls of that fact, for many suppose that spiritual matters are not something that will ever concern them. It is easy for them to believe that in times of comfort, but there will come a point when even the most cynical materialist will find themselves wondering if there really is something beyond the mundane world that they took to be the whole of reality. What often follows for such souls is the terrible realisation that they have spent their lives refusing to seriously engage with the great spiritual questions, and that it is now far too late to begin doing so.

Those great spiritual questions have been at the forefront of my mind since I was a child, and from the earliest age I would read as many books on the subject of spirituality as I could. Most of them had a very narrow scope and did not address many issues, but no matter how broad their scope, all that such books presented was a series of explanations that readers were expected to accept for little to no reason. Even in my youth I intuitively knew that there was something deeply wrong with such an approach and expectation. What I could never have known is that God would one day reveal Himself to me and that it was ultimately my destiny to help reawaken souls to the reality of the spiritual by helping them to understand the meaning and significance of ancient mystic wisdom.

I am perfectly well aware of how that latter statement sounds to most souls in the western world, even many that themselves profess some manner of spiritual belief; it is just not acceptable to use words like "God" and "destiny" in so much polite company these days, except perhaps as a punchline. The one that employs such terminology without

1

irony should fully expect to be mocked and to be regarded as very odd. But the fact is that if you are uncomfortable with a soul talking in such ways, then it is you that are the aberration; you are the conditioned product of a very young secular society, a society that will ultimately prove to be a blip within the span of human history. If you are at all concerned with truth then you should entertain the idea that your very modern perspective might be blinding you to greater realities.

The mystic message has only ever been for those souls with enough humility to receive it, and it is to the end of making mystic truth known that I have elaborated upon spiritual matters for many years now, both in person, and more recently in a weekly livestream that is also called *Experiential Spirituality*. Yet it is not merely that I have a message to share, it is that I myself am that message, in the same way that every mystic that ever lived has personified the truths that they taught. To bring spiritual understanding and to shed light on earthly mysteries is my purpose in this world. This book represents a major fulfilment within that purpose, for the more that I have interacted with souls on the subject of spirituality, the more that I have come to see the need for such books.

Different mediums have different advantages. The advantage of writing a book is that I can expound upon every relevant subject to whatever extent I deem necessary and reasonable. Therefore, making the best use of the opportunity, I have addressed as wide a range of issues as possible, yet in a measured way so as not to overwhelm. This book will answer all of the great spiritual questions, either directly or indirectly, but more importantly, it will explain the means by which you may recognise your relationship with the spiritual, and in doing so, transform your understanding and experience of reality. I have very much written the book that I would have dearly loved to have stumbled upon decades ago. May it prove as invaluable to you as it would have to me.

David McMurdo

Chapter One: Calling

There is a dissatisfaction that pervades the lives of many. For most, it will remain as just that, but for others, it becomes a strong suspicion that something is deeply wrong with the world. It suggests the need to act, yet offers no direction, leaving them with the distinct impression that they are waiting for something to happen, something that will somehow make sense of everything. Many find themselves drawn to unusual areas of interest such as the supernatural, the occult, the great mysteries of history, cryptids, and conspiracy. Such studies will often culminate in an interest in the spiritual due to a realisation—conscious or not—that the spiritual is the transcendent mystery from which all other mysteries come. Yet still, they wait expectantly for something that they cannot explain.

The Awakening

> Yeshua said, "Blessed are the solitary and elect, for you will find the Kingdom. You are from it, and to it you shall return."
>
> - The Gospel of Thomas, Saying 49

Many souls have a very strong sense that there is more to life than the mundane reality that their day to day experience presents them with, and if you are reading this book, you are almost certainly one of them. The ancient Gnostics were straightforward in their explanation of this strange mistrust of the world as it appears—we simply do not belong in this world; we do not belong in this world because we come from the Spirit above; that restlessness deep inside of us is a call to return home, and we will never be at peace until we are awakened to the reality of that Spirit and then return to it by means of a permanent awareness of its presence.

Yet the ancient Gnostics were not alone in recognising this—every major religion, every great spiritual tradition, and every genuine esoteric path originated with one that had been called to awaken to the reality of our spiritual home. Having then made the journey there, they sought to guide others, for when one has been liberated by means of the truth, one is obliged to make it available to the few ready to receive it. Therefore, first comes the calling to something higher but indefinable, then comes the awakening to that greater reality, then follows the experiential journey there, and from one's arrival, the divine mandate to testify of it.

The home that the Gnostics and others called "Spirit" is known by many different names around the world, and the means to become conscious of it has also been described in a variety of different ways such as "spiritual development", "self-realisation", a "heightening of consciousness", and an "increasing of awareness", among others. I call the journey home to Spirit "remembrance", for in truth, your calling is not beckoning you to discover something new, but rather it is beckoning you to remember that which you have forgotten. After all, no place can truly be your home if you have never been there before, and you will begin to experience (as you may have already) an odd sense of familiarity with understandings despite never having heard them before in your mortal life. The supreme spiritual state attained by having made the journey home is also assigned many different names within many different traditions. Most Christians would call it "salvation", those typically described as being "New Age" might call it "Christ consciousness", whereas those more inclined towards eastern thought might call it "nirvana". I call the supreme spiritual state "rest" just as certain ancient Gnostic groups did, for there are few words that so perfectly express the experience of it.

I am writing this book as a manual of remembrance—a guide to assist you upon your journey home to Spirit and to rest. It is a journey that I also undertook, during which I experienced the same apparent obstacles as you have and will, for such obstacles are not unique to anyone, and nor are they accidental misfortunes. It would therefore be appropriate for me to begin this work by sharing the story of my own calling and eventual awakening.

I was born in a town called Thurso within the county of Caithness in the northern Highlands of Scotland. The name of "Caithness" is derived from both its ancient inhabitants and its geography—"Caith" referring to the wild cats (or even lynx) that a Pictish tribe that once dwelt here had a particular affinity for, and "ness" referring to its status as a headland. The Norse, being aware of that Pictish tribe, referred to Caithness as "the land of the cat people". The town of Thurso is itself a Norse settlement that was established in the 13th century at the latest, its name meaning "Thor's River".

In the modern day, Scotland is a very secular country, and I myself was not raised within any religious tradition, my guardians not concerning themselves with spiritual matters. Despite this, I began to examine the great spiritual questions from my youth, called to understand our reason for being. In hindsight, I can see very clearly that I fully expected to eventually stumble upon some piece of information that would somehow make sense of everything. But although my desire for knowledge and understanding had been insatiable, in my mid-twenties I found myself relaxing into a regular life. I came to see that although I had obtained voluminous amounts of knowledge in all manner of obscure areas, that knowledge had not resulted in any great awakening, and I was no closer to understanding our reason for being.

One morning, I sat contemplating the nature of prayer; this was nothing unusual, for I had always considered such things, and on that particular day I was trying to understand what would happen if two souls, both worthy of having their prayers answered, made requests to God the honouring of which would lead to contradictory results in the world. How would God answer both of those prayers?

I know now that my consideration of that hypothetical scenario illustrated my ignorance of the spiritual, but at the time I considered it a serious dilemma, and as I sat there exerting all of my intellect into trying to work that problem out, I had what felt like an epiphany, and I was suddenly overwhelmed by a force; it was as though in attempting to resolve my hypothetical dilemma I had somehow pierced the roof of my intellect, causing a flood of what I could only have described as "power" to fill by entire being, and I became aware that the room about me was permeated by that same force, which I knew to be the essence of God—when I moved my arm through the air I was moving it through the very being of God. Yet I also knew that God had not just arrived, but that He actually permeated reality at all times, unbeknownst to most. This understanding came to me in an instant, and with it a peace and joy so absolute that words could never convey their strength.

Though that feeling of peace and joy lasted for many days afterwards, the experience of being as aware of God's presence as I was of my own lasted for only a few minutes before I was left seemingly alone again, having no idea what had just happened to me or why, but with my desire to understand our reason for being not only renewed, but more powerful than ever. I was also left with the conviction that the soul known as "Jesus Christ" had somehow been responsible for the experience, despite the fact that Christianity was to me just one tradition among many that I had no particular reason to favour.

It seemed as though God had decided to honour my former diligence by briefly making His presence known, and had then left me with Jesus Christ as my means through which to find Him again. This awakening marked the beginning of my journey of remembrance and my ultimate return to rest in the Spirit, further details of which I will expound upon throughout this book.

For many years I questioned why such an experience had fallen upon me, for I knew that many others had pondered life's mysteries just as I had, and I could see no reason that I in particular should receive such an obvious gift. What I know now, and what you will soon understand, is that such things are unimportant; what matters is that it did happen, and that as a consequence, I am where I am now.

I used to share that account of my awakening in an attempt to encourage others with a credible testimony of spiritual transformation. After all, as well as the obvious change that the experience wrought upon my life, I have never given any soul a reason to doubt my sincerity, I have no physical or mental ailments, and I do not use medications, any illegal drugs, or even drink alcohol. I have also never taken money for speaking on these matters except when material necessity demanded it, such as with the publication of this book. For all of these reasons, one cannot easily cast doubt upon my testimony, and I thought that those burdened with doubt could be heartened by that.

But while that was usually the case, it sometimes had the exact opposite effect, for some souls began to wonder why they had never experienced anything of that nature—they also felt called to something higher, and yet had never had a major transcendent experience that they considered to be an awakening. There are many such souls that come to doubt whether they are even meant to concern themselves with spiritual matters at all. Yet it is really very simple: you are here now, reading my words—do not look to your imagination to give you some expectation regarding what being worthy of spiritual understanding might look like, for be assured that your mind will give you an expectation that will never be met. You need only entertain the idea that this book might be that which serves as the conduit to your awakening, your remembrance, and your rest in the Spirit. It is to that very end that I am writing. We all come from the Spirit, and we will all inevitably return to it—it is merely a question of when.

I know very well that while some of you are merely interested in what this book has to teach you, others among you are very tired—you have wandered down so many paths, have been met with so many dead ends, and have placed your trust in those unworthy of it so many times that you are now bewildered and disillusioned to the point of frustration. Let all of that go and be comforted in the knowledge that only grace could have brought you here, and if grace has brought you here, it can only be for your benefit.

My Method

> Yeshua said, "Know what is in your sight, and that which is hidden from you will be manifest, for there is nothing hidden that will not be manifest."
>
> - The Gospel of Thomas, Saying 5

This book will naturally be written to be read from beginning to end on your initial reading, but each chapter will be divided into four clearly titled sections which can be easily referenced afterwards. Because those

7

that read my words will come from a variety of backgrounds and will have varying degrees of understanding, it would be unwise for me to assume any understanding on the part of the reader.

Whenever a mystic arose in the ancient world, it was necessary for those that were called to abandon everything else in order to follow them, since such an opportunity would almost certainly never present itself again. In the modern age, when humanity is connected like never before and where there are a diverse array of mediums for expression, the physical abandonment of one's home and dedication to a single teacher is no longer necessary, but you must still be utterly dedicated to remembrance. Different expressions resonate with different souls, and this is why mystics will arise in various times and places to teach those that are ready to hear in their own unique manner and in a way appropriate to the culture of the day. I have spoken to hundreds of souls across many years on these matters, and that experience has shaped the terminology that I employ and the way in which I express different understandings. Coherent communication is not possible if the same words evoke completely different concepts within the minds of those communicating, and when expounding upon the spiritual it is essential that we are even more cautious in our word choice, for that which is under discussion transcends all language and concept.

Even the term "mystic" requires some explanation, for to many the word is interchangeable with vague terms such as "magician", "wizard", and "sorcerer", but a genuine mystic is one that, having remembered the Spirit from which they came, lives in conscious unity with it—the state that I call "rest". This is the goal of all genuine spirituality. There are many other terms that are used to refer to individuals that have attained this conscious unity with the Spirit —"Gnostic", "seer", "sage", "guru", and "shaman" are just some terms that may be synonymous with the term "mystic" depending upon the context within which they are used. Now, when I make statements concerning "mystics" throughout this book, understand that I am not attempting to imply that I speak for all mystics or that they would all be in agreement on every issue—they most certainly would not, and my teachings are my teachings. But what all mystics have in common is an emphasis on having direct experience of the spiritual—the "experiential spirituality" that is the focus of this book.

Just as mystics may be known by many different terms, there are likewise many titles used to refer to the ultimate reality that most call "God"—"the Most High", "the One", "the Ineffable One", "the Source", "the Absolute", and "the Supreme", to name very few. I use the terms "God" and "Spirit", but do not be concerned if the meaning of those words is vague to you, for they will be fully explained. Indeed, you will be at an advantage if their meaning is vague to you, for many souls associate very precise concepts with the terms "God" and "Spirit", and thinking that they know all about them and whether or not they accept them as a part of our reality, they are no longer receptive to new understandings. I would encourage you to forget all that you know or think that you know regarding all such matters, at least for the duration of this book.

For now, it is enough for you to understand that I use the term "God" to refer to the supreme and personal intelligence from which all else comes, while I use the term "Spirit" to refer to His impersonal essence and the power through which He enacts His will. Do not be misled or put off by my use of masculine pronouns when referring to God—I use such pronouns only because it is customary; God is the source of sex and gender and transcends both of those attributes; you could therefore just as well refer to God as "She", "They", or "It", for such terms are as equally correct and as perfectly wrong as the pronoun "He" when doing so. This is a good example of the way in which the spiritual necessarily defies encapsulation within language and concept.

Jesus Christ has been central to my life since the time of my awakening and must therefore feature prominently within this book. However, when I refer to him, I will do so using his Hebrew name "Yeshua". The name "Jesus" is derived from the Latin name "Iesus" which is itself a transliteration of the Greek name "Iesous" that is used throughout the Koine Greek manuscripts of the New Testament. The name "Jesus Christ" means "Jesus the Anointed One", and in Hebrew this is expressed as "Yeshua Hamashiach", meaning "Yeshua the Messiah" ("Mashiach" being the Hebrew word for "messiah"). It matters not by which name you refer to any spiritual master, but I have discovered that many souls associate negative concepts with the name "Jesus" due to those that have acted unrighteously under it. The name of "Yeshua" evokes no such negative associations, and it is no coincidence that this original name has been so protected.

Finally, if I refer to you as a "person", you would understand me to be saying that you are a human being; you are human being, but that is only a small and very temporary extension of what you fundamentally are, and I will not subtly reinforce error through careless word choice. This is why I instead refer to individuals as "souls", the exact meaning of which will be explained within the third chapter.

Throughout this book I will use various sacred texts in order to illustrate different understandings, and this is not to be taken as an advocacy for any tradition. While mystics can arise within any tradition (or no tradition) and will express themselves in a variety of ways, true mystics are never sectarian when they are at liberty to be otherwise, and nor are they ever dogmatic. I do not belong to any spiritual collective, and nor will I ever create one. I know very well just how desperate many souls are for a guru to follow and a group to belong to, so know now that anyone that would use the content of this book to inform the founding a sect has failed to understand the book.

Because the journey of remembrance is that which gave rise to every genuine spiritual tradition, all of the world's great sacred texts teach it in their own fashion. The most ancient source that we have of these teachings are the Upanishads ("Upanishad" meaning "to sit close"), which are texts found within the ancient Hindu compilations called the Vedas ("Veda" meaning "knowing"). But while I would enjoy referencing the Upanishads as well as those other sacred texts that I prize most highly—namely the Hindu Bhagavad Gita, the Taoist Tao De Ching, and the Taoist Zhuangzi—to do so extensively would require so much explanation and clarification that a significant portion of this book would inevitably end up serving as a commentary on them. I may occasionally reference content from the Bhagavad Gita (meaning "The Song of God"), but I will primarily restrict myself to the use of excerpts from biblical texts and a single Gnostic text.

Gnosticism (meaning "to have knowledge") was fundamentally a synthesis of Jewish mysticism, Platonic philosophy, and in most instances, Christian mythology. In the vast majority of cases, those groups that we retroactively call "Gnostic" considered themselves to be the truest of Christians. Historically speaking, their beliefs are just one more expression of Christianity that lost the battle to define orthodoxy that culminated within the 4th century. There are notable exceptions to this such as the Mandeans that eschew veneration of Yeshua in favour of John the Baptist, and I write of them in the present tense because they are one of the few ancient Gnostic groups that persist into the modern day.

The Gnostics are named after the experience of "gnosis" (knowledge), which can best be described as "divine insight" or "revelation"—a knowing in your deepest being that transcends mere intellectual understanding. Whatever else they differed on, Gnostic groups always had gnosis as their central emphasis. It is for this reason that Gnosticism is often perceived as being the most mystical form of Christianity, and it is why the term "Gnostic", when not used in the strictly sectarian sense, can be understood as being synonymous with "mystic", for the experience of transcendent knowing that the Gnostics called "gnosis" is central to remembrance of the Spirit—my own awakening was an experience of gnosis, as all awakenings are.

However, despite the richness of the Gnostic tradition, I will only use excerpts from the Gnostic Gospel of Thomas throughout this book, for in its most developed form, Gnosticism involved a highly complicated cosmology and system of belief, and most Gnostic texts very much reflect that fact. As much as I would like to extensively utilise them, as with the aforementioned eastern texts, doing so would require very lengthy explanations of their meaning that would risk distracting from the central focus of remembrance. The Gospel of Thomas, however, is a simple list of one hundred and fourteen mystical sayings (at least as the text is traditionally presented), most of which can be understood in complete isolation. The Gospel of Thomas comes to us in the relatively complete form of a single Coptic manuscript that was discovered in Nag Hammadi, Egypt, in 1945. Three fragments of a Greek copy that had been found previously were only able to be retroactively identified due to the discovery of that Coptic text.

From the biblical texts I will primarily employ the books of the New Testament, including the three synoptic gospels, which are known in full as the Gospel According to Matthew, the Gospel According to Mark, and the Gospel According to Luke. I will also cite excerpts from the Gospel According to John and the epistles (letters) of the apostle

Paul, a powerful mystic that was especially beloved by the Gnostics. It is also inevitable that I will reference verses from the Hebrew Bible (the Old Testament). Biblical texts are obviously not without their own complexities, the meaning of their words having been obscured by two millennia of obtuse theologies, but they will be manageable within the scope of this book. Note that when quoting from the Gospel of Thomas or any New Testament text I will replace occurrences of "Jesus" and "Christ" with "Yeshua" and "Mashiach" respectively, for the sake of consistency and ease of reading.

The ultimate purpose of this book is not to offer yet another perspective on the teachings of Yeshua, the apostle Paul, or the Gnostics, and nor is it to embark on the kind of historical elaborations that you can read in hundreds of other works. I will also not cite sacred texts because it is necessary to so or even because I want to; I will cite them simply because most souls understandably feel more comfortable when they are able to see how what I say is reflected in the alleged words of those great mystics of the past that they are already familiar with.

Plausible Words

> I was with you in weakness and in fear and much trembling, and my speech and my message were not in plausible words of wisdom, but in a demonstration of the Spirit and of power, so that your faith might not rest in the wisdom of men, but in the power of God.

> - The Apostle Paul, The First Epistle to the Corinthians
> 2:3-5

Many souls know that something is deeply wrong with the spiritual landscape as it exists in the world, despite the vast majority of them belonging to one spiritual tradition or other. Most of you know it, for that is why you are reading a book of this nature. I will now articulate

The term "aether" refers to a non-tangible substance that is typically associated with those entities known as "ghosts", "phantoms", or "apparitions". Just as we have a material body and a mental body, so too do we have an aethereal body. Our emotions and impulses are examples of aethereal phenomenon, for it is in our aethereal bodies that emotions and impulses are felt. Many kinds of aethereal being besides disembodied souls roam the material realm unimpeded by matter itself and unseen by most souls in mortal form. There are also aethereal realms of various kinds—those that would be described as "heavenly", and those that would be described as "hellish".

The term "Spirit" refers to the perfect and eternal thing and no-thing that underlies and permeates all of reality. It is the impersonal essence of the personal intelligence that is God. Although I have referred to it as a "substance" out of necessity, it actually transcends all substance. Spirit is non-phenomenal—it cannot be perceived by the five physical senses, and its nature can only be known experientially through the transcendent experience that is the gnosis, divine insight, and revelation previously mentioned. Although they are often wrongly associated with the mind, common epiphanies are themselves minor experiences of Spirit that bestow insight.

There is a higher truth concerning the categories of matter, mind, aether, and Spirit, but for now it is only necessary that you grasp the distinctions between them, for the business of the mystic is to have direct experience of the Spirit and to then attempt to convey the significance of that experience on the conceptual level of the mind through the use of language. This is why mystics are never dogmatic, for to be dogmatic means to insist that others accept one's unprovable beliefs as though they were undeniable facts, whereas the mystic merely expounds upon experiences that any soul may undergo; one may question the interpretation of such experiences, but the experiences themselves are never in doubt.

However, the dilemma of the mystic (not that they truly have dilemmas) is that concept and language can only ever point to the spiritual and can never encapsulate it. It is for this reason that mystics so often employ allegory, metaphor, parable, and poetry in an attempt to express the inexpressible, and it is why there are so many diverse traditions based upon experiences of the same spiritual reality.

17

The majority of souls that reckon themselves to have a spirituality actually have none at all precisely because they do not understand the distinctions that exist between matter, mind, aether, and Spirit. Like the aforementioned religionists, what they actually have is an intellectual interest in the spiritual that is expressed through the study of sacred texts and the propagation of beliefs.

Material and intellectual activities may relate to the spiritual, but they are not themselves spiritual activities by definition. If such activities are not used as a stepping stone, but are instead mistaken as an end in themselves, they will prove spiritually useless. Until a soul grasps the distinction between spirituality and that which relates to spirituality, they have not yet begun to engage with the spiritual in any meaningful way, and few are they in any generation that will ever cross that threshold. If you mistake material and intellectual activities for being spiritual activities, then you must inevitably err in understanding the qualities required to know the Spirit; if spirituality is presented as a study of sacred texts and the construction of elaborate belief systems within the mind, then what matters above all else is the cognitive ability to engage in such activities. This would mean that those that come to know the Spirit are essentially an intellectual elite, and you already intuitively know that this is not so. There was never a spiritual master that emphasised the need for cognitive brilliance and that sought to appeal exclusively to those that demonstrated it, unlike a great many religionists today. On the contrary, those that became dedicated to the great mystics were invariably poor and had little education, as has almost always been the case with those mystics themselves.

I myself have no wealth or great education to speak of, though I can tell you without pride and as a pure matter of fact that I am highly intelligent; I have studied sacred texts so arduously that I could have recited them from memory; I have wrestled with the nuances of ancient and dead languages just in the hope of squeezing one more drop of insight from the words contained within wisdom literature; I have agonised over mystic texts so obscure that few know that they exist and so complicated that even though they had been translated into English they still seemed to have been written in a different language altogether —I can assure you, such activities are not the way to know the Spirit, and nor will a having great intellect help you to do so; it will actually hinder you if it causes you to become distracted by, and enamoured with, such activities.

Spirituality is not a physical journey to worldly places or an intellectual journey into sacred texts and byzantine theologies, but a journey within oneself that results in direct experience of the Spirit, and from that experience, a positive and undeniable transformation of one's state of being, a rarefied insight into the nature of reality, and good conduct. That is genuine spirituality. Yet the word "spirituality" is so misused in the modern day that I use the term "experiential spirituality" to distinguish the experiential nature of my teachings from the many counterfeit spiritualities that exist, all of which I will address.

Despite the transcendent nature of the Spirit that mystics exist to make known, the means of experiencing the Spirit are very straightforward. You need only be willing to stop pretending to know that which you do not know, to see reality as it truly is, and to put mystical claims to the test. This requires much honesty, which is why what the spiritual seeker requires is not physical prowess or intellectual brilliance, but purity of heart, which is utter sincerity.

Professor of Literature, Joseph Campbell, best known for his book *The Hero with a Thousand Faces*, is quoted as having said that "the psychotic drowns in the same waters in which the mystic swims with delight." Similar sentiments have been echoed throughout history, and as you read this book you will very quickly understand why; I will write much that, if it were stripped of its context and presented in a more haphazard fashion, could easily be interpreted as the ramblings of a psychotic. To most souls in this world, the only discernable difference between a mystic and someone afflicted with profound mental illness is how composed and coherent the former is in comparison to the latter. My point is that the mystic path is not something that should be taken at all lightly, and I most strongly advise you to read this book through to the end at least once before applying its recommendations so that you may know if you are truly prepared to do so.

This book will reveal the true meaning behind so much of what you have heard before, but never understood. However, from this point forth your focus must be upon what you experientially know to be true, with an emphasis on your present state of being and experience. While it is sometimes necessary to consider matters that are beyond your lived experience, you must always remain conscious of that experience and grounded in it. This is the way of the mystic. The only alternative is to go off on some mental flight of fancy that bears no relation to your actual state of being. Leave that to the dreamers, the religionists, the theologians, and the philosophers.

Souls embark upon the spiritual path with a wide variety of expectations and desires, and so if you were obliged to tell me what you expect or want to find through remembrance, what would you say? What should the pursuit of the spiritual (however you understand it) bestow upon you? The more emotionally inclined among you will give answers like "happiness", "peace", and "contentment", whereas those of a more intellectual disposition will respond by stating that you want the answers to specific questions, especially the answer to the question of why it is that we exist at all. What you must recognise immediately is that all such desires emerge from a sense of deficiency—you seek happiness necessarily because you perceive yourself to be unhappy, and you seek knowledge necessarily because you perceive yourself to be ignorant. Therefore, let us all agree that remembrance of the Spirit must bring contentment by removing all sense of deficiency, for no spiritual seeker supposes that experiencing unity with the ultimate manifestation of reality will leave them feeling deficient. Anything short of a removal of all sense of deficiency will leave some souls disappointed, and if even one soul is left disappointed by what they discover, then we can all agree that what they have discovered cannot be the Spirit.

Yet despite the magnitude of the matter at hand, remembrance does not require great effort on your part, for experiencing the Spirit by way of an internal journey is only possible because you have always been that very Spirit and are therefore eternally at one with God; you never truly left home at all, you merely forgot your true nature. In time and beyond time, you will know this, and your current desires will seem short-sighted—emotions will rise and fall before an equanimous you, and the questions that now seem so compelling will give way to the peace that brings perfect contentment.

Chapter Two: Identity

I have asserted that spirituality is a journey inside of yourself, and you have almost certainly heard similar assertions many times before, but without any explanation as to their exact meaning. Most souls that utter them could not tell you, for to them they are spiritual rhetoric that they have learned to repeat without understanding. Believe me, you can ruin a lot of lovely monologues on spirituality by simply asking those delivering them what exactly they are talking about. Yet understanding is necessary before one can engage in experiential spirituality, for how can you know what to do without being told, and how can you make sense of what you are doing without understanding the reason for it? This chapter will explain exactly what it means to venture inside of yourself, and where that journey of remembrance begins.

Know Thyself

> Yeshua said, "If your leaders say to you, 'The Kingdom is in the sky', then the birds of the sky will get there before you. If they say, 'It is in the sea', then the fish will get there before you. Rather, the Kingdom is inside of you, and it is outside of you.
> When you come to know yourselves, then you will become known, and you will understand that it is you who are the sons of the Living Father. But if you will not know yourselves, you dwell in poverty, and you are that poverty."
>
> - The Gospel of Thomas, Saying 3

The admonition to "know thyself" is most widely recognised as being one of three "Delphic Maxims" that is inscribed upon a column within the Temple of Apollo in Delphi, Greece, the accompanying maxims being "nothing in excess" and "certainty brings ruin". That particular temple is most famous for its oracle where—according to tradition—a chosen priestess called "the Pythia" would inhale vapours that arose from the earth and then speak on behalf of the gods. The Delphic Maxims themselves (of which there are one hundred and forty-seven in total) are attributed to the Seven Sages of Greece—an ancient selection of statesmen and philosophers renowned for their wisdom and insight.

Yet the admonition to "know thyself" is found throughout the ancient world, especially within mystic literature, for to know oneself is the beginning and the end of all spirituality. However, like so much mystic wisdom that has been filtered through the narcissism of popular culture, its true meaning is largely forgotten. As a consequence, most souls understand "know thyself" to be encouraging an exploration of one's mental body, including its preferences, habits, and quirks. It is not that such examinations are without merit, but rather that they are quite besides the point as far as spirituality is concerned. It is inevitable that profound admonitions be misunderstood in this fashion however, for souls can only understand teachings according to their degree of remembrance; if a soul is operating according to worldly assumptions, then they will reduce even the most heavenly revelation down to that same level.

Mystics are not merely psychologists operating without licence under archaic titles; they will naturally have great insight concerning the mental body, for such insight is necessary in guiding souls beyond it, but that is not their primary focus. Recall again the distinctions that I emphasised within the previous chapter and know that if teachings amount to psychology, however true and useful they may be, they are not spiritual teachings, for they explicitly concern only the mind. The Spirit that is the focus of the mystic transcends the mind and therefore psychology.

As demonstrated by the saying from the Gospel of Thomas that opened this section, Yeshua plainly taught two thousand years ago that the Kingdom of Heaven is not to be found anywhere in the external world, but rather inside of yourself, and that to remain ignorant of your true nature as Spirit is to dwell in poverty. It is that true nature that the mystical words "know thyself" are encouraging you to discover.

I find it very useful to highlight such statements within ancient mystic literature to quell any suspicion that such inwardly orientated teachings have arisen only in the modern age as a result of anticipated events—such as the coming of the Kingdom of Heaven—having failed to manifest materially. While it is true that religionists almost always await an external manifestation of such things, mystics have always understood and taught that such realities are internal.

Any bid to "know thyself" must begin with your current understanding, and so, if someone were to ask you to tell them about yourself, what would you tell them? Your name, age, and occupation? Perhaps you would reveal even more information, such as any religious beliefs that you may have, your sexual orientation, or your likes and dislikes in different areas. This way in which you understand yourself is what is known as your "egoic identity", or "ego" for short. When the biblical authors referred to "the flesh", they meant not only the physical body, but also the egoic identity with which it was associated, and even just being aware of that can greatly illuminate many wonderful verses contained within the Bible. Your egoic identity is your idea of who or what you are, and the egoic identity of the vast majority of souls will exist in the form of personhood.

While the terms "person" and "personhood" are typically understood to relate exclusively to human beings, those familiar with high theology will know that, within certain contexts, personhood can be understood as an attribute of that which is not human. For example, most Christians accept the doctrine of the trinity, which asserts that the one God is three "persons"—Father, Son, and Holy Spirit. Other Christians dispute this, correctly arguing that the New Testament authors clearly portray God as a single person—the Father alone—and that the doctrine of the trinity was a much later development. In such contexts the term "person" is used to refer to a singular intelligence with a particular character, and throughout this book I will be using that same broader definition of what it means to be a person and to therefore have personhood. Most souls understand themselves to be a singular intelligence with a particular character, and therefore they understand themselves to be a person; a person in the form of a human being, specifically.

However, while most souls would assert that they are indeed

human beings, most of them would also profess a belief in themselves as a "soul" or "spirit", which is usually understood to be some manner of phantom form that survives the death of the physical body. But regardless of what account a soul may give concerning their identity, if you were to ask them to say something about themselves, they would almost certainly respond with a series of human attributes without any reference to spiritual ideas. If pressed on the issue, they might also clarify by saying something like, "oh, well I believe that I have a soul as well." But when someone says "I have a soul", what they are saying is that they, as a human being, are in possession of a soul, which naturally places the human being as the primary identity and the "soul" as a secondary attribute.

It is because so few souls experientially know the reality of their true essence that, despite what they might profess, they betray where they really believe their true identity resides by the manner in which they speak and behave. You are almost certainly no exception to this; you may claim to believe all manner of things about what you truly are, but ask yourself honestly, what do you really know? What would an objective assessment of your experience of life lead another to conclude about your true nature? There will be few, if any of you, that can say that you have good reason to believe that you are anything more than a human being. Do not fear being honest with yourself concerning such matters, because without that honesty—without that purity of heart— you will remain in a state of delusion.

You are Spirit, eternally in union with God, and you can never be anything other than that, but you have forgotten your true nature and have come to fundamentally identify as nothing more than a human being. If you are to remember your true, spiritual nature, then you must begin to "know thyself", and that can only be done by first recognising that not only are you not fundamentally a human being, you are not fundamentally any form of person whatsoever.

Scrutinising Personhood

"Truly, truly, I say to you, unless one is born of water and the Spirit, he cannot enter the Kingdom of God. That which is born of the flesh is flesh, and that which is born of the Spirit is Spirit. Do not marvel that I said to you 'you must be born again.' The wind blows where it wishes, and you hear its sound, but you do not know where it comes from or where it goes. So it is with everyone who is born of the Spirit."

- Yeshua, The Gospel According to John 3:5-8

Consider your mortal life, who you understand yourself to be, and the ways in which you have understood yourself previously. Recognise that your personhood—your idea of yourself as an singular intelligence—has expanded and changed as you have acquired and lost attributes with experience.

There is information that you now regard as central to your personhood that you once did not because that information had not yet entered into your experience. For this reason, the "you" that you take yourself to be is not the same now as it once was. Indeed, time can bring such great change to personhood that it is not uncommon for souls to speak of themselves and others as being completely different people compared to those that they once were. Reminders of the person that a soul once was can be a source of great embarrassment, shame, or even anger, such is the change that time has wrought upon their personhood.

You are not even the same person to other souls during any one period of time—you do not express yourself to a family member in the same way that you would an old friend or a complete stranger. In each case you emphasise different aspects of your personhood depending upon what you deem to be more appropriate in those circumstances, to the extent that multiple souls might have very different perspectives on who you are as a person. Such projection is often done out of fear and as a defence mechanism, and those that project the most negative personas are invariably the most deeply insecure. Some unconsciously adopt personas that they have seen portrayed, being uncomfortable with the kind of person that they otherwise imagine themselves to be. So ask yourself, when do you present the true you? Or is the true you only present when you are not required to meet anyone's expectations? Of course, such questions assume that you are always in control of your egoic identity and how it manifests, which is not the case.

In my adolescence I perceived my grandfather to be a tough disciplinarian—he was a tall, well-built man that always insisted that my back be straight when I walked and that my appearance be clean cut. Yet in his final years he suffered from dementia, and the strong personhood that I had known for my entire life simply disintegrated until he no longer retained any knowledge of who he was, who anyone else was, or where he was. He would sit placidly, accepting any food given to him and engaging in polite conversation with those that addressed him, though those conversations were very repetitive, as he quickly forgot all reminders of his mortal life. Cases such as that of my grandfather are examples of a soul's personhood disappearing altogether within a single human lifespan.

Your personhood, being a form of egoic identity, is nothing more than an ever changing idea that exists within your mind, and like any idea, it is ultimately transitory; severe enough physical trauma can destroy it, brain deterioration can gradually erase it, and time will inevitably alter and disintegrate it. You cannot demonstrate the true you to another soul while believing yourself to be a person exclusively because personhood is a continuous cycle of attributes, and so you yourself can have only a tenuous grasp on who and what you are at any given moment. There is no attribute of human centred personhood or of any other form of egoic identity that was not acquired at some point in time, and it is a divine law that what is acquired in time must also be lost in time.

It is no exaggeration to say that every difficulty that a soul experiences during its mortal life stems from that soul's identification with an egoic identity, especially when that egoic identity exists in the form of human centred personhood. A human being is a thinking machine of flesh and blood and we are all aware of its capabilities and limitations. Even if you have a belief system that involves you being more than human, for as long as you experience reality as nothing but a creature of flesh and blood, barring a major act of grace, you will be limited by that identification and will act in accordance with it. Confused identification also inevitably confounds all attempts to understand reality; if you take yourself to be nothing more than a human being, you will almost certainly seek to understand the spiritual from an anthropocentric (human centred) perspective. This will result in backwards reasoning, as though the Spirit was created for humanity's purposes instead of the other way around. There are a multitude of supposed theological dilemmas that only have weight for as long as you assume that God is obliged to answer to humanity, but you would only assume that if you had an anthropocentric perspective due to having mistaken your own identity.

Despite this, it is perfectly natural that a soul should come to identify with its human form. Every experience that they remember having seems to reinforce that identification, and so it is useless to tell such a soul to simply believe that they are in fact Spirit and not a human being or any form of person; belief alone neither makes something so, nor does it substantiate anything to the soul that believes. If a soul were to merely assume a belief in themselves as Spirit, they would just be replacing the idea that they have of themselves as a human being with an idea of themselves as Spirit, whatever their idea of Spirit might look like. As an idea, this would still be a form of egoic identity, and all the more destructive due to its grandiose nature. The Spirit that you are is not a subjective idea that exists within the mind; it is the absolute truth that transcends the mind.

You must directly experience the Spirit so that it becomes a reality to you is and not just one more idea within the mind. However, in order to experience the Spirit, you must first find it, and a clue as to where you might begin to look lies within a concept that you are unlikely to consider related to the matter at hand.

It is important for you to know that beliefs held as central within each spiritual tradition almost always have both an exoteric meaning and an esoteric meaning. The word "exoteric" refers to that which is obvious and immediately apparent; the word "esoteric" refers to that which is hidden or secret. Religionists invariably understand the beliefs of their tradition only on an exoteric level, but as one undergoing remembrance, you will begin to discern the esoteric meaning behind such beliefs, for your experience will bestow you with the insight necessary to do so.

You have undoubtedly heard of "reincarnation". On the exoteric level it is understood as the transmigration of the soul, which is to say, the transfer of some immortal part of ourselves to another vessel of flesh and blood after the death of our current mortal form. Many souls believe that the goal of the spiritual path is to liberate oneself from this cycle of physical rebirth in order to attain the state of bliss that I call "rest", and such an understanding is very strongly associated with the Dharmic religions.

"Dharma" is a Sanskrit term meaning "cosmic law", "teaching", or "way"—as is often the case with Sanskrit terms, its meaning depends upon the context within which it is used, and so while there are many adequate ways to convey its significance through the English language, there is no definitive way. The term "Dharmic religions" is similar to the term "Abrahamic religions" in that it is a category for religions that share a certain element in common. The Abrahamic religions are those religions that trace their history back to the figure of Abraham (Judaism, Christianity, and Islam); the Dharmic religions are those religions to which the concept of Dharma is central (Hinduism, Buddhism, Jainism, and Sikhism). Although the exoteric understanding of reincarnation is associated almost exclusively with the Dharmic religions, there have been Jewish, Christian, and Islamic groups throughout history that have also come to accept the reality of the transmigration of the soul, and such groups have invariably been more mystically oriented and obscure.

It seems to be taken for granted that the Gnostics as a whole accepted the reality of physical reincarnation, but while the ancient Manichaeans and the medieval Cathars (two groups usually classed as "Gnostic") certainly maintained a belief in physical reincarnation, I have seen little evidence that ancient Gnostic groups such as the Sethians and the Valentinians did, beyond assertions made by some of their proto-orthodox Christian opponents. Having extensively studied every Gnostic text available, I would say that there is a single statement within the Sethian text, the Book of Thomas the Contender (also known more simply as "the Book of Thomas"), that could be construed as referring to the transmigration of the soul, but such an interpretation would depend upon a very loose translation, and there is an alternative interpretation that is far more natural. I rather suspect that the notion that the Gnostics as a whole accepted the reality of reincarnation is a myth that has taken root in our collective understanding, almost certainly due to the fact that, as previously stated, "Gnosticism" is a very broad umbrella term that encompasses many groups that differed from one another in some major ways, and I would contend that many souls have been a lot less sensitive to such differences than they would have been if comparing groups within the "Abrahamic" and "Dharmic" categories. I am not claiming that there were no ancient Gnostic sects that maintained a belief in physical reincarnation; I am merely stating that I have yet to see a primary source that confirms beyond all doubt that any of them did.

My own view on the exoteric understanding of physical reincarnation is a subject that I will return to later, because at the current time it can be of no relevance to you; remember to remain grounded in your immediate experience and do not become distracted by such abstract subject matter. What difference would it make to you if I confirmed or denied the reality of physical reincarnation right now? I would merely be making an assertion about the nature of reality that you have no reason to either accept or reject. It is always the esoteric understanding of any given subject that is the more immediately relevant and therefore useful, and on the esoteric level, the concept of rebirth refers not to a supposed a cycle of physical death and rebirth, but rather the very observable cycle of personhood that I elaborated upon within the previous passage. While this esoteric understanding of rebirth is not entirely unknown within religious circles, it is primarily communicated through various occult forms, such as the tarot.

If escape from the cycle of personhood within a single mortal lifetime is possible, then it can only be if we are that which transcends personhood and is constant throughout it, in the same way that the reality of exoteric reincarnation depends upon the existence of an immortal essence that persists through many physical incarnations. And so the question becomes, what are you that witnesses the cycle of personhood? It is the answer to that question that will lead you to your true, spiritual essence.

The Great "I Am"

> The disciples said to Yeshua, "Tell us what our end will be."
> Yeshua said, "Have you discovered the beginning that you look for the end? For where the beginning is, there the end shall be. Blessed is he who will take his place in the beginning. He will know the end and will not taste death."

> - The Gospel of Thomas, Saying 18

The above saying from the Gospel of Thomas is among the most mysterious within a text that contains many highly obscure sayings. Yet Yeshua was alluding to the very thing that is the object of your current inquiry—that which exists beyond the personhood that we have just scrutinised. The beginning wherein also lies the end is not some cosmic beginning quite beyond our knowing, but rather the beginning of our experience within mortal form.

When a soul finds itself within a newly born human being, it is incapable of conceiving of itself due to the limitations of their new vessel—it is merely aware of the phenomenon that it is exposed to, though it yet lacks the cognitive ability to consider and understand it. When other souls in mortal form address it by its given name, it does not recognise it as a name, but only as a particular series of sounds. In time, it will begin to understand that the series of sounds is a means by which it is identified among others. It will also begin to understand its dependence upon its guardians and their benevolence towards it, to the extent that it comes to expect to be comforted in times of distress. As its physical and mental bodies continue to develop, the soul will come to understand its relationship to its guardians. An understanding of itself as human, as male or female, as having an ever increasing age value, and its place in the larger world will all follow in short order. By the time the mortal form of that soul reaches its adolescence, the soul will have come to conceive of itself as a human being with a myriad of different attributes. In adulthood, that range of attributes is so vast that it can

30

never be fully known to any except that soul themselves.

This is the process of conditioning that every soul born into human form must naturally undergo, and it is the means by which the egoic identity of personhood is developed. A child has no conception of itself until it has the cognitive capacity to conceive, and when it does, its first intellectual recognition must necessarily be that of its own existence—the "I Am", for the attributes of any egoic identity depend upon it— "I am male", "I am tall", "I like pies", and so on. "I Am", therefore, is the first thought and that upon which personhood depends. Yet while "I Am" is necessarily the first thought, it also exists in a form far more subtle than that of thought, for it exists as the aforementioned awareness that is the child's before it has the capacity to think. During that time it simply is, without conceiving of itself being. It reacts to all phenomenon that rises and falls before it instinctively, unable to defer to critical thought. It is this unconditioned state that we call "innocence", a state that is inevitably lost as the egoic identity of personhood develops. The "I Am" thought is a degeneration of this unattached "I Am" awareness.

This state of unaffiliated consciousness is "the beginning" that Yeshua referred to in saying eighteen of the Gospel of Thomas, and that state in which we will also discover the end, for it is that state of innocence from which we emerged that all genuine spirituality seeks to return us to. It is for this reason that Yeshua often used children as an example of what his disciples should aspire to be like, even going as far as to tell his disciples in Matthew 18:3 that, "Truly, I say to you, unless you turn and become like children, you will never enter the Kingdom of Heaven."

The Christian doctrine of "original sin" negates this fundamental understanding by asserting that all humans are born inherently sinful as a consequence of Adam and Eve's fall from the the Garden of Eden, though the exact details of this idea vary. The literal meaning of the word "sin" is "to miss the mark", and in the biblical texts it means to commit wrongdoing in opposition to God's will, but the doctrine of original sin treats sin not as immoral activity, but as though it is a substance that may be physically inherited, which is false.

However, the doctrine of original sin is extrapolated from a handful of disparate biblical verses and is not something that any biblical author explicitly taught. Whereas Yeshua held children up as examples of innocence, this doctrine (particularly as it is understood within certain Protestant denominations) condemns them all as corrupt, and this results in ludicrous theological debates concerning, for example, whether or not God will damn unbaptised children to eternal hellfire; there are few religious doctrines more perverse and misguided.

As a matter of fact, the biblical scriptures themselves refer to the aforementioned state of unaffiliated consciousness—that state of innocence— prior to the development of egoic identity, most famously when, in John 8:58, Yeshua proclaimed, "before Abraham was born, I Am." Christian religionists usually interpret Yeshua's assertion that he existed before Abraham (who had died hundreds of years earlier) to be a declaration that Yeshua himself is God, connecting his "I Am" identification with God identifying Himself by saying "I Am Who I Am" in Exodus 3:14. They are right to make such a connection, but Yeshua was not declaring that he existed prior to Abraham in the form of the person Yeshua, but rather as the unaffiliated consciousness under discussion here, something that is by no means unique to Yeshua.

While that which is now considered orthodox doctrine within Christianity has raised Yeshua to a status of deity unique among souls, he did not do so himself. If you ask a Christian religionist for proof that Yeshua proclaimed himself to be God, one of the first verses that they will point to is John 10:30 in which Yeshua said, "I and the Father are one". Not that statements from sacred texts alone are proof of anything (except perhaps in historical terms), but such a citation ignores the fact that in John 17:20,21, during his "High Priestly Prayer", Yeshua, communing with God, said of the disciples, "I do not ask on behalf of these disciples only, but also for those who will believe in me through their word, that they may all be one, just as you, Father, are in me, and I in you, that they also may be in us, so that the world will believe that you sent me." Therefore, if one is to take John 10:30 as proof of the deity of Yeshua, then in order to be consistent one must also take John 17:20,21 to be proof of the eventual deity of the disciples and all that would heed their preaching, for within those verses Yeshua explicitly said that they were all to have the same unity with God that he had. But this is something that is unacceptable within the doctrinal confines of any mainstream Christian institution, and therefore they will, as religionists do, resort to convoluted apologetics in order to explain away the perfectly plain statements of Yeshua on this subject.

Be wary of souls that seek to stealthily redefine commonly used and well understood terms in order to support their arguments, for there is no surer sign that those arguments are wrong. For example, to be "deity" means to be God, but there are some that use the word "divine" as though it is interchangeable with "deity". It is not. To be "divine" means to be of heavenly origin—angels (as they are traditionally presented) are divine, but they are certainly not deity. In most circles this distinction between "deity" and "divinity" is understood perfectly well. However, the reason that some Christian religionists will pretend that the word "divine" is interchangeable with that of "deity" is that the New Testament is explicit in saying that Yeshua is divine, and if they can have others believe that being divine is synonymous with being deity, then their assertion that Yeshua is uniquely God seems to be fully reinforced by the New Testament itself when that is not the case. Such religionists depend upon those that they are talking to not being informed enough to know any better. Now I ask you, would those that act on behalf of God attempt to exploit the lesser knowledge of other souls in order to perpetuate their doctrines?

I have spent the little time that I have addressing the above biblical verses simply because while the pure "I Am" consciousness under discussion within this section would be immediately recognisable by many other terms to any serious adherent of the Dharmic religions, most would assume it to be alien to the Abrahamic religions when it certainly is not.

In the present day we are so far removed from the cultures of those that authored the world's sacred texts that few souls have any idea what those ancients were referring to when they used words like "Spirit". To the modern mind, the realities alluded to by words like "Spirit" seem very distant, in a large part due to spectacular portrayals in fiction that encourage souls to imagine such realities manifesting as some magical spectacle, as though the ancients lived a world that was somehow more supernaturally imbued than our own. As a consequence of this, souls that inquire into these matters will tend to become enamoured with highly abstract matters as they overlook the obvious.

But it is the very consciousness under discussion here—the "I Am" awareness that precedes all thought, all egoic identity, and that witnesses the rise and fall of all material, mental, and aethereal phenomenon—that is the Spirit that the ancients spoke of. It is that which, as Yeshua said, is the beginning wherein also lies the end. There really is no such thing as a person who attains enlightenment; there is only the soul behind a person remembering itself to be Spirit—pure consciousness. Similarly, while there are many people in this world that are beyond redemption, there is no such thing as a soul that is.

The common saying that "the eyes are the window to the soul" is an unwitting allusion to the effect that conditioning has upon Spirit. Observe the brightness of the eyes of a baby or a toddler—that is Spirit, pure consciousness, fully expressed through their mortal form. This aliveness in Spirit is also the reason that some children have been known to make strange statements that imply some insight concerning heaven, supernatural beings, and deceased relatives—newly incarnated souls can often remember aethereal realms and can still perceive aethereal phenomenon in the world around them. But as the mortal form develops and a soul's mind assumes more conditioning, the eyes begin to dim as the soul forgets the Spirit that they are, its focus instead being upon the personhood that results from that conditioning. Only through remembrance can that light be regained. This is why it is said that mystics and saints radiate the presence of being—of consciousness— and it is why historic art often depicts them as literally glowing. Conversely, if you have ever seen the eyes of a dead human, then you will know that they appear profoundly empty.

To many souls the idea that Spirit is nothing other than our very consciousness just seems too simple; but it is not merely simple—it is obvious, and its obviousness is the very reason that it eludes so many. Consciousness is so rarely considered within these contexts precisely because we are consciousness—it does not manifest before us as phenomenon does because it itself is not phenomenal; it is that as which we experience phenomenon. Remembrance requires that we cease looking outwards towards phenomenon, and instead look inwards to our true essence that transcends phenomenon. Historically, the recognition of this truth manifested itself within different groups in different ways.

For example, certain ancient Gnostic groups were unusual in that, unlike their proto-orthodox counterparts, they allowed women to teach. While such an allowance seemed absurd to those ancients that lived under patriarchal systems (their vision being limited to a soul's fleshly manifestation), it made sense to those like the Gnostics that understood that our true essence lies beyond the limitations of the flesh, and that it would therefore be folly to impose artificial restrictions based upon temporary fleshly attributes.

To venture into the infinite consciousness that you are is what it means to undertake the spiritual journey inside of yourself—your true self, not the false self of personhood and other forms of egoic identity. Within the Christian tradition, the process of transcending one's transitory egoic identity is expressed as "dying to self" to "live to the Spirit" or to "live to Christ". This is what it means to be "born again", "born of the Spirit", or "born from above". The crucifixion and resurrection themselves are symbolic of the need to consciously die to all egoic identity so that you may attain salvation by being made alive in the Spirit, and this shall be expounded upon within the sixth chapter of this book.

Conscience and Intuition

> You must also help us through prayer, so that many will give thanks on our behalf for the blessing granted us through the prayers of many. For our boast is this, the testimony of our conscience, that we behaved in the world with simplicity and godly sincerity, not by earthly wisdom, but by the grace of God, and supremely so toward you.
>
> – The Apostle Paul, The Second Epistle to the Corinthians
> 1:11,12

Grace is usually defined as "unmerited favour"—help that God gives to a soul even when, from a human perspective, that soul is most unworthy of it. The mystic perceives the grace of God in all things, but our conscience and intuition are two of the most obvious examples of it.

Every soul affirms the existence of the conscience, and yet most of them utterly fail to recognise its miraculous nature, for as with the Spirit itself the presence of the conscience is so taken for granted that it tends to be almost entirely overlooked. Even the greatest theologians have usually given the conscience little more than a nod—as though it was a nuisance that must be grudgingly acknowledged before more important matters are addressed. Yet the miraculous nature of the conscience is evident in the fact that it is indisputably an infallible moral guide.

Many times in your life have you employed your intellect in order to determine what the morally correct action to take in a certain situation was, and many times have you come to the wrong conclusion by doing so. But never once have you obeyed your conscience only to be led into moral error. Every soul should be in awe having recognised this. Now, it is often the case that obeying your conscience can lead to your physical, mental, or aethereal body suffering, since making the morally correct decision often involves making a form of sacrifice, but that you did make the morally correct decision is never in doubt. The conscience is a powerful example of the unmerited favour that grace is because it manifests to us even before we have the slightest concern for the Spirit or even for what is morally correct; you could be a soul that utterly rejects the idea that God exists and despise spirituality in all of its worldly manifestations, and yet still have a conscience that offers you its infallible moral guidance.

Although intuition is experienced as an inner urging just as the conscience is, it is typically understood as something distinct because it is experienced within different circumstances—whereas the conscience arises to bestow moral guidance, intuition arises to bestow practical guidance. You might consider it to be the spiritual equivalent of your physical instincts. It is interesting to note that the "pangs" of the conscience are sometimes referred to as one's "moral intuition" in a dim recognition of the close relationship between the conscience and the intuition. They are both the most consistently available comparisons to offer for the experiential knowing that we call "gnosis", "divine insight", or "revelation", for you do not hear from your conscience and

with God, and so whatever subtle understandings such a proclamation may be intended to convey will be missed by most of them. When powerful experiences of the Spirit come, it is wise to reflect upon them for a time before jumping to conclusions that may be erroneous and before making proclamations that may be foolhardy. As for the truthfulness of the claim, ask yourself, can a droplet of the ocean rightly proclaim itself to be the ocean? No, for while that droplet is of the same substance as the ocean and is necessarily at one with it, a droplet is still a droplet and the ocean is still the ocean. In the same way, as Spirit you are of the essence of God and are eternally united with God, but while you are still undergoing an experience of individuality as a soul, you cannot rightly be called "God".

It is for this same reason that there is no contradiction between being aware of your eternal unity with God and yet still worshipping God—you are not worshipping yourself in some round about way, but rather the transcendent source from which you flow and to which you eternally belong. Besides that, if even great masters like Yeshua saw fit to humble themselves before God, then there has surely been some misunderstanding on the part of those that conclude that they are above such devotion.

"Devotion" within a spiritual context means worship of and submission to a deity or deities that are in some sense understood as being "other" than oneself. Because such devotion depends upon a belief in a deity or deities that are independent, personal intelligences, not all spiritual practitioners are devotional in that way; those that believe the highest manifestation of reality to be an impersonal force will tend to express their spirituality through introspective practices, which are usually an attempt to better understand themselves and to be at peace with reality. However, these seemingly disparate approaches to spirituality will inevitably intersect in ways that few of their practitioners understand.

Because of our eternal unity with God through the Spirit, one cannot be truly submitted to God through devotion without coming to experientially know of that unity. It is for the same reason that one cannot engage in introspective practices in a bid to better know oneself without also coming to know God. Therefore, while most souls follow either a devotional path or an introspective path, both paths will lead them to the same experiential space. This is the reason for the striking similarities between the testimony of mystics from throughout history and from around the world, regardless of what tradition they adhered to and regardless of whether their practices were devotional, introspective, or a combination of both.

I am inclined towards devotion, and when I pray to God I address "Him" as "Father" just as Yeshua did, for it feels more intimate to do so. However, I have found introspection to be more immediately beneficial, both in my own spiritual life, and in the instruction of others. Because of this, and because I recognise the reality of a personal God and His impersonal Spirit, my teachings involve both devotion and introspection. Indeed, what you engaged in within the previous chapter when you were considering the various forms that your personhood has taken was a form of introspection, albeit a simple one. Introspection comes first, because it is the means by which you come to know the Spirit that you are and to therefore know God to Whom you can then be properly devoted, for how can you be properly devoted to that which you are yet ignorant of? When reading this book and applying what it says, you are adhering to my teachings and are therefore employing the arrangement of introspective and devotional practices that I deemed the most efficient within the framework of understanding that I have chosen to present. In time, however, you will come to experientially know what is more effective for you, at which point you must let go of all that I have recommended and let yourself flourish under the guidance of God, which no teacher must seek to overrule.

Just as souls forgot their most natural state through the process of conditioning into personhood described within the previous chapter, in most cases those souls will need to undergo a process wherein that conditioning is undone. While they are still bound by egoic identity their minds will perceive all kinds of apparent obstacles that, from their perspective, prevent them from recognising their true essence as Spirit. It is for that reason and for that reason alone that a conscious process of remembrance is almost always required. "But," you may ask, "if Spirit is perfect, and we are that Spirit, then how could we ever forget our true nature? Even if we are souls on a sojourn, we are still that perfect Spirit, and how can that which is perfect be vulnerable to conditioning and subject to forgetfulness?"

42

The Spirit is indeed perfect and so did not unintentionally undergo a sojourn as the souls that we are, accidentally forgetting itself in the process—there are no such accidents. Rather, Spirit chose to undergo the illusion of forgetfulness by manifesting as multitudinous souls precisely so that it could experience being other than itself. That is why souls new to mortal form are so eager to explore and to take those risks that to them are very exciting—a phenomenon that every parent experiences as a curse. The Spirit loves to experience different forms of limitation, but it cannot be truly immersed within such experiences for as long as it remains aware of its own inherent perfection and immunity to danger. I will elaborate upon this matter within chapter eleven.

Essence

"It is the Spirit who gives life; the flesh is no help at all. The words that I have spoken to you are Spirit and life."

- Yeshua, The Gospel According to John 6:63

I have explained that ancient terms such as "Spirit" are often grossly misunderstood by the modern mind, and that as a consequence, the immediate and yet subtle realities that they refer to are overlooked. I will now further illustrate this point by providing several examples that clearly demonstrate that what the ancients called "Spirit" is indeed nothing other than the consciousness that you are.

The authors of the biblical texts made all manner of assertions about Spirit, and Christian religionists, being religionists, feel obliged to repeat those assertions. Yet almost none of them could tell you what exactly those assertions mean in practical terms, and this is because almost none of them recognise the Spirit as being consciousness. But when you understand that Spirit is consciousness, every statement that the great spiritual masters made concerning it makes sense and becomes far more illuminating.

In the excerpt from the Gospel of John that opened this section,

Yeshua proclaimed that it is the Spirit that gives life, which is an assertion found throughout the texts of the Bible, and what is your life if not consciousness? Without consciousness you are dead in the truest sense, for without consciousness there can be only oblivion. A soul might be willing to trade away every possession that they own, parts of their physical body, intellectual constructs from their mind, and their ability to feel certain emotions, but they would never trade away their consciousness, for without that consciousness, all else is useless to them. Your consciousness is your life in the most profound way. When Yeshua said that the words that he had spoken were Spirit and life, he was referring to the fact that he conveyed understandings that enabled others to know Spirit and to therefore know life itself.

What of Spirit as light? This is an idea that is found throughout mystic literature, a theme that runs through the Johannine texts (those written by the apostle John) of the New Testament especially, and another notion the meaning of which becomes perfectly plain when you recognise that Spirit is consciousness, for what is the most obvious benefit of being conscious if not the fact that reality is illuminated to you? Without consciousness, there is not even darkness, for there is no awareness to perceive even that.

Now consider the biblical idea that all souls are united by the Spirit of God. If you were to compare yourself to a random soul that you encountered out in the world, it is unlikely that there would be many physical similarities between you. If you were able to compare your mind to theirs, it would be like looking into two entirely different worlds. Your emotional realities would also differ greatly. But can you say that your consciousness would differ from theirs? Of course not—consciousness is consciousness. The physical faculties of others may be better or worse than your own, they may perceive reality through a completely different mental paradigm than you do, and they may feel different emotions within different circumstances, but the consciousness being filtered through their physical, mental, and aethereal bodies is necessarily identical to that of your own.

Within chapter twenty-five of the Gospel of Matthew, Yeshua relayed a parable that featured a king who represented Yeshua himself standing in ultimate judgement on souls. The point of the parable is well summarised in verse forty when that king said, "Truly, I say to you, as you did it to one of the least of these, my brothers, you did it to me." Knowing what you do now regarding the unity of all souls in the Spirit —in consciousness—you can understand just how literally Yeshua may have intended such statements to be taken.

You cannot unsee the illusory nature of personhood and other forms of egoic identity that has already been demonstrated to you, and for a time this recognition may cause some upset. But you will soon begin to experience it as a tremendous liberation as you become increasingly acquainted with the Spirit that you are, for you will have transitioned from being a soul that took itself to be a mere human being, to being a soul that experientially recognises itself as the Spirit that manifests through all human beings. This is why I often like to say that "the one that is nobody is everybody".

Yet for as long as you live within mortal form, you will not consistently experience the freedom of Spirit in its fullness, although there are occasions where it is possible to glimpse that greater reality. For example, in particularly traumatic circumstances, your aethereal form may disassociate from your physical body, enabling you to observe it from the outside. This is grace intervening to ensure that you do not endure more suffering than is necessary for your development. Likewise, in a more extreme example of the same phenomenon, when a soul's mortal form is close to death, the aethereal body will become increasingly detached from it, to the extent that, in the later stages of the dying process, it will be free to roam, no longer constrained by the physical body. It is exceptionally rare for a soul's mortal form to survive the extensive physical damage required to bring about such an experience, but in the unlikely event that it does survive, the aethereal body will return to the mortal form, and the soul can then testify to the world of what it experienced. Such experiences are known as "Near Death Experiences". Yet, recall what I wrote about remaining grounded in your present experience; what you need to focus upon currently is coming to recognise your innate authority and power.

The most commonly accepted truth concerning Spirit is that it transcends all else, and this is obviously true of consciousness, for all else rises and falls before it. It is you that perceives the phenomenon of the material, mental, and aethereal realms—they do not perceive you.

This alone is proof that you are something greater than matter, mind, and aether. However, it is that very phenomenon that blinds most souls to their transcendent nature, for most souls are enamoured by it, and being enamoured by it, they are experientially brought down to the level of that phenomenon. This is the reason that the process of conditioning that all souls born into mortal form undergo has the effect of causing them to forget their true, transcendent status, and to dwell in such forgetfulness is what it means to be "a lost soul" or to "lose one's soul"—not that one has permanently forfeited their soul (for you cannot permanently forfeit what you are), but that one no longer maintains a conscious recognition of it.

This happens because souls do not understand the value of their most powerful asset, namely their focus, which itself stems from the Spirit that they are, for what is focus if not concentrated consciousness? When a soul bestows their focus upon anything, they empower it within their own mind. The majority of souls will spend most of their mortal lives enamoured with and therefore ensnared by phenomenon that is necessarily beneath them. You must turn your focus inwards upon your own Spirit in order to experientially enter into that Spirit.

Divine Focus

> Yeshua's disciples said to him, "Twenty-four prophets
> spoke in Israel, and all of them spoke of you."
> He said to them, "You have ignored the Living
> One in your presence and have spoken only of the dead."

> - The Gospel of Thomas, Saying 52

Consciousness is the Spirit that you are, and focus is nothing other than concentrated consciousness—it is the Spirit that you are reaching out to the material, mental, and aethereal phenomenon that arises before you. Your focus is your most powerful asset, for it empowers within yourself whatever it reaches out to, and yet, as with the Spirit, its obvious power is overlooked by most souls due to its subtly and because they have come to take it for granted.

In a world where souls are more connected than ever before, there has never been more phenomenon vying for their attention. Within an hour of waking up, a soul can be exposed to the knowledge of a dozen different atrocities that occurred around the world, and all of you have had the experience of focussing upon a particularly outrageous incident only to end up being outraged yourself as a result. For some of you this is a regular, perhaps even a daily occurrence. A soul may even watch or listen to material that is uplifting, informative, and perhaps even pertains to the spiritual, but they have focused upon that same material many, many times before—it has become the intellectual and emotional equivalent of a comfort food that they return to gorge themselves upon time and time again. This is no less a misdirection of focus, for it is in fact a more insidious form of procrastination.

In the saying from the Gospel of Thomas that opened this section, the disciples approached Yeshua to announce that they had discovered where the twenty-four prophets of Israel had prophesied of him. One can well imagine them running up to Yeshua, breathless and excited, fully expecting him to be properly impressed by their endeavours. But he is not. In fact he chastises them for a reason related to the distinctions that I emphasised in the very first chapter: the disciples believed that they had done well by being so diligent in their studies, but while they were engaging in them, they were neglecting Yeshua himself—they had forsaken the living Spirit in favour of the dead words of dead men about the Spirit. There are so many souls that believe that they are engaging in spirituality just because they spend a lot of time reading about it, thinking about it, and talking about it, but unless you are actually experiencing the Spirit you are not engaging in spirituality at all.

I once listened to a soul deliver a lecture on how to engage in mystic practices. Although that soul was factually correct in terms of the history that they relayed and the methods that they described, it occurred to me while listening that they had not mentioned any of their own experiences of the Spirit. At the conclusion of their presentation they stated that they looked forward to the day when they would have the time to put everything that they had just talked about into practice, a statement that completely undermined all that they had just said. Of course, it is possible to speak in an informed fashion on an activity even if you yourself do not engage in it, but in the case of spirituality, if you do not apply what you have learned then you cannot possibly tell anyone anything that they cannot also read in hundreds of books. More importantly, you will not benefit from whatever understandings you may have acquired, for they have remained entirely theoretical to you.

Do not misunderstand the point of this passage: for as long as you live in mortal form, there will be times when you very much need to focus on practical matters, and when you are required to do so, you should give those matters your undivided attention. This is not about being oblivious to your material needs and the world around you; this is about ensuring that you prioritise the truly spiritual, for no matter what any soul might claim, the great passion of their life is made obvious by the way that they distribute their focus, and as Yeshua said in Matthew 6:21, "where your treasure is, there your heart will be also." If you treasure the spiritual, you will focus upon the spiritual above all else.

However, souls usually struggle to have such a focus in the beginning quite simply because they are yet ignorant of the value of the Spirit, and all of the worldly phenomenon that they are already familiar with seems far more appealing. But when you begin to experience the Spirit you will treasure nothing else like it. Therefore, the more that you choose to bestow your focus upon the spiritual, the easier it will become to do so.

You may have heard it said that matter and mind are "illusory". Souls can mean all manner of things when they say that, but within the context of mystic thought, all that it means is that matter and mind are impermanent—they will disappear with the passing of time. The Spirit alone is eternal, and therefore, mystics have said, it alone is real.

Yet, time is nothing more than a measure of change. Human beings, as products of the material realm, are creatures of time, and they are bound rigidly to change. But as a soul, you are already aware of numerous ways in which you do not at all experience time as though you were inextricably bound by it; you have undoubtedly experienced time seeming to move more quickly or more slowly—when you are focussed upon something, time will seem to pass more quickly; when you are not, time will seem to pass more slowly. You completely escape time as you sleep each night, when you are no longer bound to the experience of your mortal form, which is changing with age even as it rests. Unless you witness the activity of the mind through a dream, time and therefore change no longer exist for you in any way until your mortal form reawakens and you experientially return there. Such is the relative nature of time for the one that is ultimately beyond it.

While we roam the material realm within flesh, we are obliged to note time in order to effectively function here, but if your attention is constantly being drawn through time, then you are not experiencing reality as the timeless Spirit. To understand reality as the Spirit perceives it, you must recognise that life always occurs within the present moment—whatever you did in the past was done in the present moment, and whatever you do in the future will be done in the present moment. This is what I call "the Eternal Moment", for it is the only moment that there ever is. The Spirit experiences no past or future, but only innumerable permutations of material, mental, and aethereal phenomenon within that Eternal Moment. Therefore, when you are focussed upon some endeavour and enter into the Eternal Moment, you become oblivious to the passing of time until you release your focus.

It is phenomenon that we do not intend to bestow our focus upon that consistently brings us out of the Eternal Moment, and this is primarily mental and emotional phenomenon, for you carry the source of such phenomenon with you. And so, no matter what you might be doing, if memories that arise within your mind claim your focus, you can be experientially transported into the past and spend a great portion of time remembering former events and reliving the emotions that they evoked. Likewise, if anxieties about the future steal your focus, you may begin living out different hypothetical scenarios within your mind —futures that may never come to pass. Even living in anticipation of a positive event can be a distraction as you dwell upon it and obsessively seek out fresh information on the matter, as though doing so might somehow hasten the arrival of the event. As Solomon wrote in Proverbs 13:12, "Hope deferred makes the heart sick, but a desire fulfilled is a tree of life."

If you are to remember your true spiritual nature, you must relearn how to abide within the Eternal Moment until it once again becomes your default mode of consciousness, as opposed to being something that you accidentally fall into on occasion. But with so much undesirable external, mental, and emotional phenomenon to distract you, this will prove impossible without learning how to deny that phenomenon the power of your focus. To that end, you must begin to practise meditation.

The term "meditation" is used to refer to a variety of introspective and contemplative practices, but it broadly refers to sitting quietly and engaging in some manner of mental activity, or none at all, and different "meditations" are advocated for vastly different reasons. The secular world, perceiving its benefits, often recommends meditation for all manner of mental and emotional ailments, presenting it devoid of any spiritual context. But make no mistake: meditation originated as a spiritual practice and is explicitly a spiritual practice; presenting it devoid of any spiritual framework and as a way by which souls should fixate upon troublesome phenomenon is highly destructive. When I use the term "meditation", I am only ever referring to the practice that I am about to describe unless I state otherwise.

In order to meditate, find as quiet a place as possible where you can sit down comfortably. There are meditation techniques that involve sitting in specific postures and all manner of ritualistic trappings, but that is to overcomplicate matters and is therefore counterproductive. Even audible silence is not strictly necessary, but for the soul that may be entirely unfamiliar with meditation, audible silence will certainly be more conductive to it. Physical comfort is something that will certainly be necessary for the beginner, and I would also recommend meditating when most souls in your part of the world are asleep so that their mental phenomenon does not compound upon your own by way of your shared Spirit, so either very early in the morning or late at night. The former is preferable, because that way you are giving God your focus in a refreshed state, as opposed to throwing Him the scraps of it at the end of the day when all else that you prioritised more highly has been attended to.

Remember that consciousness is the Spirit that you are, and your focus is nothing other than the concentration of that consciousness upon phenomenon. Within meditation you should allow your focus to relax back into the Spirit from which it arose. The importance of being mindful of breathing within meditation has often been emphasised, and this is because your breathing is something that is necessarily always happening within the Eternal Moment. Therefore, focussing upon your breathing can help you to remain within the Eternal Moment. You will instinctively want to try and still the thoughts that arise within the mind, but attempting to do so necessarily means focussing upon them, and so although your intent may be to diminish their disturbing effect, you can only ever empower that effect. Instead, simply let those thoughts be. Let the same be true of any audible sound, bodily sensation, or emotion that may arise. Simply sit and be. In the beginning, you will feel pulled away from this practice to do all manner of things, because your mind is not engaged during meditation, and the mind gets very restless when it does not have a project. But this pull is just one more form of the phenomenon that you must not bestow your focus upon. With experience, not only will you no longer feel pulled away in this manner, you will actually feel pulled to meditation when engaging in the very activities that once drew you from it. This happens because you have come to know something of the immeasurable value and joy of abiding in and as the Spirit.

This meditation will enable you to experience your most natural state of being in a way that most souls never do during their mortal lifetimes, having been conditioned to carelessly bestow their focus upon passing phenomenon. You are Spirit, you have always been Spirit, and you always will be Spirit. Nothing that can happen will ever change that. All that ever changes is the phenomenon that you perceive as that Spirit. Meditation is a means by which you can draw closer to the experience of your true nature and therefore to God. As you become more and more at ease coming to experience the Spirit that you are in meditation, you will find that you increasingly take the benefits of doing so into your daily life. This happens very quickly precisely because you are not acquiring some new, unnatural state, but are in fact coming to remember your truest state. You will arise from each period of meditation with a great sense of peace, and the more that you meditate, the longer that this will last. But when I speak of meditating "more", I mean more often—it is far better to meditate for short periods of time frequently than it is to meditate for long periods of time infrequently. A daily meditation that lasts for ten or fifteen minutes is a good way to begin, and you need never meditate for much longer than that; if you begin treating meditation as though it were a competition then you are indulging an egoic impulse.

The most powerful benefit of meditation is the change in the way that you will experience external and internal phenomenon in your day to day life. For most souls, the impact and the effect of phenomenon is almost immediate. And so, for example, if something angers them, that anger is felt as though it had leapt upon them, and with seemingly no time to react, they become angry. But the more that you make a point of consciously reconnecting with your true nature in meditation, the greater the distance there will be between yourself and any phenomenon that arises; thoughts, emotions, and impulses that would once have pounced upon you are now witnessed arising very slowly. This means that whenever a thought, emotion, or impulse arises, you will have ample time to recognise what it is, calmly assess the merit of it, and decide whether or not to indulge it. All of this will happen because, having disciplined your focus to not immediately jump to any and all phenomenon within meditation, you have brought yourself into experiential alignment with the Eternal Moment, and so are coming to experience reality in the way that is most natural to you as Spirit.

It is precisely because mystics experience phenomenon in this way that they are known for their seemingly unshakable equanimity. It is not that they no longer have thoughts, emotions, or impulses (they very much do), it is that they have achieved mastery over them. You must understand that there is a tremendous difference between perceiving such phenomenon and being overpowered by it—there is a tremendous difference between recognising the presence of fear within oneself, and being afraid, for example. But this distinction is subtle and is known only to those that have either considered the subject deeply, or that have consistently engaged in the kind of introspective practice that I have just elaborated upon. When you have attained to such a degree of remembrance, you will no longer have to force yourself to meditate, for it will be a joy to you, and rather than having to engage in it according to a strict schedule, you will do so spontaneously.

The Tree of Duality

Yeshua said, "This heaven will pass away, and the one above it will pass away. The dead are not alive, and the living will not die. In the days when you consumed what is dead, you made it alive. When you come to dwell in the light, what will you do? On the day when you were one you became two, but when you become two, what will you do?"

- The Gospel of Thomas, Saying 11

The Book of Genesis within the Hebrew Bible is best known for those narratives concerning the Garden of Eden, the Tower of Babel, and Noah's Ark. It is the first of the five books that make up what is called "the Pentateuch" (meaning "the five books"), the other books being those of Exodus, Leviticus, Numbers, and Deuteronomy. According to the Abrahamic traditions, those five books were written by Moses himself. To introduce the subject of duality, I will begin by expounding upon the significance of the story of Adam and Eve within the Garden of Eden, and their fall from that paradise as it is related within the Book of Genesis.

According to the narrative, God created the first humans, Adam and Eve, and they lived together as a married couple among a variety of animals within a paradise garden called Eden. They were free to do as they pleased within the garden, but God warned them not to eat the fruit of the Tree of the Knowledge of Good and Evil, or else they would die. However, a serpent convinced Eve that God was not telling them the truth, and that she and her husband would not in fact die if they ate of the fruit. And so Eve ate of the fruit and convinced her husband to do likewise. As punishment for this, God cast the couple and the serpent from the Garden of Eden, condemning Adam to have to work for his food, condemning Eve to be subject to her husband and to endure pain during childbirth, and condemning the serpent to slither along the ground as the eternal enemy of humankind.

This story, like so many that are contained within the biblical texts, is purely allegorical, and until you recognise that you will never understand the lessons that it was intended to impart. Should you bestow the biblical texts with any kind of authority and yet take such narratives literally, you are likely to find yourself involved in misguided discussions concerning such matters as how one might substantiate the existence of Adam and Eve, where the Garden of Eden was, and how there could ever have been a talking snake.

The Garden of Eden does not represent a material place, but an aethereal one. Adam, Eve, and all of the animals of Eden were aethereal beings with no physical form—they were the heavenly counterparts of the creatures that we find upon the earth. This is why the narrative portrays Adam and Eve as living in constant communion with God, for they existed in a realm closer to that of Spirit. To eat of the Tree of the Knowledge of Good and Evil is symbolic of choosing to enter into stark duality apart from God through mortal incarnation, something that God in the Genesis narrative is opposed to, representing how detrimental to the experience of Spirit such a sojourn is. The serpent is symbolic of the whispering mind, tempting souls to do even that which they know they ought not do. This is why it is indeed the eternal enemy of all souls that dwell within mortal form.

The consequences of Adam and Eve eating from the Tree of the Knowledge of Good and Evil have proven to be an endless source of bafflement for theologians, annoyance for philosophical materialists, and amusement for comedians. Many souls have pointed out that a man being made to work by the sweat of his brow, a woman enduring pain in childbirth, and a snake being made to slither along the ground are silly punishments because such is the lot of those beings by nature. They will also point out that the serpent seems to have been more truthful than God, for Adam and Eve did not in fact die having eaten from the Tree of the Knowledge of Good and Evil.

But when you understand that the Garden of Eden represents an aethereal realm and not a location that might be found in the world, the punishments received by Adam, Eve, and the serpent make sense, for they are the consequences of being bound by their respective mortal forms having chosen to undergo incarnation within flesh. God did not lie to Adam and Eve by saying that they would die upon eating the fruit of the Tree of the Knowledge of Good and Evil, and nor was the serpent telling them the truth by saying that they would not. To understand why you must be aware of the multiple meanings of the word "death" within the biblical texts.

In the Gospel of Matthew, a disciple, though eager to follow Yeshua, asked that he first be allowed to attend the funeral of his father, to which Yeshua responded in Matthew 8:22 by saying, "Follow me, and leave the dead to bury the dead." The second instance of the word "dead" in that statement obviously refers to the corpse of the disciple's father, but the first instance refers to the ones burying the corpse. This is because, throughout the biblical texts, there are three kinds of death: the physical death that all souls are familiar with, the "dying to self" that is the transcending of egoic identity described within the previous chapter, and the spiritual death that is to lose one's relationship with God. It is this latter meaning that Yeshua is referring to in saying that those burying the corpse are dead—they are spiritually dead because they do not know God. There is an echo of this meaning in modern parlance: if a soul describes another as being "dead" to them, it means that they no longer desire to have any form of relationship with them. It is precisely that form of death that God was referring to when He warned Adam and Eve not to eat from the Tree of the Knowledge of Good and Evil, and it was precisely that form of death that Adam and Eve endured, for to be cast from the Garden of Eden and incarnated into mortal form is to lose one's relationship with God through the process of conditioning that I described within the previous chapter.

Of course, what I have just presented you with is nothing more than my interpretation of a particular biblical narrative, and while I could expound upon even more of its details and argue at length that my interpretation makes more sense than any other, there is no need, for beyond how convincing you may or may not find my explanations, you ultimately have no reason to accept my interpretation as being accurate. This is fine, for is enough that you know what my interpretation is.

The material realm, as well as being the realm of change and therefore time, is also a realm of duality—up and down, left and right, hot and cold, pain and pleasure, good and evil, and so on. These dualities do not present only two possible positions, but rather a variety of positions upon a spectrum between two opposing poles. Because matter is subject to duality in this way, the mortal forms that souls find themselves within having incarnated into the material realm are also subject to it, with the division of male and female being the most obvious example of such a duality.

As a soul undergoes conditioning it is increasingly exposed to duality in its many manifestations and its developing personhood will gravitate towards different poles within those dualities, thereby adding to its list of attributes. Order and chaos, quiet and loud, political right and political left, and introverted and extroverted are just some random examples of the dualities that personhood will be inclined towards the different poles of. But because the inclination towards the different poles within such dualities emerges from personhood, it is inevitable that the one that transcends all egoic identity and comes to know their true nature as Spirit will be free of the grip of duality, even while still being exposed to it. The story of Adam and Eve demonstrates that this is possible, for although the Tree of the Knowledge of Good and Evil is symbolic of the decision to enter into stark duality here within the material realm, duality necessarily already existed within the Garden of Eden itself, for the moment that there is more than one of anything, there is duality. Therefore, duality is inherent to the very act of creation, something that is hugely significant in regards to the purpose of creation, as will be explored within chapter eleven. The important point is that it is only the conscious awareness of God through direct experience of the Spirit that enables us to resist the pull of duality if, unlike Adam and Eve, we ultimately choose to do so.

Sensitivity to the detrimental effects of the opposing poles within dualities of all kinds is the reason that mystics have sometimes talked of the poles of dualities ultimately being the same. And so, it has been said (much to the confusion of most), that pleasure and pain are the same thing. This is because, while the former is certainly experienced as positive and the latter as negative, both represent poles of a duality and therefore both will experientially take a soul away from its balanced equanimity as Spirit. Mystics have been known to make statements that imply that they are indifferent even to good and evil, something that seems appalling to most souls. Let me be clear that the outrage that souls feel in the face of evil is not some kind of dysfunction. On the contrary, the fact that it is felt tells us something about God's own disposition towards that which we call "evil", for it is the conscience itself that is troubled when we behold evil. But mystics also understand that, although not the source of evil, God uses the evil enacted by lost souls towards His own ends. To fully elaborate upon that issue now would be premature, but it is not that mystics would have you believe that you might as well commit acts of evil as acts of good, it is that they have the insight and wisdom to understand good and evil in a way that allows them to retain their peace. Most importantly, they recognise that, as is the case with the poles of most dualities, becoming focused upon and emotionally invested in the presence of either good or evil will rob them of their equanimity while doing nothing to alter the realities of either good or evil.

However, there is a unique duality the experience of which was perfectly expressed by Yeshua himself when, in the synoptic gospels, he prayed to God in the Garden of Gethsemane immediately before his arrest and crucifixion: in Matthew 26:39, Yeshua said to God, "My Father, if it be possible, let this cup pass from me. Nevertheless, not as I will, but as you will." Yeshua knew that it was the will of God that he be crucified—that was the "cup" that he was to drink from. Yet in his personhood, Yeshua most certainly did not want to die such a torturous death. Even so, he demonstrated true virtue by surrendering his egoic will to obey God. It was soon afterwards in Matthew 26:41 that he uttered a famous statement that succinctly illustrates the dilemma that this duality highlights: "the Spirit is willing, but the flesh is weak." The duality in view is experienced by all souls that live in mortal form, most commonly in the decision that they face to either obey the voice of their conscience—the voice of God—or to do that which will be of practical benefit to them. What makes this duality unique is that we must always make the choice to gravitate towards one particular pole—the Spirit, for it alone is perfect, and it is the means by which we return to the paradise represented by the Garden of Eden. In this way, we are all Yeshua in the Garden of Gethsemane every single day.

Within the next three chapters I will be focussing upon subject matter that, while still relevant to your direct experience, will not require you to engage in any specific activities. This is therefore a good time for you to reflect upon all that you have read thus far. Despite elaborating upon some of the highest subjects, have I asked you to

57

accept anything without evidence or to speculate about abstract matters? No. Rather, I have pointed to common phenomenon, explained its true significance, and recommended practices that will allow you to experientially verify whatever claims I have made. This book will continue in that fashion, but until you actually do verify all that I have said, my words will be of no spiritual worth to you.

Chapter Four: Matter

Matter is the lowest substance that is to be found within creation, and therefore the material realm is in essence the lowest of all of the realms, though the mental and aethereal realms can be experienced as far worse. Few souls need any convincing of the deficiencies of the material realm, and no soul would need any convincing of the deficiencies of their own material bodies, for such deficiencies become apparent very early on in a soul's mortal sojourn. However, it is the suffering that results from these deficiencies that can trouble souls, especially in light of God, for they cannot reconcile the presence of such suffering with the existence of a God that is said to be both infinitely benevolent and all powerful.

Mortal Life and Suffering

> Yeshua said, "I took my place in the midst of the world and I manifested to them in flesh. I found all of them intoxicated and none of them thirsty. My soul became afflicted for the sons of men, for they are blind in their hearts and do not have sight. Empty they came into the world, and empty still they seek to leave it. For now they are intoxicated. When they shake off their wine, then they will repent."
>
> - The Gospel of Thomas, Saying 28

All mortal life is driven by its physical instincts to ensure its own survival and that of its offspring. Human beings are no exception to this, for they are one more form of mammal. Because of this, human behaviour is every bit as predictable as that of any other mammal, though this is no longer true when the soul indwelling a human being remembers its divine origin, for from that point forth its motivations are

59

supernatural and not natural. The human being has proven itself to be a highly effective creature in material terms, for it has come to dominate all other forms of mortal life.

What has truly given human beings the ability to dominate in this way is not just the form of the human vessel, but also the cognitive capacity of that vessel, which has allowed humans to innovate and overcome their physical limitations through technology. This has left animal life increasingly at the mercy of human beings. But the soul that has remembered its divine origin will not abuse their dominance over animal life—you can be certain that the soul that is neglectful or cruel towards animal life will inevitably be neglectful or cruel towards human life, and such callousness is a sure sign that a soul dwells within the deepest ignorance. There is a powerful statement within the Gnostic Gospel of Truth that describes certain souls as being "creatures of forgetfulness who will die as such." The Gospel of Truth is a Valentinian text said to have been written by Valentinus himself (the founder of the Valentinian sect). Although in context he was not referring specifically to those that are cruel to animals, there is nonetheless no better description of their status.

As to the often asked question, "Do animals have souls?", the answer is that they are Spirit and are therefore souls that have aethereal forms, having been part of God's initial aethereal creation. Having aethereal forms, animals experience emotions, but because they never develop the cognitive capacity to acquire conditioning, the souls within them never become lost within any form of egoic identity. Animals are therefore never ensnared within the cycle of physical reincarnation that results from a soul having failed to remember its true nature.

The truth of our unity in Spirit with even animal life manifests itself in many subtle ways that run contrary to purely materialistic assumptions. For example, souls are often more distraught at the suffering and death of animals than that of humans, and while this is a phenomenon that has often been met with disgust (being perceived as a sign of inverted morality), it is actually virtuous. This is because, being Spirit and yet not having the cognitive capacity to contemplate themselves, animals share the exact same innocence as children. This is why, like children, animals can often perceive aethereal phenomenon in the world around them that a conditioned soul simply cannot. The difference between animals and humans is that animals always retain that innocence and all that comes with it. Therefore, not only is it natural for the suffering and death of such beings to affect a soul more powerfully than the suffering and death of many fully developed human beings, there would be something amiss if it did not.

Contrary to souls in human form being divinely licenced to enslave other mortal beings, they instead have a sacred duty of care towards them, and this is especially true of those that, through the process of remembrance, have come to recognise that all life shares the same Spirit, for one can be more easily forgiven for wrongdoing having acted in ignorance. Most of us do not have the influence to effect widespread change as far as animal welfare is concerned, but it is good for those of you with pets or livestock to remember that those mortal forms have a considerably shorter lifespan than you do, and that while their mortal existence will ultimately be a short-lived phenomenon within your own, your existence is everything to them. Whatever treatment you bestow upon them will almost certainly be the only treatment that those souls will ever know within mortal form, so be sure to treat them well.

However, any soul that would choose to read a book of this nature almost certainly already has a profound empathy with animal life, and if anything is far more likely to resent human life for the destruction that it has wrought upon the natural world. Such resentment is understandable from a certain perspective, but ultimately not justifiable, and it will only hinder your remembrance. Everything within reality serves a particular function, and this is just as true of human beings, regardless of how lost the souls dwelling within them become.

Having said that, if you assume that human life is valuable in and of itself, then the history of the world thus far cannot reasonably be seen as anything other than a great tragedy, for it is obvious that not only do humans display a cruel disregard for other humans, reality itself seems to be utterly callous towards them.

Human beings of every age suffer and die in terrible and apparently meaningless ways every single day all over the world. From an anthropocentric perspective, such human beings have been cruelly robbed. It is little wonder then that so many souls come to doubt the character or even the existence of God; many fall away into apathy and nihilism, and even those that profess a belief in God will often describe their faith as being "tested". Because all material things are subject to change, all material things will pass away. Those periods of time most cherished by a soul will pass into memory, which itself will inevitably deteriorate. The strength that a soul experiences during its mortal youth will give way to frailty, and the mortal forms of beloved souls may come to endure great suffering, and will inevitably perish.

You may also recognise the transitory nature of matter on a greater scale by observing the way in which the world operates in cycles of numerous kinds. As surely as a human being in its prime will inevitably age and deteriorate if its life is not cut short, so too does every great civilization that arises eventually degenerate and disappear, if it does not collapse due to internal or external strife beforehand. The same great debates that are now had within great halls have been had in many other great halls throughout history, and they will be had again by souls that have likewise long forgotten any lessons that were learned by previous generations. If a soul comes to recognise such things while still fully identifying as a human being, despair is often the outcome, and understandably so, for the obvious impermanence and apparent futility of the material realm is necessarily of deepest consequence to the one that believes it to constitute the whole of reality. To merely hope that there is something more than material reality or to simply assume a comforting belief to the same effect will never enable you to escape that despair, for hope and belief alone cannot bring certainty.

As stated within the second chapter, souls that are still bound by a human centred personhood will invariably seek to understand reality from an anthropocentric perspective. Believing themselves to be human, they will assume that human life is important for its own sake and that humans are collectively working towards a better future that may ultimately result in some manner of utopia. If the souls within cats had the physical capacity to contemplate such things, they would make similar assumptions about themselves, and they would be just as wrong.

It is when you recognise that human beings exist only to serve as vessels for souls that you can begin to make sense of the suffering that characterises human existence, and it is then that you can begin to perceive purpose in the repetitive cycles that can be observed on both an individual and on a civilizational level.

The same change that cause periods of happiness to be lost in time also prevents mistakes and their consequences from lingering. The same change that causes a soul's mortal form to weaken with age also brings strength to those mortal forms that are developing. And the same change that brings the destruction of one soul's mortal form will also bring life to that of another. It is no great observation that the material realm can only continue to function because of this duality, for the survival of both the natural world and human civilization depend upon such a balance.

Spirit descends into the material realm and forgets itself by identifying with personhood so that it might know the experience of doing so, and then the experience of ultimately transcending all egoic identity and remembering its true nature and origin. Spirit comes to play, and therefore souls will be enamoured with the world for a time, but it is precisely the deficiency of matter—that which from a human perspective is negative—that will eventually lead those souls to seek the Spirit, for there is nothing that brings about a greater desire for change than the experience of suffering. Sometimes ancient Gnostic groups would describe the accumulation of conditioning and the transcending of it as "forgetting" and "remembering" just as I do, but at other times they would instead compare the accumulation of worldly conditioning to becoming drunk and the transcending of that conditioning to becoming sober again, as in the saying from the Gospel of Thomas that opened this section.

It is suffering that ultimately brings about the calling and awakening that initiate remembrance. This is because, in its various forms, suffering weakens a soul's identification with egoic identity by exposing its flaws to that soul: physical suffering is pain, and it reveals to us the frailty and fallibility of our mortal forms; mental suffering is psychic anguish, and it demonstrates the utter folly of the way that we were conditioned to understand ourselves, and our ultimate inability to control even our own thought patterns; aethereal suffering is emotional turmoil, and it is that which proves to us that no matter how physically or intellectually capable we may be, we can be rendered functionally useless by feelings that are seemingly beyond our control. It is because suffering is that which will free a soul from its delusions that so many spiritual awakenings occur during particularly testing periods in a soul's experience—suffering has finally caused their egoic identity to crack, allowing the light of grace to shine through and provide the soul with a miraculous opportunity to begin the journey of remembrance. A degenerated understanding of this truth is what lies behind so many ascetic practices within religious traditions that involve inflicting pain upon one's own mortal form. Such practices are utterly useless in terms of spiritual development because the suffering that they bring carries with it no lessons, except perhaps the lesson that mutilating oneself achieves nothing. It would be best to heed what I have said and avoid having to learn that particular lesson.

From an anthropocentric perspective, it seems grossly unfair that one human being should be born into poverty and have to toil for all of its life while another is born into extreme wealth and never have to work even a single day. In truth, it is the same Spirit—the same consciousness—that is undergoing every experience that human beings have. Therefore, there is nobody that is being short-changed—there are merely different souls undergoing different human experiences depending upon the kind of lessons that they have yet to learn before they can embark upon the journey of remembrance.

The material realm can never be perfect because it is material and is therefore deficient by its very nature. But if the material realm could be perfect then souls would certainly be trapped within it, for without the suffering that comes from the experience of deficiency they would have no reason to search for something greater. In this way, the material realm, while not experientially perfect, is functionally perfect, for it perfectly fulfils its purpose in enabling souls to experience its stark dualities while also ensuring that they will not do so indefinitely.

Counterfeit Spirituality

If with Mashiach you died to the elemental spirits of the world, why, as if you were still alive in the world, do you submit to regulations—"Do not handle, do not taste, do not touch," referring to things that all perish with use— according to human commands and teachings? These indeed have an appearance of wisdom in promoting self-made religion and asceticism and severity to the body, but they are of no value in stopping the indulgence of the flesh. If then you have been raised with Mashiach, seek the things that are above, where Mashiach is, seated at the right hand of God. Set your mind on things that are above, not on things that are on the earth.

- The Apostle Paul, The Epistle to the Colossians 2:20-3:2

The word "idolatry" is often taken to refer only to the literal worship of physical idols that represent deities other than the one true God, but within the Abrahamic traditions, idolatry is the act of venerating anything that is not God as though it were God (including that which was intended to depict God), whether or not it is a physical idol. I alluded to this within the very first chapter when I emphasised the importance of distinguishing between matter, mind, aether, and Spirit.

A major source of conflict between Christianity and Islam is that, while most Christians believe Yeshua to be God, the second person of a triune being, Muslims identify him as being another human prophet of God, and so from an Islamic perspective, most Christians are guilty of idolatry by worshipping Yeshua as God. Within Islam, idolatry is known as "shirk", and it is the one sin that is unforgivable. Therefore, this theological divide cannot easily be bridged. The one unforgivable sin within Christianity is known as "blasphemy of the Holy Spirit", and it could be considered a compliment of shirk, for to blaspheme the Holy Spirit means to attribute the activity of the Spirit to evil forces.

Unfortunately, most religionists have an extremely crude understanding of the ways in which souls engage in idolatry, and they are usually entirely incapable of explaining why it is wrong, besides uselessly asserting that the jealous and petty god that they imagine exists is angered by it. Because religionists only recognise idolatry in its most obvious forms, they themselves unwittingly engage in it.

Idolatry always arises from mistaking material, mental, or aethereal phenomenon to be the highest manifestation of Spirit and engaging with it as such, but some forms of idolatry are more subtle than others. The religionist that esteems their ideas about God as if they encapsulate God is effectively making them God and is therefore committing idolatry as surely as anyone that bows down to a stone idol, and most religionists do that very thing. The ancient Gnostics always used terms like "Living Father", "Living One", and "Living Christ" to emphasise that the spiritual realities that they wrote of were alive and active, unlike the intellectual constructs that theologians conjure within their minds and codify in doctrines. You will have already seen several instances of such terms within the excerpts from the Gospel of Thomas that I have utilised thus far.

The reason that idolatry is so dangerous is not because God is so petty as to be angered by it, but because for as long as you identify matter, mind, or aether as being the highest manifestation of reality, you will not seek for anything beyond it. Likewise, if one interprets spiritual forces as evil, thereby committing "blasphemy of the Holy Spirit", one would certainly shun those forces, and in this way also make remembrance impossible. This is why the ancients, in keeping with their anthropomorphising of God as a zealous judge, deemed both of these errors to be unforgivable—it was their way of illustrating that they would keep a soul from the presence God indefinitely until repented of, which is to say, until that soul recognised their error and corrected their approach accordingly.

Due to the ways in which idolatry is misunderstood, I refer to it using the term "counterfeit spirituality", the meaning of which is far less ambiguous to the modern mind. There are two primary forms of material counterfeit spirituality, and the first is the most crude form of worshipping the natural world, or the products of the natural world, as though they are the highest manifestation of reality.

There is nothing wrong with having reverence for the natural world—I myself very much enjoy being close to nature, and there is so much that we can learn from it regarding how best to live in the material realm that entire books can and have been written on the subject. But this book is not one of them, and the problem, as stated, is that if a soul takes the material realm to be Spirit (the ultimate manifestation of reality) then they will not seek for anything beyond the material realm. Therefore, have respect for the natural world, but do not lose sight of the fact that Spirit transcends it. There is more to say regarding the Spirit and the natural world, but it would be premature to do so at the current time.

The second of the material counterfeit spiritualities is the belief that bloodlines, whether they be familial or that of a larger collective, are in some way innately superior to others in spiritual terms. This notion, while relatively rare in the modern world, can still be found in many forms. Within the western world, it is most commonly found within "neo-pagan" and "heathen" movements, the entire "spirituality" of which is often centred around a national, ethnic, or racial collective. There is no denying that in worldly terms it makes sense to prioritise one's own tribe, whether it be one's family, nation, or anything else, for the tribe that does not demonstrate preference for its own interests will certainly lose out to those that do. Any mythology or idea that helps convince that tribe of its own superiority will therefore be hugely beneficial to it in practical terms. It is also true that, like individual souls, larger collectives have a specific part to play in the great drama of worldly life. But this is just another example of how worldly wisdom almost always runs contrary to spiritual wisdom.

For the individual soul, matters of tribal identity relate to egoic identity and are therefore not only useless for the one that seeks to undergo remembrance, but detrimental if there remains great attachment to them. You should appreciate where your mortal form comes from, for it is unique to you, but as with reverence of the natural world, you must not become enamoured with it, thereby blinding yourself to the transcendent.

Renouncement

> Yeshua said, "The heavens and the earth will be rolled up
> in your presence, and the one who lives from the Living
> One will not see death." Does not Yeshua say, "He who
> finds himself is greater than the world"?
>
> - The Gospel of Thomas, Saying 111

Renouncement is something that features prominently within the history of every great spiritual tradition, and there are two forms of renouncement: there is the outer renouncement that involves physical isolation from the world, and then there is the inner renouncement that involves the retraction of one's focus from external phenomenon as described within the previous chapter.

Outer renouncement in the form of abandoning civilization to live alone in the wilderness is something that almost every mystic desires, but few are actually called to, for having come to know the Spirit, they are then obliged to make it known to others, and this responsibility keeps them within civilization. However, every great mystic had an extended period in isolation. For example, Yeshua was led into the wilderness by the Spirit for forty days, and when he returned and began his ministry, he would continue to ensure that he spent much time alone with God, rising early in the morning to visit a desolate place. If Yeshua, experientially aware of his unity with God, still needed that time of communion with Him, then you that are not yet experientially aware of God most certainly do.

The soul that has come to recognise its unity with God has no need to hide from the things of the world, for they recognise themselves as infinitely more powerful. This is why spiritual masters like Yeshua did not hesitate to interact with those that were still enamoured with the world in order to share the truth with them. More than that, you must learn to appreciate the function of every soul as it exists in mortal form. God has ensured that few in any generation are called to become mystics, for civilization could not function otherwise. And so while a focus on material affairs almost exclusively is indicative of a soul in a

68

state of spiritual development comparable to human infancy, they are still nonetheless still playing just as essential a role in the world as the mystic, and the one that undergoes remembrance must always be conscious of this and remain humble. One activity that I enjoy is free climbing, and if I were to one day fall from the side of a cliff and break my back upon the rocks below, it would not be a team of mystics that came to my rescue.

Many of the statements that sacred texts make concerning inner renouncement can often be mistaken for statements relating to outer renouncement, and this is especially true when it comes to Yeshua's teachings concerning material possessions. The best known of Yeshua's statements on the subject of wealth came when, in Matthew 19:24, he said, "It is easier for a camel to pass through the eye of a needle than for a rich man to enter the Kingdom of Heaven." What lesson are you meant to derive from such statements? That God frowns upon souls that acquire great wealth, thereby making wealth itself evil? No. The point is that the more wealth a soul has, the more that there is to distract them from seeking God. Therefore, it is very difficult for them to enter the Kingdom of Heaven. And so, although from a human perspective to be born into less wealthy circumstances is to be born into misfortune, from a spiritual perspective, it could be most auspicious. If you consider the matter, you can easily imagine how much easier your own spiritual progression might have been without so many material luxuries being there to distract you from it.

Mystics will invariably be relatively poor, materially speaking, due to their focus on spiritual affairs, yet if wealth should come, there is nothing inherently wrong with that provided that the mystic does not misplace their focus as a consequence, and I say that as one that is always likely to be poor by modern, western standards. But while outer renouncement of the world is something that only a few are ultimately called to, inner renouncement is mandatory for any soul that would undergo remembrance, for it is the disentanglement of one's focus from external phenomenon. Now is the time for you to understand the full scope of this renouncement.

I have seen many souls fall away from the path of remembrance, and the vast majority of them do so because their investment in some aspect of the material realm proves too strong. Most often, they are unable to detach from their political concerns and, having become unduly invested in those affairs, their desire to argue for what they see as the correct perspective overwhelms their desire to know God. Therefore, where once they restrained their lower impulses, being focussed upon knowing the Spirit, they began to indulge those lower impulses, feeling fully justified in doing so.

There are undoubtedly many worldly affairs that you take to be of the utmost importance; it may even be that those matters really are of the utmost importance in worldly terms. The question is, will you be one that is focussed upon worldly affairs, or will you be one that seeks to know God? You cannot be both, for as Yeshua said in Matthew 6:24, "Nobody can serve two masters, for either he will hate the one and love the other, or he will be devoted to the one and despise the other."

The great spiritual masters have always been unanimous in teaching that being enamoured with worldly affairs is detrimental to one's spirituality. Yeshua himself could not have been more plain on the subject when, in John 18:36, he said, "My Kingdom is not of this world. If my Kingdom were of this world, then my servants would have been fighting, so that I might not be delivered over to the Jews. But my Kingdom is not from this world." There were few mystics that emphasised this point as strenuously as Yeshua. If you were to search the gospels, canonical or non-canonical (contained within the Bible or not), you would find Yeshua having said in dozens of different ways that one must renounce worldly concerns, and not a single statement to the contrary. It is a sad irony then that the name of no other spiritual master has been so misused in order to further worldly agendas.

You are perfectly at liberty to disregard the testimony of every spiritual master that ever lived and behave in as worldly a fashion as anyone else in pursuit of your material goals, but do not deceive yourself into believing that you are on any kind of spiritual quest as you do so. At least have the decency to not evoke the names of the great spiritual masters during your worldly pursuits having ignored their clear teachings. They did not care about worldly affairs during their mortal incarnations, so it is the height of arrogance to suppose that they would take an interest in your petty material concerns now that they are free in and as the Spirit. In many cases, in order to justify themselves, those souls that become enamoured with worldly affairs will accuse those that are not of being negligent. Statements like "you may not care about politics, but politics cares about you" are commonly uttered. Yet such statements only reveal how spiritually ignorant the souls that make them truly are. Of course I understand that as a soul living in human form I am impacted by what goes on in the world, but what they do not understand, being ignorant of the Spirit, is how utterly trivial their worldly concerns are by comparison to the majesty of God.

Those souls that become invested in worldly agendas consider themselves strong, when in fact they are weak, for it is fear and faithlessness that causes them to turn from the spiritual path to become enamoured with the world once more; they fear for the well-being of their flesh and do not have faith enough to trust that everything happens according to the will of God. Make no mistake, all that such souls have done is scumble to the most base of temptations, and having done so, they will twist anything, even their own sacred texts that warn them against what they are doing, to justify themselves. They want to present themselves as spiritual souls while also having the exact same worldly concerns as everyone else. Be assured that when you choose to prioritise worldly affairs above God, you reject your calling, and the only destiny in store for you from that point forth is the suffering required to bring you into a recognition of your folly. It is easy to perceive the ways in which souls that focus on worldly matters having overtly reject the spiritual have gone astray, but never be so gullible as to believe that a soul likewise focussing on worldly matters is any different because they happen to be evoking the name of a spiritual master at the same time. It is actually worse, because it necessarily involves considerable pretence and hypocrisy.

The last thing that the world and the souls in it need is one more ideologue providing simplistic answers to highly complicated issues. Such ideologues are themselves the source of the vast majority of the problems that consistently blight the world. If the world needs anything at all, it is souls that have surrendered their egoic desires to know themselves, and that having done so, live in accordance with the will of God.

Understand that every soul gravitates towards one pole of each duality within their personhood, and therefore every soul has opinions about all manner of worldly affairs. There is something in the world that is hateful to almost every soul and that tempts them to become embroiled in controversy, but not every soul indulges themselves in this way— some exercise restraint for a higher purpose. I am not suggesting that you should never have an opinion on worldly matters, for historical mystics certainly did, and indeed, your conscience may well lead you to take a particular stance and to advocate it; the problem arises when you become intellectually and emotionally entangled with the subject and so begin to prioritise it over God.

Contrary to being brave, becoming enamoured with worldly concerns to the point that everything else ceases to matter is the easiest thing that any soul can do. But not only will scumbling to such a temptation be detrimental to your remembrance, it will also taint any effort that you make towards sharing whatever insights you may have gained with others, for when you are zealous concerning a worldly affair, you naturally set yourself up in opposition to those that have taken a different stance. If you have a position, it is best to state it and let others freely agree or disagree as they may. Demonstrating a sense of humour can help to ease tensions when strong disagreements exist.

There are some that attempt to discern a soul's political persuasion and overall worldview by observing those that the soul interacts with, but to do so with me is utterly impossible precisely because I interact with souls of all manner of political persuasions and that belong to every kind of collective that you can imagine. For me, a soul's worldly attachments (including their religious attachments) are as the biblical "dirty rags" that I overlook in order to engage with them, knowing that they are the same Spirit that I am, regardless of how oblivious they are to that fact. If I was prejudiced against souls due to their worldly inclinations, I could not effectively speak truth to them. Therefore, eschewing worldly attachment is as important to me as eschewing pork is to the adherents of the Jewish and Islamic religions.

To some of you, the renouncement of worldly concerns will seem like an impossible task, and I can tell you that in the beginning it was not easy for me either, for be under no illusion, in my personhood I am more opinionated than most on worldly affairs. In former times I would not hesitate to respond in as harsh a fashion as I felt necessary

72

when another soul shared an opinion on worldly affairs that I found disagreeable. But I began to stop myself, withdrawing my focus from such affairs to the glory of God. In time, I no longer felt constrained by doing so, but rather liberated—I was liberated from being so intellectually and emotionally entangled in so many worldly matters, the vast majority of which would never have a direct bearing on my mortal life anyway. It is far wiser to be able to engage with any soul because you no longer have artificial barriers raised against them. Of course, there are souls that will assume all manner of things about you regardless, as well as souls that will be hostile no matter what, but in such cases the problem lies with them and so does not concern me.

There is a saying in the Gospel of Thomas that addresses this issue of worldly investment beautifully: in saying forty-two, Yeshua simply said, "Be passers-by." This means that one should regard the world as though it were a town that one were passing through; if you were passing through a town, while you might have opinions on what you see and may even voice those opinions, you would not stop to interfere in the local politics, for you would know that you were only visiting very briefly.

Reincarnation and Karma

> "Come to terms quickly with your accuser while you are going with him to court, lest your accuser hand you over to the judge, and the judge to the guard, and you be put in prison. Truly, I say to you, you will never get out until you have paid the last penny."
>
> - Yeshua, The Gospel According to Matthew 5:25,26

This book would seem incomplete if I did not address the exoteric understanding of reincarnation, which is to say, the transfer of the soul to a new mortal form after the death of its previous mortal form. Of all the many subjects that I have addressed and will address within this

73

book, the exoteric understanding of reincarnation is the most difficult to substantiate through experiential spirituality. In every other case, I can simply point to a common experience or tell you of a particular practice that will enable you to experientially verify what I am saying, but the reality of reincarnation can only be confirmed by the one that has already attained rest. However, not only does that fact not trouble me, I am actually very grateful that it is so.

In the very first chapter I said that I was mostly asked "weak questions", which are questions that have nothing to do with a soul's immediate experience—which is the focus of experiential spirituality. Many of those weak questions relate to the exoteric understanding of reincarnation in some way, and so while the subject will be highly intriguing to most of you, to me it is a huge distraction from those matters that are of far greater importance. Not only does physical reincarnation not make any difference to your immediate experience of reality, it is also not something that you would want to be distracted by whether it did or whether it did not in fact occur. If those that fail to attain rest are indeed subject to a cycle of physical rebirth, then you will only escape it by making the best use of your present experience in order to enter into that rest; if there is in fact no cycle of physical rebirth for any soul, then you must still make the best use of your present experience, because it is the only one that you will ever have here in the material realm.

But while physical reincarnation is simply beyond your ability to immediately confirm, I will nonetheless matter of factly explain how it works and why the cycle of material rebirth is indeed a reality, for without such an explanation a degree of uncertainty will remain concerning separate, but related issues. In giving such an explanation I am trusting you to be mindful of the fact that you cannot verify my words, and to remain grounded in what your immediate experience teaches you.

Souls are incarnated within human form to experience the stark duality and extreme limitations that are found only within the material realm, but having forgotten their true nature and origin through the process of conditioning into egoic identity, they are unable to return from whence they came upon the death of their human form, and are instead drawn to whatever aethereal realm is appropriate for them.

Physical reincarnation occurs because, having become lost within worldly conditioning and enamoured with the material realm, souls will be drawn back here repeatedly until they learn to overcome that conditioning through the transcendence of all egoic identity. But note that it is not physical addiction that will draw a disembodied soul back to the material realm, for they no longer have the body that was so addicted. Rather, it is mental and emotional addiction to material experience, and here again you can see why inner renouncement is of the utmost importance. If souls were not reborn within the material realm, then they would remain forever trapped in whatever aethereal realm they went to after the death of their first human vessel.

The mind retains all memory of a soul's previous incarnations within the material realm, but as with memories of aethereal realms, while they may still be accessible to a soul in the infancy of its mortal form, conditioning will soon cause them to be forgotten. Even so, the focus that a soul had within previous incarnations will manifest in the form of innate inclinations and abilities. It is why, for example, souls such as myself have an interest in the spiritual from childhood despite our secular upbringing, while others will live the entirety of their mortal lives without concerning themselves with such matters. But those souls that do concern themselves with spiritual matters have a habit of becoming distracted from remembrance by speculation concerning the details of their former mortal incarnations, which is ironic because the only way to be able to recall past incarnations is through the very process of remembrance that they neglect on account of those past incarnations.

Physical reincarnation also serves justice, for from a human perspective, it seems that people so often die never having had to account for their wrongdoing in life. In reality, no soul can ever escape the consequences of their wrongdoing. This is the significance of the excerpt from the Gospel of Matthew that opened this section: Yeshua was using a judge to represent himself and "prison" as a metaphor for life here in the material realm, his point being that, despite how things may seem from a human perspective, justice will ultimately be served. A soul's mental body will exhibit whatever strengths and weaknesses it had developed within previous incarnations, their aethereal body will retain emotional dispositions, and the form of their physical body can be shaped by their actions within those former sojourns. Although that latter fact has often been construed as a form of punishment, it actually occurs in order to teach a soul the lessons that it still has to learn before it can embark upon remembrance—the "prison" referenced within Yeshua's allegory is a place of rehabilitation, not punishment.

The concept of "karma" is strongly associated with this aspect of physical reincarnation, but many souls understand "karma" to mean that the exact wrongdoing that one soul inflicts upon another will in turn be inflicted upon them within their current mortal lifetime or within their next. In fact, "karma" is a Sanskrit term that simply means "action", and it refers to nothing more than cause and effect, whether it is cause and effect in material, mental, or aethereal terms. Therefore, the fact that you will get hungry if you do not eat food is just as much an example of karma as the fact that a soul's physical body can be shaped by their actions within former mortal incarnations. This is why there is also such a thing as "collective karma", whether that collective be a family, a political party, a religion, a nation, or a civilization.

While karma is not something that is associated with the Abrahamic religions, and is in fact often thought to be contrary to their outlook, when the concept is properly understood it is obvious that, far from being contrary to the outlook of the Abrahamic religions, it is actually innate to it. The apostle Paul wrote in Galatians 6:7, "Do not be deceived: God is not mocked, for whatever one sows, that he will also reap." This is a sentiment that you will find repeated many times within the primary sacred texts of the three Abrahamic religions, and you could hardly ask for a more succinct description of karma.

Chapter Five: Mind

If an emphasis on material matters is indicative of a soul in a state of spiritual development comparable to mortal infancy, then an emphasis on mental matters is indicative of a soul in a state of spiritual development comparable to mortal adolescence, and whereas everyone that would seek to learn from a book of this nature will have developed beyond infancy, almost all of you will still be in this state of adolescence. This is nothing to be ashamed of—no more than being a physical adolescent is; there were many that remembered the truth before me, and there will be many that remember the truth after you. But if you are to transcend the mind, then you must first understand the mind.

The Deficiency of Mind

> Do not be conformed to this world, but be transformed by the renewal of your mind, that by testing you may discern what is the will of God, what is good and acceptable and perfect.

> - The Apostle Paul, The Epistle to the Romans 12:2

The mind is widely revered as the most wondrous, mysterious, and powerful tool that mankind has at its disposal, while simultaneously being widely recognised as the greatest single source of suffering for souls. There are few subjects around which there is more confusion than that of the mind.

The mind is so often credited with abilities that it is actually incapable of. For example, souls associate "psychic powers" almost exclusively with the mind, but while the information bestowed by these "psychic powers" is conveyed to the mind, it not bestowed by the mind, but by the Spirit, for it is through the Spirit that we are united with all other life. What most souls call "psychic power" is a soul hearing from the voice of God just as they do in the form of their conscience and intuition, the distinction being that the information received through "psychic powers" pertains to something beyond their immediate experience, but it still comes from the same source. However, the most important thing to recognise concerning the mind is the way in which it seeks to direct your focus towards negative phenomenon.

Those of you familiar with different spiritual traditions and teachers may be confused by the fact that some (usually those influenced by eastern thought) speak of the mind as if it is the highest manifestation of reality, whereas others like myself say that it is not. There is actually no contradiction between these outlooks: those that speak of the mind as being the highest manifestation of reality will nonetheless still acknowledge that it is a source of great suffering and will insist that it therefore must be refined. What I call an experience of "Spirit" is what they would understand as the experience of a refined mind, and so we are merely defining and understanding the same transcendent experience in different ways, an experience that is ultimately beyond definition. You will notice that we otherwise differ little on outlook. However, I will explain my use of the word "Spirit" to refer to something beyond the mind, for with my reasoning comes observations that are simple and yet powerful.

Any soul with a spiritual outlook that involves a belief in God rightly assumes God to be perfect and that His Spirit is therefore also perfect. Those that say that all of reality, including God, consists only of mind have a dilemma, for even in their own view most souls experience the mind as a source of great suffering, and that is why it needs to be refined. But to say that the perfect needs to be refined is a paradox. Therefore they must explain why the mind—that which to them is the highest manifestation of reality—would need correcting in the ways that they acknowledge that it does. They have their answers, of course —they will speak of different levels of mind, or of its imperfection being an intentional part of its perfection, but I feel that it is far more straightforward to understand the mind—and especially the conditioned mind—as something inferior to the Spirit that is consciousness. It is certainly far more consistent with direct spiritual experience, for none would ever undergo a transcendent experience and attribute it to the mind that they are familiar with unless they had already accepted a framework that encouraged them to do so. Indeed, mystics have always struggled to convey the understandings derived from such experiences to the mind; are we to believe that the mind is bestowing revelations of a nature that it cannot comprehend?

I hope that I have made the reason that I do not portray the mind as the highest manifestation of reality clear. I was reluctant to even address this issue, for I know that by doing so I risk confusing those unfamiliar with it, and when you address such highly complicated subjects so briefly there are inevitably going to be those that take issue with how you summarised the matter. Nonetheless, I have encountered enough souls that are confused about this apparent contradiction within the history of mystic thought to make me feel that it was worth giving at least a brief explanation of it. This also serves as a perfect example of how systems of belief can be different in terms of their outward form, and yet still be based upon the same transcendent experiences.

There have been those that, having recognised the obvious deficiency of the mind and the suffering that it brings, have gone so far as to personify it as an evil being. I do not share such a negative disposition towards the mind, for it is undeniably a wondrous tool that we cannot function in the world without, and although it is indeed a great source of suffering and delusion, even in that it is serving its purpose for reasons explained within the previous chapter.

Yet those that characterise the mind as though it were a separate and malevolent entity do not do so without justification, for as with the physical body, it can be observed that the mind operates according to its own rules, rules that are far more vague than those that govern the body. The mind is very much set upon its own course, and this is most easily perceived as your mortal form falls asleep, for during this transition you experience your awareness slipping away not just from the activity of the material realm, but also from the activity of the mental realm, which can be observed to be continuing without your input.

As stated, that which is perfect does not need to be refined, and nor can it be transcended, but the mind must certainly be transcended, otherwise its maelstrom of thoughts, concepts, and narratives will prove abrasive to our experience of reality. Just as the mortal body yearns for physical sustenance, so too the mind yearns for intellectual sustenance, and just as the mortal body will invariably grow hungry again, the mind is likewise never sated for long. If allowed to do so, it will lead a soul on a never ending journey to obtain new identities, ideas, beliefs, narratives, and problems. As Spirit, you are the eyes, and the mind is as an ever changing lens through which you perceive the phenomenal realities of the material and aethereal realms. The stream of intellectual constructs within the mind are comparable to dirt on that lens, and the more that you focus upon them, the less clearly that you can see reality as it truly is.

Why do you fear phenomenon? It is because the mind invents a fearful narrative concerning it. But the fearful effect of that narrative is dependent upon it speaking to that which has reason to fear. A human being has reason to fear much in the material realm and beyond, for it knows its own vulnerability. Therefore, fearful narratives within the mind must necessarily induce fear in the one yet bound in human centred personhood. Why do you desire endlessly? It is because, believing yourself to be a human being, you are obviously deficient in so many ways, and therefore the mind will insist that you seek out that which might supplement your existence, be it material gain, relationships with other souls, or intellectual understanding. Such ideas can only drive one that fully believes that they can be improved by acquiring such things. Why do you utter foolish statements? It is because you perceive yourself to be in a situation where your identity as a human being is threatened if you remain silent; a human being is a social creature that seeks to convey a particular idea of itself to other human beings so that they do not take it to be weak in any regard. Being poised with such a defence mechanism, the one that identifies as a human being will often utter whatever arises within the mind without due consideration of its merit or of the consequences of doing so.

These are just a few examples that illustrate the relationship between the egoic identity and other phenomenon that may arise within the mind. The mind has power over you precisely because of your erroneous identification as that which should heed it. Any form of egoic identity is an intellectual construct that itself resides within the mind, and you cannot overcome mental phenomenon if you are bound by another form of it. That which is deficient cannot be the solution to its own deficiency—the mind cannot refine the mind; only the Spirit that transcends it can do that.

In the excerpt from the Epistle to the Romans that opened this section, the apostle Paul (who naturally acknowledged the existence of the Spirit and its superiority to the mind) wrote of a "renewal" of the mind. This "renewal" occurs when a soul is liberated from egoic identity, for when a soul experientially recognises its nature as Spirit, it recognises the way in which it transcends the mind. This does not change the fundamental nature of the mind (although it will result in an increase in positive mental phenomenon), but rather it changes a soul's experience of the mind so that it may be more effectively utilised towards God's ends, as opposed to the ends of an egoic identity such as personhood.

Heaven and Hell

Yeshua said, "A vine has been planted outside of the Father, but being unstable, it will be pulled up by its roots and destroyed."

- The Gospel of Thomas, Saying 40

There is little that has preoccupied souls more than questions regarding what their fate will be when their mortal form perishes. Most spiritual traditions assert that those that have done what is right will receive some form of reward, whereas those that have done what is wrong will receive some form of punishment. It is the notion of an eternal bliss called "heaven" and an eternal torment called "hell" that has dominated Christian and Islamic thought historically.

Most souls have understood heaven and hell as places that one enters into only upon the death of the physical body. As a consequence, there are many theologies that assert that one's state of being and the deeds that follow from it are entirely irrelevant to one's fate in the afterlife. In this they are catastrophically mistaken; heaven and hell are

81

states of being that souls will enter into during their mortal lifetimes, and I will begin by expounding upon hell as a state of being.

You must distinguish between those souls that endure a brief hellish experience due to circumstance and those souls that enter into a continuous hellish experience as a consequence of their own folly. Egoic identity is the root cause of all hellish experiences, even those involving the most sympathetic soul. Consider a mother whose son dies —why does she suffer? It is because her motherhood is central to who she takes herself to be as a person and the son is essential to that identification. Therefore, the loss of the son deeply fractures that personhood, generating a profound feeling of loss. When, in such circumstances, souls say, "it feels like a piece of me has died", they have no idea just how right they are. In this way, when we mourn, we mourn for ourselves. I myself have not felt grief for many years, despite several relatives and friends having died during that time. That may seem strange and perhaps even abhorrent to you, but I have said that we are truly immortal Spirit and can never be anything else; if I really know that to be so as I claim, then why would I mourn for any human that dies? Consider the possibility that you have become so accustomed to inconsistency between the words and the behaviour of those that profess spiritual belief that you now perceive consistency as folly. But while there is no need to mourn for anyone, it is right that dead humans be honoured, for their particular expression of humanity was wholly unique and will never be repeated.

Regardless, souls do not at all like to hear that those suffering are in fact the cause of their own suffering, because they naturally have great sympathy for them, but do not let an emotional reaction to what may seem like an unpleasant proposition blind you to the obvious truth of it; it is easy to be sentimental and utter flowery rhetoric, but doing so does not help anyone. Speaking truth is hard, and yet it is truth that will set souls free from the anguish that they ultimately choose to endure by being attached to various forms of egoic identity. But while every soul will endure relatively brief hellish experiences at one time or another, a soul is only condemned to a continuous hell by consistently ignoring their conscience and by consistently dishonouring truth, because doing so results in them acting erroneously in a way that incurs karmic suffering. If a soul's physical form dies while they are in such a hellish state, then that state will thereafter be experienced as a hellish aethereal realm. Therefore, a soul's consistent state of being while they exist in mortal form is the greatest indicator of their destination after the death of their mortal form.

There are those that cite the works of Shakespeare as though they were sacred texts, such is the great wisdom and insight that can be derived from his words. *The Tragedy of Julius Caesar* and *The Tragedy of Macbeth* are my favourite of his plays, and the latter concerns the 11th century figures of Macbeth and his wife Lady Macbeth who plot to murder the king of Scotland so that Macbeth might take the crown. Although they succeed, Macbeth grows more brutal in his attempts to secure his power, while Lady Macbeth slowly descends into madness. During her breakdown in the first scene of act five, she utters the words "hell is murky", seemingly at random. It is not a statement that receives a great amount of attention, and yet it is amazingly profound, since there could hardly be a more fitting description of what it is to experience hell, for hell is anxiety, fear, doubt, and confusion. Recalling again my comparison of the mind to a lens through which our perception is filtered, understand that hell is "murky" because the minds of those in hell are clouded by so much negativity. They are unable to observe reality clearly because their perception is obscured by such phenomenon, and that phenomenon also provokes a host of negative emotions within their aethereal bodies.

You may feel pity for those enduring such suffering, but in many cases any attempt to help them will be met with an aggressive response, for despite their wretched condition, many such souls are fully convinced that there is no error in their approach to life, and they would remain so convinced even if the whole world were to tell them otherwise. It is such hubris that led many of them to where they are, and it is such hubris that will drive them deeper into that dark pit. As strange as it may seem, there is a perverse way in which some souls enjoy their suffering, because it has become central to their egoic identity; to lose that suffering would mean undermining the way in which they understand themselves. Their personhood, having assumed a mantle of victimhood, then seeks affirmations of that status which, while soothing to such an egoic identity, keep the soul in bondage to it.

However, here again we have an example of how even the most

negative experience is ultimately for our betterment, for no matter how central to a soul's identity a source of suffering is, they simply will not endure that suffering forever. In this lifetime or another, they will grow weary of it and seek the understandings that bring remembrance. Therefore, the wise will not allow their mind to superficially assess such suffering as being wholly negative.

Just as we must distinguish between those souls that endure a brief hellish experience due to circumstance and those souls that enter into a continuous hellish experience as a consequence of their own folly, so too must we distinguish between those souls that undergo a brief heavenly experience due to circumstance and those souls that enter into a continuous heavenly experience as a consequence of their wisdom. A soul that obeys their conscience and honours the truth will enter into a heavenly aethereal realm after the death of their physical body, but unless they have also transcended all egoic identity it will not be the true heaven.

While a soul remains bound by some form of egoic identity they are also bound by their mind, and regardless of how pleasant the state of that mind may be, it cannot take a soul to the true heaven because that state is of the mind. A mind well ordered with positive constructs, while preferable to the alternative, is always going to be vulnerable to being overturned by a change of external circumstances or increasingly negative mental activity. If a soul depends upon a pleasant state of affairs within the mind for their contentment, then it is only a matter of time before phenomenal reality shifts in a way that causes that pleasant state of affairs to crumble, at which point that soul will be cast out of their heaven once more. For as long as a soul remains bound in personhood or any other form of egoic identity, they are subject to their mind, whether it be positively or negatively.

Up until a major cache of documents was uncovered at Nag Hammadi, Egypt in 1945 (the find that resulted in the discovery of the mostly complete Coptic manuscript of the Gospel of Thomas), academics were almost entirely reliant upon the historical opponents of the Gnostics for their information about Gnosticism, information that there is good reason to doubt. For example, a 4th century Cyprian bishop known as Epiphanius of Salamis claimed that a Gnostic group called the Borborites drank the menstrual fluid of its female members and consumed foetuses with honey, pepper, and spices. You would struggle to find writings that exude as much zealous hatred as his do, so much so that it is hard to imagine anyone ever believing them to be trustworthy. But of course, there are plenty of Christian religionists even now that will cite them as if they are just that. This is of no surprise to me, because I have yet to encounter a Christian religionist that knows anything about the Gnostics beyond that which such blatant propaganda asserts, but they readily accept such obvious nonsense simply because it suits their primitive and spiritually bereft sectarian tribalism to do so.

Regardless, although it is difficult to speak of ancient Gnostic belief in absolute terms because Gnostic groups differed from one another in so many regards, many of them, informed by the New Testament writings of the apostle Paul, divided humanity up into three categories: the "hylics", the "psychics", and the "pneumatics". These are Greek terms: the word "hylic" refers to material substance, and the Gnostics held the hylics to be those enamoured by the material realm and the most common kind of soul; "psychic" refers to the mind, and the psychics were said to be those souls enamoured with the intellect and were thought to be far fewer in number than the hylics; "pneumatic" refers to Spirit and air, and the pneumatics were said to be those enamoured by the Spirit and were thought to be the rarest among souls. The Gnostics naturally took themselves to be pneumatics, and as earlier stated the word "Gnostic" in the non-sectarian sense has the same significance as the word "mystic" in the way that I use it. It seems that most Gnostic groups considered the hylics to be utterly unable to escape from their material disposition and to therefore be doomed from the very beginning. In some cases, however, it was believed that the psychics could attain to a lower form of heaven after the death of their mortal form. The lower form of heaven that the Gnostics wrote of is in fact a recognition of the heavenly aethereal realms that souls still bound by egoic identity (and therefore by the mind) will find themselves in after the death of their mortal form.

I call the "afterlife" destinations of souls still bound by egoic identity "artificial afterlives", because whether heavenly or hellish, they are highly individualised aethereal realms informed by the egoic identity that the soul is still bound by, and they are only ever temporary abodes until the soul is reborn within the material realm once again; they are the vines planted outside of the Father that Yeshua mentioned within the excerpt that opened this section. The true heaven is an aethereal realm designed by God—it is that written of in the biblical narrative of the Garden of Eden. It cannot be reached by any soul that is still bound to an egoic identity, whether that identity is positive or negative.

Dreams and Hallucinogens

> Let nobody disqualify you, insisting on asceticism and the worship of angels, going on in detail about visions, puffed up without reason by his sensuous mind, and not holding fast to Mashiach, from whom the whole body, nourished and knit together, through its joints and ligaments, grows as God causes it to grow.
>
> - The Apostle Paul, The Epistle to the Colossians 2:18,19

The counterfeit spiritualities of the mind are far more insidious those of the material realm, for they are far more subtle, and yet they are also far more powerful. Whereas any soul knows when they are enamoured with things of the natural world, most souls are completely unaware of being devoted to false gods within the mind, and whereas any soul may simply walk away from an earthly idol, they always carry the idols of the mind with them.

As with all counterfeit spiritualities, the counterfeit spiritualities of the mind stem from the category error that I highlighted within the very first chapter: having mistaken the mind as the means by which spiritual truth is arrived at, souls assume that this truth is therefore a series of intellectual conclusions and concepts concerning the nature of reality. These become their false gods—intellectual idols that they mistake for God. I will say again that ideas and beliefs are intellectual constructs developed by and retained within the mind, and as such they are by definition not God. That they relate to spiritual subject matter does not change the fact that they are intellectual constructs. Intellectual constructs may be stepping stones to truth, but in the "spiritual" and religious world they are almost always taken to be truth itself. A series of ideas and beliefs about the nature of reality, when mistaken for truth itself, become false gods of the mind. Never, ever forget this.

The consequences of such counterfeit spiritualities are plain for all to see: why is it that so many souls take their ideas and beliefs about spiritual realities so seriously that they will hate, fight, and kill those that disagree with them? It is because merely believing certain things to be so bestows no certainty whatsoever, and the spiritual quest therefore becomes a matter of making an educated guess as to what the truth is. An element of doubt will therefore always remain, and with that doubt comes insecurity and the need to convince yourself that you are right and that every other soul is wrong, violently if necessary. This problem is only exacerbated when a soul believes that being wrong will result in some form of eternal damnation. Believing that the accumulation of knowledge pertaining to the spiritual is itself a spiritual activity has also caused many spiritual seekers to abandon the spiritual path altogether, for they suffered from mentally exhaustion having acquired so much information, and the more that they acquired the more disheartened they became as they realised just how massive their assumed task of working out the truth really is. Genuine spirituality is never exhausting, for it involves experiencing the Spirit that you are, that which is nothing other than life itself.

However, in many cases a soul's religious convictions do not even rise to the level of the above form of counterfeit spirituality, which while misguided is at least serious. You do not have to search for a long time to encounter those that very clearly love the imagery of the stern theologian, the zealous crusader, the pious Templar, the ferocious Viking warrior, the mysterious pagan priestess, the elusive mystic, or whatever it might be, their "spirituality" being nothing more than an obvious egoic effort to project such well known images as being representative of themselves.

Just as there are two forms of material counterfeit spirituality, so too are there are two forms of mental counterfeit spirituality, the first of which involves dreams. Dreams have historically featured very heavily in spiritual traditions of all kinds due to the notion that we can extrapolate valuable insight about our lives from them and that they are essentially coded messages sent to us for a purpose.

The idea that we can extract valuable insights concerning our lives from dreams is actually true, but it is true in the same way that it is true that one can determine what an animal digested by examining the content of its stomach, for just as the physical body processes matter ingested by a creature, so too does the mind process information retained by a soul, and this includes information retained from former incarnations. On those occasions when we remember witnessing this process during sleep, we say that we had a "dream" or a "nightmare", depending upon the emotions that the experience provoked within our aethereal bodies. Insight regarding a soul can be obtained from dreams simply because they contain such information.

Despite this, I would recommend against placing such a high importance on dreams and the interpreting of them, for dreams are ultimately one more form of mental phenomenon, and you are able to witness them because as Spirit you transcend them. Indeed, it is possible, and not even particularly difficult, to have power over your dreams even as you experience them, just as one can interfere with the body's digestive process. I will give a testimony of having power over dreams within the tenth chapter. But it is not just that dreams are subject to interpretation, it is that they require interpretation to be perceived as conveying any kind of coherent message at all. What you are doing when you attempt to interpret a dream is using the mind to interpret mental phenomenon, and so whatever conclusion you come to is necessarily a conclusion of the mind that is by nature deficient. This is why attempts to establish belief systems and collectives on the basis of dreams have never worked and can never work.

Similar things may be said of those experiences that are induced through the use of hallucinogens. Within the New Testament, the use of hallucinogens is condemned, it being referred to in the majority of English translations as "sorcery", which is a translation of the Greek word "pharmakia" from which the modern word "pharmacy" is derived. Since this issue concerns experiences provoked by the use of chemicals, one might argue that this could be classed as another form of material counterfeit spirituality, yet the focus of those that use hallucinogens is not the physical materials they consist of, but the mental phenomenon that they induce. Many souls can get very defensive about their use of hallucinogens, something that itself betrays the true nature of their usage. However, I am not at all concerned with their legality, any potential health risks, or their impact upon society, nor am I interested in telling anyone what they can and cannot do; I am only interested in explaining why I do not recommend the use of hallucinogens to those undergoing remembrance. I do not deny that the experiences evoked by hallucinogens are real and that they can have a positive and lasting impact on the way in which a soul perceives reality, but they can never bestow the kind of profound insight that a consistent effort to know the Spirit does. Excessive use of hallucinogens may also fracture your mind and render you incapable of conscious remembrance within this lifetime precisely because they propel you into very powerful experiences that considered methods such as my own would ease you into.

What it comes down to is that a spirituality that is dependent upon something other than yourself is no spirituality at all. Consider the absurdity of Spirit incarnating within the material realm and then coming to believe that its "spirituality" was dependent upon a product of that realm. Even if the use of hallucinogens was a legitimate form of spirituality, why would you want to engage in it knowing that you would be entirely dependent upon access to certain substances? Would you not rather that your spirituality was something that you could engage with at any time? Well it is.

You must also consider your own testimony. When you come to know yourself as Spirit, you will be obliged to testify of what you know. If your testimony involves heavy use of hallucinogens, there are many souls that will reject your experiences outright as the result of substance abuse. You can choose to see that as their failing, but it is a reality nonetheless. You will be a much more efficient messenger of God if you do not compromise your testimony in such ways.

Harnessing the Mind

> The peace of God, which surpasses all understanding, will
> guard your hearts and your minds in Yeshua Hamashiach.
> Finally, brothers, whatever is true, whatever is honourable,
> whatever is just, whatever is pure, whatever is lovely,
> whatever is commendable, if there is any excellence, if
> there is anything worthy of praise, think about these
> things.
>
> - The Apostle Paul, The Epistle to the Philippians 4:7,8

The mind cannot liberate a soul from its sense of deficiency because it
itself is deficient; more than that, it is intentionally deficient. Direct
experience of yourself as Spirit will enable you to recognise your
invulnerability to the mind, and yet there is still much useful that can be
said in terms of effectively utilising the mind, for it will always act
according to its deficient nature.

There is a certain exercise practised most famously among
certain Dharmic sects whereby, in order to combat lustful desires, the
practitioner will dwell upon the fact that the human that is the object of
their desire is fundamentally composed of bone, blood, gristle, and
everything else that makes up the physical body. By focussing upon
these less appealing realities the practitioner hopes to douse the fire of
their lust and thereby overcome it. Such exercises are merely a
conscious effort to do what most souls will do instinctively when
negative thoughts arise within their mind, which is to combat them with
other thoughts. This can often be successful, and yet such a solution can
only ever be temporary, for it is only a matter of time before the
prevailing intellectual constructs are themselves overturned.

As a general rule you should be mindful of the nature of the
information your mind takes in. Most souls understand that they should
not have their mortal form eat rotten food, for the detrimental effects of
doing so are obvious. While the detrimental effects of filling your mind
with negative information may be more subtle, they are actually far
more damaging. I am not saying that you should avoid facing certain

realities as though you were fearful of them, only that, as the apostle Paul recommended in the excerpt that opened this section, you should ensure that you primarily focus upon positive phenomenon, for just as empowering negative phenomenon through your focus will bring you experientially low, so too will empowering positive phenomenon uplift you. This guarding of the mind is the reason for the much maligned prohibition on music within certain forms of Islam and other traditions. To the secular world, such things seem baffling, but they are rooted in sound reasoning, even if that reasoning is conveyed in terminology that is alien to the secular world or has even been forgotten entirely. If any soul claims not to understand the value of being selective regarding the influences that one absorbs, then the most generous conclusion that I can reach is that they are being deliberately obtuse, which is a very common approach to religious notions within the secular world.

As my own spiritual awakening indicates, it is possible to use positive intellectual constructs to transcend the mind in an experience of divine insight. This is achieved through contemplation, which means to intensely consider a spiritual mystery, or to simply enter into a gentle reflection upon something of the Spirit. In the case of the latter, more gentle form of contemplation, you might do something as simple as consider the majesty of God, and this milder consideration is done more in wonder and appreciation, as opposed to the intense intellectual scrutinising of the subject that is the alternative form of contemplation. Note that what I call "contemplation" many others would call a form of "meditation". Most English translations of the biblical texts consistently admonish the reader to "meditate" upon a particular subject, often the glory of God, and this is especially true of more reflective texts such as the Book of Psalms. When such texts advise the reader to "meditate" upon a subject, they are advising them to engage in contemplation as I have just explained it.

Contemplation can be tremendously beneficial and can result in many wonderful insights and experiences, to the extent that it tends to be the practice that excites souls the most, but it is meditation (in the form that I detailed within the third chapter) that is the superior practice, for whereas within contemplation you are operating within the mind in a bid to focus upon higher thoughts, within meditation you are simply abiding as the Spirit that you are within the Eternal Moment.

You do not engage in contemplation in a bid to overthrow the mind, for you do not need to overthrow that which you, as Spirit, are already superior to.

When mental phenomenon that has the potential to disturb you arises, recall that you transcend it by the mere fact that you are perceiving it; it exists within you and its existence is therefore dependent upon you. Without you, it could have never been, and without your focus, it cannot continue to exist. Having recognised the obviousness of this, the next time that such abrasive phenomenon arises within your mind, say to yourself, "what a wonderful thing this is", knowing that it exists only to test and strengthen you. And then let it be.

Your mind could be an absolute maelstrom of highly negative phenomenon and it should make no difference to you. Why would it? You will think of all manner of reasons why those thoughts matter, but all of those reasons are themselves thoughts—the mind is attempting to justify the effects of its own activity to you. Let it do so. If you buy into those justifications by bestowing them with your focus, you will be pulled into that mental maelstrom as surely as if you had consciously focussed upon that negative phenomenon in the first place. When you experience being oppressed by mental phenomenon, you may say to yourself "I am losing my mind", but the truth is the opposite—you are fully investing in your mind. You all know very well the ways in which the mind whispers doubt to you at the beginning of any endeavour, so I will use an endeavour—specifically that of the writing of this book—to illustrate my current point.

I set out to write this book, and the mind whispered, "This is too great a task. Give up." I ignored it and chose to proceed, bestowing my focus upon the task at hand and planning out a structure for the book, and the mind whispered, "See? This challenge is insurmountable, for such a book can be written in so many different ways. Give up." I ignored it and eventually settled upon what I deemed to be the most effective structure. Having done so, I began to write the first draft, and the mind whispered, "Your writing is both crude and incomprehensible to all but you. Give up." I could see that the mind was not wrong in its assessment, yet I proceeded to write many more drafts, after which the mind whispered, "This is much improved. Even so, you lack the talent to present such a broad array of subjects coherently. Give up." I ignored the mind and began revising my work over and over again. I can tell you now that when I am finished writing this book, the mind will whisper, "This has shaped up well. I never doubted you."

The mind will always be there providing its commentary on whatever is happening and on whatever you are doing; it is as an impatient child upon a long journey and you have no reason to heed it whatsoever. The choice for you is plain: do or do not. The mind's commentary is irrelevant, even if it happens to have merit at times. Ignore that commentary and you may harness the power of your mind towards whatever you are attempting. Any struggle that you might have with your mind is an imaginary struggle brought about by an erroneous belief that you are not greater than it. This is why identification with an egoic identity is so devastating, for it ensnares you within such a belief.

As you will increasingly see, the mind can be very subtle in the ways that it tries to lure you into empowering it. Be aware of the fact that what you are doing throughout this book is not attempting to resist undesirable mental phenomenon by merely thinking "as Spirit I transcend this phenomenon", for that thought is itself mental phenomenon. Rather, you are overcoming such mental phenomenon by entering into the experiential recognition of yourself as the Spirit that necessarily transcends such phenomenon. Negative phenomenon cannot be detrimental to your experience of reality unless you consciously choose to allow it to be. It really is as simple as that. Any other notion is pure imagination, and imagination itself, as a product of the mind, can be dismissed.

Chapter Six: Religion

A book of this nature would be incomplete if it did not address the subject of religion. Because of the centrality of Yeshua to my own life and my decision to primarily employ Christian sacred texts throughout this book, I will use the Christian religion to illustrate my points throughout this chapter. This should not be taken to mean that the faults that I highlight are unique to Christianity or that it is uniquely deficient, for that is certainly not the case. The vast majority of questions that I receive pertain to religion and its faults, and so this chapter will explain what the purpose of religion is, why it inevitably fails to fulfil that purpose, and what some of the most dire consequences of that failure are.

The Function of Religion

> What then is Apollos? What is Paul? Servants through whom you believed, as the Lord assigned to each. I planted, Apollos watered, but God gave the growth. Neither he who plants nor he who waters is anything, but only God who gives the growth.
>
> - The Apostle Paul, The First Epistle to the Corinthians
> 3:5-7

Religions are ideologies that centre around the teachings of a mystic. Ideally they should preserve the teachings of that spiritual master, but all too often they corrupt and abrogate them. Ideally they should be environments within which the spirituality of souls is fostered, but all too often they suffocate and suppress that spirituality. Ideally they should by the guiding light of the societies within which they exist, but all too often they oppress and degrade those societies. In order to understand why this is, you must understand the process by which

94

religions are created and the inevitable degeneration that follows it.

Historically, a mystic may have been well known or obscure within their lifetime, but either way, those that truly grasped their teachings were always few. After the death of a mystic's mortal form, those followers that truly understood their message would continue spreading it, preserving their master's teachings orally, and sometimes in written form. If those teachings became widespread enough, their adherents came to be recognised as a distinct religious collective. However, the vast majority of souls that are attracted to any belief system are attracted due to the external trappings of that belief system and not the mystical essence that lies at the heart of it. Therefore, when a belief system becomes popular enough, its adherents will primarily be religionists enamoured with counterfeit spirituality, and opportunistic materialists that seek to exploit the power of that belief system for their own ends.

Degeneration is inevitable whenever a mystic's teachings become the central tenants of a worldly institution, because worldly institutions require worldly means to sustain them, means that are almost always going to be contrary to the original teachings of that spiritual master. Therefore, the ignorant souls that so often rise to power within them concoct doctrines and theologies that exist specifically to justify such obvious contradictions. The enshrinement of those very doctrines is also essential to the survival of such institutions, for they are all that ultimately distinguishes one from another; if the acceptance of a certain degree of dogma is not made mandatory and portrayed as being crucial to one's spiritual security then there is little to compel souls to be part of one institution instead of any other.

As a consequence of this degeneration, profound teachings are understood and conveyed in a crude form that contains none of their original relevancy, immediacy, and vitality. What were once profound understandings to be confirmed through direct experience of the Spirit become dogmatic statements concerning the nature of reality that must be adhered to if one is to be considered a true follower of the mystic in question. In this way, religion promotes a crude form of tribalism that genuine spirituality would liberate souls from. Understanding all of this, what soul can be surprised that the religious institutions of the world are rife with corruption and abuse? What soul can be surprised that souls struggle to find spiritual sustenance within them? And what soul can be surprised that the self-appointed representatives of mystics like Yeshua so often not only bear little resemblance to them, but in many cases behave in the exact opposite fashion?

Yeshua warned of those that take pride in their religious authority, such as in Mark 12:38-40 where he said, "Beware of the scribes, who like to walk around in long robes and like greetings in the marketplace and have the best seats in the synagogues and the places of honour at feasts, who devour widow's houses and for pretence make long prayers. They will receive the greater condemnation." Despite this, some religionists will do all of those things, will openly tell you that they are "proud" to have their position of authority, and that such a position means something in the sight of God. They think that the worldly authority bestowed upon them by their religious institution is an acceptable substitute for genuine spiritual insight because it appeals to the egoic identities that they are bound by. The vast majority of leaders within any religion engage in the counterfeit spirituality of the mind, bowing down before the theological idols of their tradition. This is why even the greatest among them are reduced to delivering obvious sentiments and trite rhetoric; if the best that a soul claiming spiritual authority can do is state that it is nice to be nice in fifty different and increasingly poetic ways, then that is simply insufficient—anyone can formulate such rhetoric. Where is the substance? Where is the insight?

Philosophical materialists have a habit of caricaturing religions and religious souls, but I am always conscious to never unfairly characterise any soul or collective of souls. Even so, many of you will think that I am being harsh in my assessment of religionists, perhaps because you are imagining your friendly local priest or pastor as you read my words. If so, then you are simply unaware of the consequences of their counterfeit spirituality. The average religionist themselves is certainly very benign, but every abuse and atrocity committed in the name of spirituality stems directly from their false teachings. Many adherents of the major religions would have you believe that the worst abuses are exclusive to the smaller sects that they would call "cults", and while the most extreme manipulations typically occur within such groups, the exact same behaviour patterns can be observed within most religious institutions. If you understood the sheer magnitude of the horror that results from the ignorance and the arrogance of religionists then you would know that I am actually being exceedingly restrained in the manner in which I am articulating their faults.

It is precisely because their fruits are so destructive that Yeshua was harsher with nobody more than the religious leaders of his day, for they—the Pharisees, the Sadducees, and the scribes—had likewise utterly failed to comprehend the great revelations that they had been entrusted with, and in accordance with their ignorance, had warped them, and had begun to use them as a means to bully and oppress, abusing the privileges that their religious authority had bestowed them with.

It took only three hundred years for the message of Yeshua to be almost entirely lost in the rush to secure the worldly power and authority of the emergent Catholic Church. In the 4th century Yeshua was deified above all other souls, the doctrine of the trinity (something that Yeshua and his apostles had never even conceived of) was finally formulated, and there was the establishment of a canon of sacred texts.

Although it is commonly believed that it was the early 4th century Roman emperor Constantine that made Christianity the state religion of the Roman Empire, he actually only made it legal to practice Christianity; it was the Emperor Theodosius, ruling decades later, that not only made Christianity the state religion of Rome, but also defined it as Trinitarian, thus ensuring the dominance of Trinitarian Christianity even up to the present day. Before Christianity became the state religion of the Roman Empire, Christians had been the despised and the persecuted, but after that point, those Christians that acquired worldly authority very quickly became the persecutors.

As well as the material effects of the wrongdoings of religious institutions down throughout history, there has also been a more subtle effect of such destructive behaviour, namely that many souls that would otherwise have been open to the spiritual turned away from it having come to see that the very institutions that claim to represent it are so often deeply malevolent. It is true that such souls should not be so foolish as to dismiss the spiritual due to the behaviour of the obviously unspiritual, but it is equally true that those that abuse spiritual matters for their own selfish ends will pay a heavy price for doing so, for as the apostle Paul wrote in Romans 2:24 when citing the Hebrew scriptures against the religionists of his day, "'the name of God is blasphemed among the nations because of you'".

Religionists often highlight all of the good works carried out by their chosen religion and argue that it has been a stabilising influence in the world, and yes, religions have conducted many good works and have helped to usher in great societal advancements, and yes, religion can be a tremendously powerful unifying force that provides a vital cohesion to society without which it would surely disintegrate. But so what? Is this book about the best way to manage a civilization? No it is not, and such considerations have nothing to do with my current point, which is that religion as a whole largely fails to meet the needs of those souls that are seeking spiritual sustenance. Until religionists, and particularly Christian religionists, recognise this and seek to reform their institutions, they will continue to watch in bafflement as the number of souls attending their places of worship dwindle.

However, despite all of the criticisms that I have levelled at religion and religionists, the philosophical materialist that dreams of a day in which religion dissolves as the souls of the world embrace a practical materialism are doing just that—dreaming. I can assure you that such a day will never, ever come, for although most souls are unconscious of the fact that they are actually Spirit, they nonetheless are, and this will inevitably drive them to seek the transcendent. Different religions will rise and fall, but religion itself will always be, complete with its deficiencies.

I use the term "philosophical materialist" to indicate one that has thoughtfully rejected the existence of anything beyond the material; most would use the term "atheist", but that is not precise enough—an atheist is merely a soul that does not accept the existence of any deities, and so it is perfectly possible for someone to be an atheist and still maintain a fruitful spirituality centred around introspection, even if that spirituality would be lacking without devotion. Philosophical materialism is simply not something that I deem important enough to address at length, but I will say this much: if a soul consciously rejects all forms of religion and spirituality, far from being "liberated" from their trappings, they will inevitably find a far worse worldly substitute, almost always in the form of political ideology and state power. This is why those that outwardly reject spirituality propagate worldly causes with what can only be described as "a religious zeal". As the carnage of the 20th century demonstrated, the fruits of such false gods are the most rotten of all.

There are some souls that are so utterly entrenched within their ideology, whether it is religious or secular, that they have become a prisoner of it and can no longer think outside of its confines. As a consequence, you may perceive when talking to them that they are not at all present in the conversation, but are instead passively running through a mental script. This phenomenon is most often seen among the adherents of particularly controlling cults, though is far from exclusive to them. Be very wary of such souls.

Given my assertion that all major religious traditions stem from an experience of the same spiritual truth, the most common questions that I am asked concerning them are why it is that they are so many in number and why it is that in many cases they seem to teach entirely contradictory things about the nature of reality and the way in which one should conduct oneself in the world.

You must distinguish between temporal wisdom and eternal wisdom. Whenever a spiritual collective arises, it will inevitably contain elements that are specific to the time and place in which it arose. This is unavoidable. The eternal wisdom is easily discerned not by a study of the material form that a religion takes in the world, but by discerning the most prevalent commonalities between all of the great spiritual teachers. Religions are as wells all drawing from the same source of water—the form of the wells will inevitably differ having been constructed in different times and places and by different souls, but the source of water that they were designed to draw from is the same. That source is the Spirit. To be enamoured with and dogmatic about the form of the well rather than focussing upon reaching the water is to tragically miss the point, and yet every religionist does this, for it is what defines them as a religionist.

Sometimes souls feel attracted to more obscure traditions, and in many cases they are so obscure that we really have no idea what their historical adherents actually believed in any great detail. As stated, before the discovery of the Nag Hammadi library in 1945 there were tremendous gaps in our knowledge concerning Gnosticism, and within spiritual circles, such gaps are invariably filled with all manner of ideas that would typically be described as "New Age". This is still very much the case when traditions that yet remain shrouded in mystery are resurrected in various forms. Druidism is just one example of such a tradition: all we really know about the belief system of the ancient Druids is that it probably involved reincarnation; our understanding is so lacking that one cannot truly restore Druidism, but must instead reimagine it. However, do not think that by adhering to a more fringe tradition you will escape the controlling behaviour of souls still bound by egoic identity, for believe me, no matter how far from mainstream religion you may wish to venture, you will encounter that same behaviour, for it is present within all collectives, spiritual or otherwise —even within the collective of those that reject collectives. It can often be worse in the more fringe collectives, for souls can more easily convince themselves that they somehow own a tradition when its institutional presence is small or even non-existent. There are those that seem to spend all of their time seeking to ensure that others are articulating their shared beliefs in a way that they deem acceptable.

Despite all that I have said, do not be under the impression that I do not understand the allure of religion and collectives generally. On the contrary, I understand it perfectly well. You see, immediately after the spiritual awakening that I described within the first chapter, I was left without any direction, but since I had the impression that "Jesus Christ" had been responsible for the experience, it seemed that the logical thing to do was to try and read the Bible again and to become a Christian. And so I did—I became a member of a local church, and was soon overtaken by what I call "the zeal of the convert" (though I would be surprised if I was the first to call it that). I became the very kind of religionist that I have criticised throughout this book—arrogant and yet ignorant. In my case it was simply because I had never before had anything to believe in, and having now obtained such a thing by way of an experience that was undoubtedly genuine, I was prepared to defend it at all costs, even when I knew deep down that I really had no good reason to believe the ideas that I was espousing with such certainty.

But by the grace of God my sincere desire for truth could not be suppressed for long, and I soon began to question the dogmas that I was expected to believe in and to be honest with myself about why I had become so utterly zealous and obnoxious. I began to realise that I had failed to appreciate the nature of my spiritual awakening, and that instead of seeking that pure experience of God once again as I should have, I had instead lowered my focus to become enamoured with doctrines, creeds, and theology. This realisation was the beginning of the end of my brief period as a religionist, a period that was actually very necessary for my development, for without it I would not have the intimate knowledge of Christian theology that I do now. Even so, those that have likewise stepped away from an ideology, religious or not, will understand what I mean when I say that it is hard for me to believe that I was ever such an ideologue—it was like being in the grip of a form of madness.

However, I can honestly say that my experience with religious souls (including religionists) during that period was mostly positive. On my insistence, the minister of the aforementioned church spent many hours patiently answering my questions about Christian theology, despite his ridiculously busy schedule. I will always be grateful for the efforts of such souls. And so, do not think that my criticism of religion and religionists is born of any kind of animosity, for that is far from the case; I met many souls during that period that I am still tremendously fond of, even though to them I am now a heretic of the worst kind. So be it—my only duty is to honour God by honouring the truth.

You can certainly remain part of a spiritual collective and come to know the Spirit, as was the case with the Catholic mystic Teresa of Avila, the Muslim mystic Rumi, the Hindu mystic Ramana Maharshi, and many others, but what you cannot do is know the Spirit while being dogmatic about the theology of one's tradition, for knowing the Spirit requires, among other things, letting go of the idea that you can encapsulate God within doctrines and creeds. This is why, whenever a mystic has arisen within a religious tradition, they have always been treated with at least suspicion, if not outright hostility and persecution by their religionist brethren. Mysticism is considered heresy in many religious circles even now, which is a testimony to the sheer ignorance of those circles, given that mysticism is nothing other than spirituality itself.

Crucifixion and Resurrection

If anyone would come after me, let him deny himself and take up his cross daily and follow me. For whoever would save his life will lose it, but whoever loses his life for my sake will save it. For what does it profit a man if he gains the whole world and loses or forfeits himself?

- Yeshua, The Gospel According to Luke 9:23-25

Given that Yeshua is so central to my own remembrance and therefore to this book, I must address the significance of those incidents that are widely seen as being paramount in his life, namely the crucifixion and the resurrection. It is especially important that I do so given that, while all that I have said concerning the need to transcend egoic identity is easily recognisable within the Dharmic religions, its presence within the Christian tradition has been obscured by two millennia of misguided theology.

The New Testament texts themselves are reasonably clear regarding the theological significance of Yeshua's crucifixion: Yeshua was the messiah of the Jewish people, and as their messiah he represented them before God. He was not the first to do so: King David, for example, also represented Israel before God, to the extent that he was even described as sitting on the throne of God. Because of this, when King David behaved righteously, Israel as a whole benefited from it, but when he behaved unrighteously, Israel suffered for it. It is because Yeshua represented Israel before God in this same way that he was able to die for the absolution of the sins of the Jewish people. The New Testament portrays Yeshua as having represented the sacrificial lamb of the Jewish Passover Feast, and within his epistles, the apostle Paul sought to explain how and why the power of Yeshua's atonement had been made available to non-Jews.

But if the theological significance of the atonement is so clearly explained within the texts of the New Testament, then why have theologians endeavoured to concoct their own theories across the last two millennia? The simple answer is that, in the hands of non-Jewish theologians, Christianity very quickly became disassociated from its Jewish origins, a process exacerbated by the anti-Jewish sentiment that has infamously haunted much of Christian history. Therefore, the explicitly Jewish biblical explanation of the atonement was deemed insufficient, if it was heeded at all. What non-Jewish theologians within the early centuries sought was an explanation of the atonement that was more appropriate for the multicultural force that Christendom was quickly becoming.

There is the Christus Victor theory which states that the death of Christ overthrew the powers of darkness, and the specifics of the theory will depend upon the views of the theologian that is espousing it. There is the Ransom theory that states that because of what happened in the Garden of Eden, Satan owned mankind—or at least that mankind owed a debate to Satan—and that the death of Christ is that which liberates mankind from Satan. There is the Penal Substitution theory, which states that, due to its sin, mankind deserves punishment (usually eternal torment in hell), but that Yeshua took that punishment upon himself upon the cross, thereby sparing those that believe in him from it. There is also the more grounded Moral Influence theory of the atonement, which emphasises understanding the crucifixion of Yeshua in light of his ministry and not as an isolated incident. In this view the crucifixion is the culmination of a ministry of self-sacrifice and is the ultimate example of self-sacrifice, something that the followers of Yeshua are to be inspired by. Because of its simplicity, the Moral Influence view is sometimes held alongside other atonement theories. These are just some of the more popular understandings of the atonement that have developed across the last two millennia.

But what you should notice about all such atonement theories, including the biblical view, is that none of them make the slightest bit of difference whatsoever. Let us say that you become convinced of the Christus Victory theory of the atonement. What would that mean for you? It would mean that you have a certain idea within your mind concerning the significance of the atonement. If you were to be later convinced of the Penal Substitution theory, then you would merely be replacing one idea with another. Because all of these atonement theories present entirely abstract ideas about what the crucifixion meant, they make no difference whatsoever in the immediate lives of those that adopt them; they merely feed the minds of those that have fallen foul of intellectual idolatry.

However, alongside the theological understanding of the atonement contained within the New Testament texts, there is also an esoteric, mystical understanding. It is this mystical understanding that the Valentinian Gnostics clearly grasped in asserting that the deepest significance of the crucifixion lay not in it being an event in history, but in it being symbolic of that which we all must endure if we are to be raised to spiritual life as Yeshua was in his resurrection.

Throughout his ministry and in a variety of different ways, Yeshua taught that his followers must die to themselves if they were to find true life. One of the most explicit examples of this comes in John 12:25 where Yeshua said, "Whoever loves his life loses it, and whoever hates his life in this world will keep it for eternal life." To die to self is to transcend the egoic identity in the way that I have been describing within this book, and Yeshua's teaching on the subject was not merely one teaching among many, but the teaching upon which the whole of his ministry stood. If you overlook or misunderstand it as mainstream Christianity invariably does, then everything else that Yeshua said is rendered insignificant. The crucifixion and the resurrection are that very same central teaching demonstrated in the most extreme way possible.

The apostle Paul fully accepted the historicity of Yeshua and that of his crucifixion and resurrection, but he also knew well the more important mystical significance of the crucifixion, that which makes the crucifixion directly relevant and effectual in the life of every soul. He demonstrated such an understanding many times in his epistles, such as in Galatians 2:20 where he wrote, "I have been crucified with Christ. It is no longer I who live, but Christ who lives in me." If you do not understand the mystical significance of the crucifixion and instead only understand it to be a historical event that involved some manner of abstract metaphysical transaction, then you have no way of making sense of the apostle Paul's teachings on the subject and you have no way of explaining why it is that the crucifixion liberates souls from their sin or why it is immediately relevant to anyone at all.

The resurrection is symbolic of new spiritual life—being "born again", attaining "Christ consciousness", "nirvana", or what I call "rest"—but there can be no resurrection without crucifixion. This is why Yeshua's teaching that one must die to self to truly live was central to his ministry, and it is why the apostle Paul considered himself crucified with Christ and therefore alive with Christ, and it is why he insisted that others likewise crucify themselves and die with Christ so that they might live with him. And so it is that, not only is the notion of overcoming egoic identity to attain spiritual bliss that is so apparent in the Dharmic religions not absent from the Christian tradition, it was in fact the very essence of Yeshua's ministry and the very lesson that the narrative of his life and death were intended to convey.

If this truth had been widely recognised from the beginning, then Christianity would have developed as a far more introspective religion. But there are those that will do everything within their power to deny this mystical understanding of the crucifixion, and the reason is perfectly obvious: the mystical understanding of the crucifixion and resurrection actually demands something of us. Most souls would prefer to continue behaving in the lowly manner that they always have and then soothe their conscience by telling themselves that they are free of the consequences of doing so because Yeshua died to absolve them of culpability in some abstract way. There are many reasons that the history of the Christian religion—whether Catholic, Protestant, or Orthodox—is so full of misdeeds, but this misunderstanding of the significance of the crucifixion is the primary reason.

Sacred Texts

"You search the scriptures because you think that in them you have eternal life, and it is they that bear witness about me, yet you refuse to come to me that you may have life. I do not receive glory from people, but I know that you do not have the love of God within you. I have come in my Father's name, and you do not receive me. If another comes in his own name, you will receive him. How can you believe, when you receive glory from one another and do not seek the glory that comes from the only God?"

- Yeshua, The Gospel According to John 5:39-44

Sacred texts are those works of literature held in high esteem within religions. These are often called "scripture", though that word carries with it specifically Christian connotations and so I have avoided using it in favour of a broader term until now. Sacred texts exist in many forms and are regarded as being authoritative for a variety of different reasons.

In some cases, texts came to be regarded as sacred for historical reasons, such as the belief that they were composed by a direct follower of a religion's founding mystic, or perhaps even by that mystic himself. In other cases, texts came to be revered simply because they could be interpreted to share the view of the prevailing orthodoxy of the day, and it was convenient to be able to reinforce the authority of that orthodoxy with such a text. Within the religious sphere, beliefs are typically formed on the basis of words found within the pages of such sacred texts. The fact that those words must be subjectively understood is the reason that diversity inevitably develops even among those groups that hold exactly the same texts to be scripture.

But what exactly is "scripture"? The definition may differ from group to group, but generally speaking, scripture is a text that is held to be inspired or dictated by a divine source, and it is important to distinguish between inspiration and dictation. Muslims believe the Quran to have been dictated by the angel Gabriel to the Prophet Muhammed. This means that every single word is taken to be holy and inerrant. In the modern day, one might refer to such writings as "channelled material". Inspiration is different in that, while a divine source is believed to have guided the author of the inspired text to write, they were still writing according to their human limitations, instead of being compelled to write by a being without such limitations.

The scriptures contained within the Bible are regarded to have been inspired, and yet very few Christians understand what that means even according to their own tradition; it is very common to hear them talk of the Bible as though it was dictated by God in the same way that Gabriel is said to have dictated the Quran. You cannot help but get the distinct impression that many of them believe the Bible to have fallen wholesale from the sky one day. And so, before many souls even begin to read the texts of the Bible, they already misunderstand the nature of the book. However, it is important to know that most souls that adhere to a religious tradition do not read the sacred texts of that tradition. As stated within the first chapter, the souls that adhere to religions are mostly nominal and are not overly concerned with their tradition. What little understanding they do have will almost always come from casual oral transmission, as opposed to a rigorous study of their sacred texts or the works of the theologians of their tradition. When such souls do employ excerpts from their sacred texts, they will almost always be ignorant of the contexts from which those excerpts come.

For example, Christians will often quote Yeshua as having said "judge not", and take that statement at face value. But the full statement is "judge not that you be not judged", and if you read the context from which it comes within Matthew 7, you will see that Yeshua was not condemning all judgement, but hypocritical judgement. Indeed, in John 7:24 Yeshua said, "Do not judge by appearances, but judge with right judgement." The idea that one could go through life never judging is pure foolishness; you cannot function in the world without making judgements, and the very reason that those aforementioned souls quote Yeshua as having said "judge not" is because they themselves have judged another to be in error and are seeking to correct them by doing so.

The Bible is a compilation of writings belonging to a various different genres and that were written mostly by different authors across a period of at least six hundred years. They were assembled together because certain individuals concluded that they had been inspired and thought that it would be useful to have a canon (a list of texts taken to have been inspired) to distinguish them from those writings that they did not consider to have been inspired.

Serious problems arise when souls begin to believe that any book or any collection of writings are the epitome of spiritual truth, because that is idolatry. The irony is that not one text contained within the Bible makes such a claim about itself, nor would any of their authors have ever made such a claim about any text. Firstly because they were spiritually aware souls free of any delusions about a text serving as an infallible guide to life, and secondly because not one of those authors had any idea that their work would one day be included in a compilation called "the Bible".

The New Testament consists of twenty-seven books, thirteen of which are epistles attributed to the apostle Paul, and I will use those epistles in order to illustrate how we came to have the New Testament texts in the form that we do today. Quite simply, the New Testament texts were successfully passed down through history due to their popularity within the early church. And so, for example, the apostle Paul wrote twice to a church at Corinth, advising and chastising them on a number of matters, and those letters were then collected by Christians, copied, and distributed for the edification of Christian communities. It was eventually decided that they were inspired, were therefore scripture, and should therefore be included as part of the official canon of the Catholic Church.

The modern academic consensus is that the epistles that are known as "the pastoral epistles" (namely the First Letter to Timothy, the Second Letter to Timothy, and the Epistle to Titus) were almost certainly not actually written by the apostle Paul. It should also be noted that in the early centuries a Christian community would have been very fortunate to have access to even a single text, and that most communities were wholly reliant on oral teaching. There were all manner of Christian works in circulation at that time, some of which were later deemed to be scripture and some of which were later condemned as heretical. If a community did have access to one or more texts, the content of those texts naturally did much to shape the details of that community's theology, if they accepted them as having been authored by a legitimate source.

The apostle Paul himself could never have anticipated the way in which his simple epistles would come to be used, and had he been able to—had he known that for over two thousand years souls would take his letters as infallible truth—he would have written them very differently, or perhaps not at all, since he was wise enough to understand the devastation that would be caused by souls ignoring the original context and intent of his words and believing them to be representative of ultimate spiritual truth. Indeed, the very fact that he was evidently unable to anticipate this should tell you a lot about the true nature of his writings. I love the apostle Paul and I value his writings, but he was ultimately a soul living its own human experience and was limited by that experience as we all currently are.

To have a collection of writings to derive wisdom and insight from is a wonderful thing, and it is generally accepted that the 2nd century proto-Gnostic, Marcion of Sinope, was the first to conceive of and assemble a canon of Christian works. But to accept a contrivance that asserts that such works are infallible and that you should read them as though they were written directly to you is a grievous mistake that will not only lead the one that makes it astray, but will also prevent others from seeing that such texts have any worth whatsoever. Here is a scenario that I have seen play out time and time again: a religionist will insist that the Bible is "the Word of God", by which they mean infallible truth. A sceptic that is more informed will dispute that claim, citing the historical record demonstrating the manner in which the biblical scriptures were written and assembled. The religionist will then grow frustrated at the overwhelming evidence that contradicts their view of the Bible, and the sceptic will leave the exchange more convinced than ever that the texts of the Bible are taken seriously only by the ignorant.

The Bible having come to be called "the Word of God" is truly one of the most disastrous developments within Christian history. It not only reinforces all of the errors that I have just described, but it also usurps the title of the true Word of God, ironically the very one that the writings of the New Testament themselves identify as Yeshua. When, for example, the Johannine texts use "Word" to refer to the Word of God within their English translations, it is being translated from the

Greek "Logos", which is an important concept within Platonic thought where it meant "divine reason"—the means by which man might know God. An extensive exposition on the meaning of the Logos within Greek philosophy is unnecessary, for you should already have an idea as to why this "divine reason"—that which united man with God—was associated with Yeshua who was said to be the mediator between man and God. But if you are led to believe that "the Word" referenced within the New Testament refers to a scriptural compilation that would not exist for centuries after such references had been made, then your focus will not be upon "divine reason" as personified by Yeshua, but rather mundane reason exercised in the form of the study and interpretation of texts. This is why the Bible having come to be called "the Word of God" is responsible for untold numbers of souls being misled into a fruitless counterfeit spirituality.

Of course, the elevation of certain writing to the status of "scripture" necessarily involved the condemnation of other writings, to lesser and greater degrees. But which soul told you that you should restrict your reading to a certain selection of texts? It was not God, and it was not Yeshua or any other mystic; the idea emerged from worldly souls that wanted to control the information that others had access to for the sake of their own religious power and authority. To the end of securing that power and authority they have, through the centuries, suppressed and burned any works deemed heretical, and punished those found in possession of them. This is not the behaviour of the spiritual; it is the behaviour of the ignorant. The one that abides in truth through the Spirit has no cause to fear examination or opposition.

Many of you will be familiar with the ancient myth concerning the figure of Midas who gained the ability to turn objects into gold by touching them. The story was first related within the Roman poet Ovid's work, *Metamorphosis*, and most of you will vaguely recall the narrative as going something like this: there was a man called Midas who desired that everything that he touched would turn to gold. He got his wish, but the story ended tragically when he embraced his daughter, accidentally turning her into gold. Thus, what we have is a nice little fable about the folly of greed. But in actual fact, Midas' daughter was only added to the narrative in a rendition of the tale contained within *A Wonder-Book for Girls and Boys* that was written by the novelist Nathaniel Hawthorne in the mid 19th century, nearly two thousand years after Ovid's original account. Despite this, Hawthorne's addition of Midas' daughter to the story is such an obvious improvement that the original narrative seems somewhat pointless by comparison, and there are few that know any version of the tale but Hawthorne's.

Most sacred texts likewise come down to us having undergone a period of revisions, whether they occurred over a period of years or decades. The biblical texts were not even divided into the chapters and verses that souls are familiar with today until the 16th century. I am not suggesting that sacred texts as we have them now should continue to be altered—I am merely highlighting one more problem for the notion that they are inerrant or were classically held to be so. Religionists approach sacred texts backwards by first concerning themselves with a text's origins and then afterwards with the usefulness of the information that it presents. But if any text provides valuable insights then it does so regardless of whether or not the source is approved of by any given soul or tradition and regardless of the history of its development.

The degree to which a soul esteems a sacred text will tell you a lot about their level of awareness. Any soul that regards a work of literature as being an infallible guide to life and that which represents the pinnacle of spirituality must necessarily be completely ignorant of the spiritual, for no soul having so much as glimpsed the awesomeness of Spirit would be capable of retaining such a disposition.

It was for this reason that the apostle Paul observed in 2 Corinthians 3:6 that "the letter kills, but the Spirit gives life". The fact that those words are contained within a compilation of texts that is esteemed by many in a way that both Yeshua and the apostle Paul warned directly against is just one more example of the kind of pitiful irony that can be easily observed within organised religion. This is why I earlier asserted that the apostle Paul would have been repulsed if he could have foreseen the ways in which his innocent letters would be used in the two millennia that followed their creation. His writings and those that accompany them within the Bible have become that which souls will deliberately heed over the voice of their own conscience, which is how you end up with religionists committing atrocities even as they feel sorrow for doing so—their conscience condemns them, but their mind tells them that they are doing the right thing because they are obeying their holy book. The truth is that they are consciously ignoring God as He seeks to guide them through their conscience and are instead using their lowly understanding of their chosen sacred text as an excuse to do that which, on an egoic level, they very much want to do.

No matter how inspired a sacred text is taken to be, it is the work of a soul living a human experience and it is therefore necessarily shaped by that experience. Sacred texts should be taken seriously, but not bestowed with an undue level of authority. As I stated within the first chapter, I employ sacred texts throughout this book only because I know that others feel more comfortable when I do so, and that is precisely because they do view them as having such authority. I myself make no claims about their authenticity or authorship—I merely highlight what is written within them.

Besides around ten letters that were almost certainly written by the apostle Paul, we have little to no evidence regarding which souls authored most of the biblical texts. Even the four gospels are only named as they are according to tradition, their authors never having named themselves internally. This lack of historical data is not helped by the fact that ancient Christian writers would often attribute their own works to well known Christian figures in order to bestow their words with a greater degree of authority; the Epistle of Second Peter was almost certainly written by a soul doing that very thing. Indeed, it is highly unlikely that either of the epistles attributed to the apostle Peter were actually written by him.

But regardless of which souls did author any given sacred text, we must always be honest about what they were attempting to convey within their writings, for it is very easy to interpret their words according to our own desires and inclinations. For example, in Psalms 46:10, David quoted God as having said, "be still and know that I am God." Those words are often cited in isolation as an example of an Old Testament introspective teaching, the assumption being that the "stillness" encouraged is of the kind that one seeks during meditation. But anyone can open a Bible, read the verse in its context, and see that it has nothing whatsoever to do with introspection. Its context is one of many in the Hebrew Bible where God is emphasising the superiority of His power and authority; far from being a verse that is encouraging

112

introspection, the actual meaning of "be still and know that I am God" can be accurately conveyed as "shut up because I am God and you are not." You may be disappointed to learn this, but we must always honour the truth, even if it is not to our liking on a personal level.

It is very common for religionists familiar with the biblical texts, seeing that I will often employ them, to attempt to use their content against me, and often in very petty ways. For example, I have long hair, and such religionists will sometimes point to 1 Corinthians 11:14,15 where the apostle Paul wrote, "Does not nature itself teach you that if a man wears long hair it is a disgrace for him, but if a woman has long hair it is for her glory? For her hair is given to her for a covering." Their expectation is that such verses will present a dilemma for me, but my response is always, "yes, and that is one of several foolish things that the apostle Paul wrote." Such religionists are so used to souls deferring to the biblical writings that they cannot understand how one can value and derive insight from them without also making themselves their prisoner. I know of so many ways in which Christian religionists twist and contextualise inconvenient verses into irrelevancy. It is the reason that, for example, women are allowed to talk in most Christian churches, despite the apostle Paul insisting that they should not in 1 Corinthians 14:34. The difference between myself and such religionists is that I do not claim to be bound by the alleged authority of such sacred texts and I therefore have no need to play games with their content in order to make clear inconsistency of application seem like genuine submission to "the Word of God".

Sacred texts exist to point readers to the spiritual. If they are understood to be an end in themselves then they are being misused in the worst possible way. Therefore, concern yourself first with a direct experience of the spiritual. Then, and only then, do you have a chance of properly understanding what the authors of the world's sacred texts were attempting to convey within their writings.

Biblical Prophecy

> Yeshua's disciples said to him, "When will the Kingdom come?"
>
> Yeshua said, "It will not come by waiting for it. None shall say, 'here it is', or, 'there it is.' Rather, the Kingdom of the Father is spread out upon the earth, and men do not see it."
>
> - The Gospel of Thomas, Saying 113

Among the most devastating religious ideas are those that relate to the supposed future fulfilment of prophecies. The tragedy of this when it comes to biblical prophecy is that not one of those prophecies has any fulfilment beyond the 1st century, something that is acknowledged even within mainstream Christianity itself by those that advocate what is known as a "fulfilled eschatology" ("eschatology" meaning "the study of the end times") or simply "preterism". This is as opposed to the traditional "futurist" eschatology, which refers to the belief that the biblical "end time" prophecies have yet to be fulfilled.

Even those that maintain a futurist view of eschatology must confront the fact that, when it comes to the prophecies of Yeshua and his apostles concerning the coming of the Kingdom of Heaven, two thousand years have elapsed without them having come to pass in the way that they anticipate them manifesting. Even the renowned writer and theologian Clive Staples Lewis (more widely known as "C.S. Lewis") conceded defeat on the issue in his essay *The World's Last Night* in which he described Matthew 24:34 as being "certainly the most embarrassing verse in the Bible". Within that verse, Yeshua told his disciples that their generation would not pass before the end of the age and the coming of the Kingdom of God: "Truly, I tell you, this generation will not pass away until all of these things take place."

There are no shortage of verses that Lewis could have cited to the same effect, because Yeshua and his apostles make over a hundred such "time statements" within the New Testament, statements that place "the end times" within the 1st century, and they make not a single one that suggests that they might extend beyond it. Lewis, a Christian himself, felt forced to conclude that Yeshua was simply in error, though he uses this to argue for the legitimacy of the gospel accounts—after all, why would anyone record Yeshua as having made such an obviously false statement if not for the sake of preserving history as it actually occurred? But of course, Yeshua was not wrong, and nor were any of his apostles; the error lies with the worldly souls that have erroneous expectations concerning how such prophecies were to be fulfilled.

To the ancient Israelites there were two ages: the age in which they lived and the coming "Messianic Age" (what Christians refer to as "the Old Testament period" and "the New Testament period" respectively). When Yeshua spoke of "the end of the age", he was referring to the end of the former age and the beginning of the next, everlasting age—not the end of the world (despite what certain English translations may suggest). The apocalyptic imagery that colours his description of this transition from one age to the next is typical of Hebraic hyperbole and idiom, and you can find similar descriptions of proven historical events within the Hebrew Bible.

In chapter twenty-one of the Gospel of Luke, Yeshua explicitly tied his "end time" prophecies with the destruction of Jerusalem and concluded by saying that "these are the days of vengeance, to fulfil all that is written." Right there Yeshua explicitly stated that the destruction of Jerusalem signified the fulfilment of the Hebraic prophecies that are contained within what we now call "the Old Testament". Jerusalem was destroyed in 70 AD, around forty years after Yeshua is said to have spoken those words; that was the time in which he returned for those that waited for him, as he promised that he would. But because most do not understand the Hebraic manner of expression and take biblical prophecies hyper-literally, they are incapable of seeing that Yeshua and his apostles were absolutely correct in stating that "the end" would come within the lifetime of those that lived within the 1st century, and that there is therefore no longer any biblical prophecy that has yet to be fulfilled.

However, no book of the Bible has manifested more dread anticipation of the future than the last within the New Testament, the Book of Revelation. Even as I write these words there are souls all over the world feverishly tying its predictions into all manner of current events. Yet as with every book of the New Testament that contains prophetic warnings, the text itself makes perfectly clear that its prophecies do not have any application beyond the generation for which it was written. The Book of Revelation was composed towards the end of the 1st century by an individual that called himself "John". Tradition asserts this to be the same John that wrote the Gospel of John and the first, second, and third epistles of John, but most historians and textual critics would agree that this is almost certainly not the case. Regardless, the Book of Revelation is a letter that this "John" wrote to convey a message delivered to him by Yeshua, a message that was directed to seven churches that existed at the time. The letter begins with Yeshua speaking directly to the individuals within those churches, warning them to make certain changes before the end of the age comes or face dire consequences. This fact alone means that the prophecies contained within the Book of Revelation could not possibly have any application beyond the 1st century, not least because not one of those churches has existed for nearly two thousand years.

None of this is to say that even a text as laden with prophecy as the Book of Revelation is entirely useless to us in the present day. On the contrary, the Book of Revelation also contains many profound truths concerning remembrance. But we must always be informed and honest about which soul wrote such texts, why they were written, and which souls they were written to. It is good that we can derive understanding from letters such as the Book of Revelation, but they were written to souls living mortal lives two thousand years ago, and their warnings of near-future events are simply no longer relevant to us.

There are many reasons that biblical "end time" prophecies have been propped up as future events despite the overwhelming evidence to the contrary, not least of which is the fact that most Christian institutions depend upon them being understood as such. It must be remembered that while Christianity has been something that souls can freely criticise for all of our mortal lives, this is actually a relatively recent liberty; it was only within the last three centuries that it became possible to question Christian dogma without risking ostracisation or persecution for having done so.

But now that it is possible to question Christian dogma without risk, the Christian institutions of the world will increasingly face the choice of either acknowledging that even some of their most central dogmas are wrong, or dying as souls that recognise the truth abandon them. This is occurring even now, but those in power within such institutions have repeatedly demonstrated that they would rather engage in disingenuous apologetics or even accuse Yeshua of being in error than simply correct their doctrines and adapt accordingly. Yet there are others within such institutions that recognise the need for change and are working to effect it. But concern for the fate of religious institutions is a worldly concern, and therefore not my concern.

Contemplate this very carefully: in every generation for two thousand years there have been souls utterly convinced that events occurring in their day were signs that the world was about to end, and every last one of them was utterly wrong. That alone should give you some perspective. I have known souls that lived their lives utterly crippled by fear because they were certain that they lived in "the end times", and such souls would awaken gripped by terror should so much as a loud noise disturb their sleep, the threat of Armageddon being ever present within their minds. There are also those that delight in believing in and perpetuating such ideas because they are fantasists that enjoy the thrill of indulging their paranoia; they delight in assigning biblical significance to current events because it gives them a sense of having secret knowledge, even though they are demonstrably just as spiritually ignorant and as powerless as most others. And when their predictions inevitably fail, they will simply begin devising a new one, in many cases without even offering an explanation as to why they were wrong. There are some souls that make a fortune in such ways, for prophecy is a big industry indeed.

Yet so much of what passes for "prophecy" today is not at all reflective of prophecy as it existed in the ancient world, and especially not biblical prophecy. Biblical prophecies were not so hopelessly vague that they could have meant anything. For example, Yeshua said in Luke 21:20, "When you see Jerusalem surrounded by armies then know that its desolation has come near." Any soul that heard those words would have been left in no doubt as to what to expect, and when the Romans began to besiege Jerusalem decades later, any of those souls that still lived in mortal form would have known that Yeshua's prophecy had begun to unfold and that Jerusalem was therefore about to be utterly destroyed. Yet despite the clarity of biblical prophecies, even biblically literate souls can be convinced into bestowing utterly ambiguous "prophecies" with legitimacy.

I suspect that the reason for this lies with the figure of Michel de Nostredame, better known as "Nostradamus". Nostradamus was a 16th century French astrologer that is more widely known for being a prophet. In fact, the name of "Nostradamus" has become almost synonymous with the very concept of prophecy, and therein lies the problem, because the "prophecies" of Nostradamus were delivered through quatrains (stanzas) that are so ambiguous that they could be interpreted as having been fulfilled in a thousand different ways with every passing year. The only real insight that the quatrains of Nostradamus have to offer is that souls living in the 16th century were no less sensationalist and excitable than souls living today. But even now the name of "Nostradamus" carries with it a powerful aura, and he is so strongly associated with the very concept of prophecy that many now believe it to be perfectly acceptable when alleged prophecies could mean absolutely anything. What it comes down to is that a prophecy that cannot be understood by anyone except in retrospect is a worthless prophecy, for the very purpose of a prophecy is to bestow insight concerning events that have not yet transpired.

This was not so in the ancient world, and ancient peoples did not humour souls that claimed the gift of prophecy and then fell short in their ability to accurately and consistently foretell events. The authors of the Hebrew Bible repeatedly proscribed the death penalty for false prophets that attempted to lead souls astray. That may seem harsh to many souls living now, but I would suggest that it is not harsh at all; even in the modern, western world, souls have had their material lives all but destroyed because they believed in the prophecies of those that ultimately turned out to be wrong. A fragile Iron Age culture such as ancient Israel could easily have been utterly destroyed by such a false prophet if enough souls believed in them. False prophets were potentially more dangerous to such a society than an invading army, and they were certainly more insidious.

Yes, the world will one day be destroyed, for such is the destiny of all matter, but as Yeshua repeatedly made clear, the Kingdom of

Heaven is not something that will manifest materially, for it is an aethereal realm that can be experienced only by those that have attained rest. Those that fail to do so as they wait for a dramatic manifestation of the Kingdom of Heaven within the material realm, or for the fulfilment of any other prophecy, are neglecting that which is most important while waiting for something that will simply never come. Do not follow such souls in their costly error. Instead, make use of the opportunity that God has graciously given you here and now while you still have it.

Chapter Seven: Silence

Silence is a subject that is often alluded to, but rarely elaborated upon within mystic literature, for it is truly one of the great spiritual mysteries. If I could distribute just one chapter of this book, it would certainly be this chapter, but I will tell you now that most of you will not immediately understand what I am about to write, because of all subjects related to spirituality, silence is among the most difficult to articulate a coherent explanation of. If you apply enough focus, your mind will certainly grasp what I am pointing to here, but it is only when you put what I say into practice that the meaning of my words will be truly illuminated.

The Mystery of Silence

> I know a man in Mashiach who, fourteen years ago, was caught up to the third heaven—whether in the body or out of the body I do not know, God knows. And I know that this man was caught up into paradise—whether in the body or out of the body I do not know, God knows—and he heard things that cannot be told, which man may not utter.

> - The Apostle Paul, The Second Epistle to the Corinthians
> 12:2-4

To convey information we must employ words and concepts, but the problem with this within the context of a discourse on spirituality is that the subject matter by definition transcends both word and concept. As I have stated, words and concepts can only ever point to the spiritual, they can never encapsulate it. Only through direct experience can one know the spiritual.

If I am to refer to your true essence as I must, then I have to

120

choose a word by which to do so. The word that I chose is "Spirit", for it is a word that is used universally. But words naturally evoke concepts, for having a shared idea of what concept each word refers to within different contexts is the only means by which we can communicate. But since Spirit itself transcends the mind and therefore concept, whatever concept the word "Spirit" evokes within your mind is necessarily wrong; you can only know Spirit by experiencing Spirit, and yet the word "Spirit" itself does not point to a widely recognised experience. The word "silence", however, while also necessarily evoking a concept, does point to a widely recognised experience.

Most souls understand silence to be nothing more than the absence of sound. It is that, but it is infinitely more than that, for what does sound emerge from if not silence? Audible silence is not merely the absence of all sound, but also the potential from which all sound emerges. Likewise, mental silence is not merely the absence of mental phenomenon, but also the potential from which all mental phenomenon arises. You know something about this from all manner of mundane experiences—if you approach a soul that you have fraught relations with and they greet you warmly or dismiss you harshly, they will have made their disposition clear within your mind. But should they ignore you, they will leave you considering all manner of reasons why they did so, because their silence is laden with possibility in a way that anything that they might articulate is not.

The word "silence" and the conception of silence are not the experience itself. This is true of anything: the word "cat" is not itself a cat, just as the concept of a cat is not itself a cat. What is unique about silence is that words and concepts not only are not the thing itself, but they also negate the thing itself in its different forms: if you speak any word you obscure the experience of audible silence, even if the word that you speak is "silence", and if you conceive of any concept, you obscure the experience of mental silence, even if the concept that you conceive of is silence.

You already know that creation is composed of matter, mind, and aether, yet within each of those realms, some forms are more subtle than others—rock and water are both tangible, material substances, but water is obviously more subtle than rock. Silence is the most subtle form in all of the realms. Material silence, for example, is the most

121

subtle form of matter, to the extent that it cannot rightly even be described as a form, but is more accurately described as the absence of all forms.

The 13th century Catholic mystic, Meister Eckhart, wrote that "there is nothing in all creation so like God as silence". Sometimes the word "silence" in his statement is translated as "stillness", which conveys the same experiential idea. The term "emptiness" that is more commonly used in connection with the Dharmic religions (and particularly Buddhism) is also a term that may be used interchangeably with those of "silence" and "stillness". Others may use the term "nothingness". But whatever term a soul may employ to this effect, it is vital to recognise that it refers not only to the absence of all form, but also to the potential for any form.

Despite the fact that the mysteries of silence have always been acknowledged to be among the most profound, there has been relatively little written on the subject within mystic literature, and this is precisely because its subtle nature means that, while an explanation of silence is useful, the more that one says, the less true that explanation becomes. That is why I fully expect this to be the shortest chapter of my own book. The subject of silence is so important that I would even be so bold as to say that it is only when you can speak with insight on the subject of silence that you have something to say worth hearing on the subject of spirituality—just do not say too much on the matter.

Consider what I have already explained about silence in relation to God. The first obvious comparison is that both elude encapsulation within concept—one's concepts of God necessarily cannot adequately represent God, just as one's conceptions of silence necessarily cannot adequately represent silence. An understanding of both God and silence can only be gained through direct experience, and such experiences can never be conclusive, for they will only reveal the infinite depths of both. Just as God and His Spirit are the source of all phenomenon and are not themselves phenomenal, so is silence less phenomenal and more that from which phenomenon emerges. The line between God and silence can never at all be clear to the mind, and therefore the most that mystics like Meister Eckhart could say of silence was that there is nothing else in creation so comparable to God.

122

It is certainly through silence that we experience God, and that is the reason that devotional, introspective, and contemplative practices are ideally done in silence. Yet while there is audible silence and conceptual silence, there is also always a deeper silence that is the way in which you will commonly experience the Spirit that you are. If you have been engaging in the meditation that I taught within chapter three, you will already know something of this silence. All such practices are ideally engaged in when there is physical, mental, and aethereal silence, and in this way, audible, conceptual, and emotional silence, because they are the most subtle manifestations within their respective realms, serve as gateways through which souls might more easily consciously reconnect with God—they are the experiential bridge between realms, from the material realm to the Spirit. Truly, God speaks through silence in wordless words.

However, although the silence of Spirit can more easily be experienced if the material, mental, and aethereal realms are also silent, it is not dependent upon them being so, and the more that you abide within the Eternal Moment the more that you will be aware of the silence of the Spirit that is the essence of both you and God. The Hindu mystic, Ramana Maharshi, would sometimes respond to questions posed to him by sitting in silence; since to speak is to limit potential by obscuring silence, just as to conceive, by remaining audibly, mentally, and emotionally silent, you allow for the inner silence of Spirit to speak in its wordless conveyance. Yet to merely be acquainted with the inner silence of your Spirit is insufficient to allow for this; you must consciously become the inner silence of Spirit so that you may manifest it.

Being Nobody and Nothing

> Yeshua's disciples said, "When will you be revealed to us
> and when shall we see you?"
> Yeshua said, "When you disrobe without being
> ashamed, take up your garments, place them under your
> feet like little children, and trample on them. Then will
> you see the son of the Living One, and you will not be
> afraid."

> - The Gospel of Thomas, Saying 37

Dying to self as Yeshua taught means to live free of the erroneous belief that you are limited to personhood or any other form of egoic identity. An identity will naturally still be present within your mind as a necessary intellectual construct that enables you to interact with the human world as a human being, but you will no longer identify as it exclusively. In this way you will have died to self.

In the second chapter I explained the manner in which a soul begins to identify with personhood—it is a very gradual process of conditioning that occurs as the egoic identity grows ever more complex with the development of the soul's mortal form. I also stated that since it was a gradual process that led the soul to identify with personhood, more often than not it is a gradual process that liberates them from that identification. When Yeshua referred to "garments" in the above excerpt from the Gospel of Thomas, he was referring to the very layers of conditioning that form egoic identity. In doing so, Yeshua was alluding to the nakedness and innocence of Adam and Eve within the Garden of Eden prior to the fall, the significance of which I elaborated upon within the third chapter. Just as Adam and Eve made the decision to enter into stark duality and to therefore acquire an egoic identity, to strip off one's garments and trample them is to free oneself from such an egoic identity and assign it to its proper place. In this way, one returns to their original state of innocence, the only state in which it is possible to know God by knowing the Spirit that you are.

I do of course mean experientially and not intellectually—it is

124

not difficult to intellectually grasp all that I have said concerning the Spirit that you truly are and the fact that the details of your egoic identity were obtained after you knew what it was to dwell as that pure consciousness, but if that understanding remains only intellectual, then it is only theoretical, and it is therefore useless to you; Yeshua did not tell his followers to merely understand what it would mean to die to themselves, but to actually do it.

Many are they that, having received these understandings, fully accept the truth of them, and yet never apply what they have learned. This is because they have been tricked by the mind: they constantly tell themselves that they will soon begin to engage in spiritual practices, but they never do, and so in this way the mind continually fools them into settling for intellectual understanding until another day, but that day never comes. Souls put off all manner of things in this way, but because in this case it is the supremacy of the egoic identity that is being challenged, the compulsion to do so is particularly strong. Quoting from the prophet Isaiah, the apostle Paul made a wonderful statement in 2 Corinthians 6:1,2 when writing to the Corinthian church for the second time: "Working together with God, we appeal to you not to receive the grace of God in vain. For He says, 'In a favourable time I listened to you, and in a day of salvation I helped you.' Behold, now is the favourable time. Behold, now is the day of salvation."

Now is indeed the day of salvation for those that are willing to embrace it. You can allow your mind to fabricate all manner of excuses that will make you feel better about delaying should you accept them, but if you take so much as a cursory glance inside of yourself, you will know that those excuses are just that. You are either ready to undergo remembrance or you are not. No soul that committed themselves to applying these understandings ever regretted it, but many are they that regretted not having done so.

However, it is not uncommon for the spiritual seeker to fall into the trap of replacing their personhood with another form of egoic identity while convincing themselves that they have escaped egoic identity. The most common form of this is to begin conceiving of yourself as one that is attempting to overcome egoic identity—to conceive of yourself as a "spiritual seeker". But this, of course, is still a form of egoic identity.

A misunderstanding of the correct application of spiritual names can also lead one into the same error. Most souls acquire a spiritual name at what they regard as a "spiritual threshold"—a point where they feel that they have acquired enough of a greater understanding of reality to justify regarding their old understanding and manner of living as being redundant. Therefore, they take a new name under which to live according to their greater understanding. This is a fine thing, and it is a practice that is found throughout the spiritual traditions of the world, but spiritual names serve a very specific purpose that the vast majority of souls are unaware of.

Your birth name is that upon which all conditioning is heaped. Therefore, to evoke your birth name is to evoke the whole of your egoic identity—the way in which you understand yourself. The purpose of spiritual names is to help souls disassociate from their former egoic identity by abolishing the old name that evoked that identity. By discarding that name and acquiring a new one, you are disassociating from your former personhood in a powerful way. I myself have a spiritual name: Druce Gildas—"Druce" being a Celtic name meaning "wise", and "Gildas" being a Celtic name meaning "servant of God". However, I long ago returned to using my birth name because my spiritual name had already served its purpose of helping me to liberate myself from my former identity, to the point that I may now use my birth name without it ensnaring me within the personhood that was constructed atop it.

The mistake that most souls make when taking spiritual names is to build up a whole new egoic identity around it. They believe this to be an improvement because it is a more spiritually orientated identity than their former identity, but it is still an egoic identity, and for as long as one identifies with such, no real progress has been made. Therefore, spiritual names must be understood as temporary tools that help souls disassociate from their egoic identity and must not be taken as the foundation for a new identity.

Similarly, throughout this book I have said that you are not merely a person, but actually Spirit. It could be that someone, having read all that I have written, begins to let go of the idea that they have of themselves as a human being, only to begin to identify with their idea of Spirit instead. They will believe themselves to have made progress, but

126

they are still identifying with an egoic identity, it is just that they call this egoic identity "Spirit" and conceive of it differently than they did their personhood.

This is not as complicated as it may seem. All that you need know is that for as long as you are identifying with an idea that exists within your mind, no matter how grandiose it may be and no matter how finely arrayed in spiritual garb it is, you are still bound in egoic identity, and it is identification with egoic identity that gives rise to all sense of deficiency. I have told you how to come to know the Spirit that you are and to begin to transcend all phenomenon within the Eternal Moment, but the only way to be permanently liberated from egoic identity is to begin making a conscious effort to defer to silence in all matters.

Your mind will always insist upon having an answer to everything. To the mind, an obviously wrong answer is better than no answer at all. Nowhere is this more true than when it comes to the question of who and what you truly are. The mind will insist upon an answer to this, even if it knows, as you now do, that any answer that it may conjure can only be an idea—an intellectual construct—and is therefore necessarily false. From this point forth, whenever your mind grasps for identity, defer to silence; silence is your new identity—the absence of all things and yet the potential for all things. It is this silence, this emptiness, that you must consciously abide in and as.

Many souls have visited me in my home, and most of them have commented upon how silent it is. You will now understand the reason that this is so, but most souls are deeply uncomfortable with silence of any kind, sometimes to the extent that they will openly admit to "needing" some form of background noise at all times, even as they are attempting to sleep. There is no greater indication of how tightly bound in egoic identity a soul is than how uncomfortable they are in silence, for they have strayed so far from knowledge of themselves that the experience that should feel like home to them has come to be disconcerting. Yet there is an obvious contradiction in their disposition, for even they love dreamless sleep, which for most souls is the ultimate experience of silence, and that into which no soul may bring anything, not even their idea of themselves.

Although I have referred to "mystics", "spiritual masters", and similar terms throughout this book because I must use terms of that nature, some of you may have noticed that I have not once assigned myself such a title. This is because, if I call myself anything at all, I am inviting the mind to form a new egoic identity. I would also be helping your mind to form an idea of who and what I am. So instead, I defer to silence in the exact same manner as I have just explained, even while engaged in writing a book that requires the use of words. If asked to describe my role, I will describe myself as "a spiritual teacher", for that speaks to my function without bestowing myself a high status.

You must never bestow yourself with a grandiose title or seek to conform to a particular image, or else your mind will make full use of the opportunity to begin investing in a new egoic identity. Before you know it you will be dressing in robes, establishing a "mystical order" for "initiates", and in all kinds of ways projecting that new egoic idea of yourself out upon the world. If you truly have wisdom and insight, then it will be obvious to all without such superficial displays which, to those that actually do have wisdom and insight, will be seen as the desperate projections of a fragile ego that they are. It is understandable that you might seek to, for example, emulate the behaviour of a spiritual teacher that you particularly admire, but that too would be to attempt to create a new egoic identity for yourself to invest in.

What we are is beyond all words and beyond all concepts; we are that which perceives all human activity, all egoic identity, all mental phenomenon, all aethereal phenomenon, and everything else that can be encapsulated within word and concept. Therefore, regarding ourselves, let us remain silent, audibly and mentally. Then we are as Spirit— formless and infinite. You will experience this as a liberation, and so it is, for you are free of the concepts that you have been a prisoner of for most of your mortal life, those things that gave rise to every sense of deficiency that you have ever felt. Having experientially verified the power of silence as your identity, you will naturally find that it begins to permeate your existence until you not only abide in and as silence, but also exude it in your day to day life.

Manifesting Silence

Yeshua said, "The man aged in days will not hesitate to ask a small child seven days old about the place of life, and he will live. For many who are first will be last, and they will become one and the same."

- The Gospel of Thomas, Saying 4

Your focus dictates the actions that you will take in the material realm. The soul that is bound by their egoic identity will act according to that egoic identity and the ways in which the mind pulls it to and fro. But the soul that has surrendered their identity to silence, and therefore to God, will be liberated from the influence of all phenomenon, and their actions within the material realm will follow from that.

To surrender your identity to silence and to therefore have your speech, actions, and thoughts be permeated by silence is the greatest peace that any soul can consistently know while they still exist in mortal form. But to the one yet bound in egoic identity, abandoning oneself to silence in this way may seem like a foolish or even terrifying prospect. After all, how can one possibly function in the world if one is consistently deferring to silence? Surely there is so much that needs to be acted out, considered, and discussed.

It is obvious that for as long as we exist in mortal form there will be times when we need to act, times when we need to speak, and times when we need to think. If I believed otherwise, I would not now be writing a book in order to convey understandings to your mind. But actually, the vast majority of souls act, speak, and think far in excess of what is needed to function in the world and fulfil their obligations. They act too much because they believe that their destiny, and sometimes that of the whole world, is dependent upon them forcing their will upon reality. They talk too much because they feel that they must give voice to the chaos of their minds, especially if the alternative is the silence with which they are deeply uncomfortable. And they think too much because they live in the past and in the future, and rarely the present. All of this stems from identification with some form of egoic identity, an identity that is necessarily insecure because it understands itself to be detached from, and to a large extent, at the mercy of the rest of creation. Most souls believe that their noise is strength, when in fact it is a testimony to their great weakness and as sure a sign of suffering as a cry of pain, for despite all of their acting, talking, and thinking, they are unable to simply be. Despite this, most souls will resist letting go of their own idea of themselves because they dread any alternative and fear that it will result in them becoming entirely inactive.

Yet, does my writing this book suggest that I do not act? Does my experience in discussing these matters suggest that I do not speak? Do my words suggest that I do not think? When you abide in silence and as silence, you will find that, contrary to doing nothing at all, you will do exactly what is needed, and you will do it far more efficiently, for you are no longer bound by the egoic identity that is so vulnerable to phenomenon, and particularly that of the mind which will cast doubt on all that you have done, are doing, and will ever do.

There are very many souls in this world that claim to be living under the guidance of God, but if a soul is still bound by egoic identity, then it is necessarily that egoic identity that is dictating their actions.

Worldly wisdom will insist that you should come into a better understanding of yourself as a person, and that you should carefully chart your course through life and force reality to conform to whatever vision you have for your future. Mystic wisdom says that you must surrender all conceptions of yourself and therefore all intent to silence, for when you surrender to silence, you surrender to the Spirit. Only when you have surrendered yourself in this way can you live out the destiny that God has in store for you, and whereas the guidance of the mind is insistent, the guidance of God is a silent, effortless guidance that, due to its grace, will not impose itself upon your life, but rather will wait for you to consciously surrender to it. When you have done that, you will find that life simply begins to unfold in your favour.

I am not concerned with what I take myself to be, what others take me to be, or what I will do in the future. Having surrendered my identity and intent to silence, I simply am, and when I act I act, for as the apostle Paul wrote in 1 Corinthians 15:10, "by the grace of God, I am what I am." Although that verse is often used to cheaply excuse immoral behaviour, you should now have at least an idea of its deeper significance: when we surrender to the Spirit in silence, we drop all egoic ideas about what we are and what we should be and so no longer carry the burden of deciding our own destiny. Instead, it is the Spirit of God that guides us, and therefore, whatever we become, it is by the grace of God.

Not only will all of the disparate elements of your experience begin to fall into place, other souls out there in the world, regardless of their own state of remembrance, will perceive the change in you. This is because, having surrendered your identity to silence, you have returned to the state of innocence that I elaborated upon within chapter two, and the Spirit that you are will begin to radiate as silence. There will be times when another soul feels an urgent need to ask a question of you, but upon meeting you, they suddenly no longer feel that need, because although they do not recognise it, your very presence has brought them peace. But there will be other souls that will become every bit as uncomfortable with you as they are with silence itself for this same reason; they will either believe that there is something wrong with you, or they will be intimidated by you, because they cannot relate to being at such peace in circumstances within which their minds are so chaotic.

There is also no pretentiousness in surrendering to silence—you should not expect to spend your days meditating upon a mountaintop or behind a waterfall in a continuous bid to demonstrate how spiritual you are. On the contrary, your life may continue to be relatively mundane in terms of the worldly activities that you engage in. The difference is that no matter what you end up doing, you do it in the peace of the Spirit that you are. There is a wonderful saying—allegedly a Zen saying—that goes, "before enlightenment, chop wood; after enlightenment, chop wood." I am unsure of where that statement originates, and one must always be wary regarding the true origin of such quotations, especially when they are attributed to Siddhartha Gautama—souls have a habit of erroneously attributing all manner of statements to him, almost certainly because he is so highly respected. But regardless of what the true origin of that alleged Zen saying is, it refers to the reality in view here.

Purpose

> "I can do nothing on my own. As I hear, I judge, and my judgement is just, because I seek not my own will, but the will of Him who sent me. If I testify about myself, my testimony is not true."

> - Yeshua, The Gospel According to John 5:30,31

For many souls the most troubling aspect of my teachings on the subject of silence is the fact that in renouncing one's intent in all areas, one is seemingly also renouncing their purpose. Meaning is very important to any soul, and yet meaning is derived from that very purpose. Therefore, it would seem that to suggest that a soul should abandon all purpose is to essentially ask them to surrender their reason for being.

The only purpose that most souls conceive of themselves as having emerges from the responsibilities that they obtain throughout the course of their mortal life. For example, the only purpose that most parents perceive themselves as having is to ensure the survival and happiness of their children. Such a purpose emerges from natural and healthy instincts and is not at all what is under discussion here. When I use the word "purpose" throughout this book, I am specifically referring to a soul's perception of itself as having a task to effect great change in the world or to otherwise be something very specific in the world.

I will begin by pointing out that the purpose that souls decide for themselves is not usually the wonderful thing that most would make it out to be. Indeed, the grander the purpose that a soul believes itself to have, the more dire the results usually are. Every atrocity in history was committed by those that either sought to hurt the world that they perceived as having hurt them, or that fully believed that their purpose was to make the world a better place. Not even the most evil human in all of history believed themselves to be evil. Rather, they fully believed that they were fulfilling a greater purpose. Has your own experience not taught you that those that are content in life are far easier to get along with than those driven by some self-determined purpose? Of course, there are those that have effected great and positive change in the world through their belief that it was their purpose to do so, but such souls are very much the exception.

Any idea that a soul may have of themselves as someone that must have a purpose or that must make a difference in the world is just that—an egoic idea, and believe me, within every killer there is a personhood bulging with self-importance, self-righteousness, self-pity, and weak sentimentality. It is almost always the case that those that are the most determined to change the world are the least fit to do so, being crippled by all manner of mental and emotional ailments. Indeed, determination to "correct" the world is often nothing but an avoidance strategy: it is far easier for a soul to direct their focus upon the problems that they perceive with the world rather than upon the very obvious problems within themselves. In many cases the problems that souls perceive in the world are nothing more than projections of their own miserable state of being.

The reality is that all of us make a difference in the world every single day in ways that most never consider through the simple ways in which we interact with others within our sphere of direct influence, however small that sphere may be. A pleasant smile or a kind word to another soul can transform their immediate experience and therefore their future in ways that few could imagine. But I have never known anyone that was determined to change the world that was not also wholly negligent in their dealings with those closest to them; their egoic desire to enact great change and for the recognition of having done so blinds them to the obvious difference that they can make with whatever influence they already have. More than that, such souls are highly likely to justify neglect and abuse in seeking to fulfil their purpose.

Spirit manifested as innumerable souls so that it might know duality and limitation. Therefore, all souls are fulfilling God's general purpose merely by undergoing their experience of individuality. However, God also has a specific purpose for each soul within that experience of individuality, but it is not a purpose that can be fulfilled for as long as those souls seek to create their own substitute for it.

Even Yeshua never had a purpose that he consciously crafted for himself—he made clear on numerous occasions that he did not, in any circumstance, do his own will, but only the will of God who had sent him. Being aware of this, do you honestly believe that while Yeshua understood himself to be unfit to decide his own purpose, you are fit to decide yours? Do you believe that in doing so you will somehow create for yourself a purpose that is greater and more fulfilling than the purpose that God has in store for you? The reality is that when souls craft a purpose for themselves they are doing so based upon their own idea of who and what they are, which is to say that they are doing so according to their egoic identity. This is why such a self-determined purpose will almost always lead a soul astray and cause them to be a detriment to themselves and to others.

When you first surrender your identity and intent to silence, you will initially feel somewhat lost, because you have been habituated into following the whims of your mind, including those whims that relate to your destiny. But what you will find is that, day after day, you will do exactly what you need to be doing. This is the way that God's destiny for us manifests—not as a vision within our minds of what we should be and what we should be doing in this world, but as a reality that manifests effortlessly before us every day. It is for this reason that while we will certainly have peace in living out this destiny, we can only see the true brilliance of it in hindsight—God's plan is one that, due to our limited perspective, is only understood as perfect in retrospect. This is why surrendering to God through silence in this way requires a high degree of faith on our part, and the true meaning of faith will be elaborated upon within chapter nine.

Many of you are reading a book of this nature because suffering has brought you to a place of seeming desperation, and this is to your advantage, for having walked down so many different paths in this life through your own initiative, you have come to know of the folly of doing so. Therefore, you lose nothing by putting what I say here to the test and, for once, properly acknowledging that God knows best how to chart the course of your life. There is also nothing to say that God's purpose for your life will not involve activities that you are already inclined towards; when souls imagine God giving them a purpose, they typically imagine living a life comparable to that of a prophet from the Hebrew Bible, but that is rarely the case. If, for example, you are particularly talented at music, it is highly likely that God's purpose for your life involves you employing that talent; for all of my life I have been fascinated by the paranormal, cryptids, and ancient mysteries, and God has me pursue them even now. When you are doing what God intends you to be doing in life, you will know it without doubt, and you will strive with God to fulfil your true purpose.

There are many ways that one might describe what spirituality is to a soul that is not at all familiar with any spiritual ideas. The best way to describe spirituality is with the word "surrender", for spirituality really is a process of continuous surrender: you surrender your false ideas of self so that you might know your true self, you surrender your ideas about God so that you might know God, and you surrender all intent so that your life may be guided by the divine will. This is why I wrote earlier that if I could distribute only one chapter of this book, it would be this chapter, for while many important understandings that will make remembrance easier lie outside of it, that spirituality is a continuous process of surrender to silence is all that any soul need ever know.

Chapter Eight: Adjustment

As you seek to surrender all identity and intent to silence, you will feel a tremendous amount of resistance within. This arises from the duality innate to being a soul in mortal form that I elaborated upon within chapter three, and the egoic identity will fight for its supremacy even as you come to experience the reality beyond it. Of course, as an idea within the mind, the egoic identity has no power in itself; rather, it is your attachment that gives it power. For as long as we exist within mortal form, we will experience this duality, as is evident from the way that Yeshua had to choose to surrender his fleshly desires to do the will of God right up until the end. But it is not only this internal duality that you will experience—it will seem that all of reality is conspiring to hold you in forgetfulness.

The Sifting

> Yeshua said, "Simon, Simon, behold, Satan demanded to have you, that he might sift you like wheat, but I have prayed for you that your faith may not fail, and when you have turned again, strengthen your brothers."
>
> Peter said to him, "Lord, I am ready to go with you both to prison and to death."
>
> Yeshua said, "I tell you, Peter, the rooster will not crow this day until you deny three times that you know me."
>
> - The Gospel According to Luke 22:31-34

As you consciously surrender all identity and intent to silence, not only are you likely to experience much of the phenomenon addressed within this chapter for the first time, but even familiar abrasive phenomenon will come to be experienced more strongly than ever. This experience of

136

negative phenomenon suddenly seeming to conspire against you is what I call "the Sifting" based upon Yeshua's statement to his disciple Simon Peter in the above excerpt from the Gospel of Luke.

Peter is well known for having been zealous and yet foolhardy in his devotion to Yeshua; he was always the first one to assert his loyalty to Yeshua and to insist that he would follow him, even if doing so meant death. And yet, he is also infamously the disciple that betrayed Yeshua by denying knowledge of him three times in order to save himself while Yeshua was away standing trial before the Jewish religionists. This test that Peter ultimately failed was part of the very "Sifting" that Yeshua warned him of. But what conclusions can we draw from the existence of this Sifting? If everything in reality has a specific purpose, then why does this Sifting come about and on behalf of whom? In the excerpt from the Gospel of Luke that opened this section, Yeshua attributed the Sifting of Peter to Satan, so are you meant to conclude that there is some malevolent force that is set against souls remembering their true spiritual nature? The answer is "yes", and the answer is "no".

The figure of Satan is nothing more than a personification of egoic phenomenon that arises to tempt, distract, and otherwise be detrimental to our experience of reality, and especially our journey of remembrance. This can be plainly seen within the texts of the New Testament where, for example, the narrator of the Gospel of John tells us in John 13:27 that Satan entered into Judas immediately before he left the last supper to betray Yeshua to the religious authorities, thus conveying that Judas surrendered to an egoic desire, namely that of greed. This is something that Judas had clearly struggled with for some time, for John 12:6, in explaining why Judas objected to money being spent on ointment for Yeshua instead of the poor, tells us that, "He said this, not because he cared about the poor, but because he was a thief, and having charge of the moneybag he used to help himself to what was put into this." The synoptic gospels also tell us that Judas ultimately betrayed Yeshua to the Jewish religionists for thirty pieces of silver, something that he quickly regretted doing, but too late to stop the events that would follow. And so it was through the common allure of greed that "Satan" gained victory over Judas, a soul that would later destroy its own mortal form, being unable to find peace afterwards.

There are similar personifications of these egoic forces within other traditions, such as the demon "Mara" in the Buddhist tradition who fulfilled the exact same function in Siddhartha Gautama's life as Satan did in Yeshua's life. Anyone that has studied the mythology surrounding the great mystics of history will know that there are many commonalities in their stories, and this is especially true when it comes to the stories surrounding Yeshua and Siddhartha Gautama, so much so that there have been attempts within academia to try and establish a historical link between the early Christian tradition and Buddhism, the assumption being that they must have had significant contact for such similarities to exist.

Yet such a historical link is not at all needed to explain such commonalities, for the ultimate purpose of such mythologies, whether or not Yeshua and Siddhartha Gautama actually existed within mortal form, is to convey universal spiritual truth. The testing of the central mystic by an adversary portrayed as being supernatural is among the most common motifs, yet in no case is such an adversary the clear cut personification of evil that so many perceive them to be.

There are several mentions of Satan throughout the New Testament that make no sense until you understand that Satan is a personification of our own egoic desires. For example, in 1 Corinthians 5:1-5, the apostle Paul addressed the misconduct of a member of the Corinthian church and concluded that the soul should be cast out of the church "to Satan for the destruction of his flesh". This pronouncement naturally causes much confusion for those in the modern day that understand Satan as nothing more than an evil entity that stands in opposition to God, and it would seem to cast the apostle Paul himself in a very negative light.

But when you understand that Satan is nothing more than a personification of egoic impulses you can understand the apostle Paul's pronouncement and reasoning: since that member of the Corinthian church would not conduct themselves properly, the apostle Paul knew that it would be best if they were abandoned to their carnal desires, for sating them would invariably lead to suffering (the "destruction of their flesh") and then perhaps their repentance. The apostle Paul understood that, as I explained previously, suffering is ultimately for our own benefit, for it weakens and undermines our egoic identity, which is why it is always suffering that will cause souls to turn to God.

But although the figure of Satan, whether he is understood literally or metaphorically, is typically understood as opposing God, this understanding can only be maintained if New Testament references to him are being considered in isolation from the texts of the Hebrew Bible that themselves were the sacred texts of the authors of the New Testament. When one looks to the Hebrew Bible, one will find some apparent oddities, such as the much marked fact that Satan sits upon the Divine Council of God and acts only at God's behest, and it is this detail that is the key to understanding Satan and therefore "his" conduct from the highest perspective.

It is commonly observed that so often it seems that just as one is "getting somewhere" in life, something will go wrong to ensure that the process is not as smooth as it otherwise could have been. This observation is often made in a joking fashion, and yet the phenomenon being commented upon is indeed very real, for the purpose of the material realm is to put us to the test so that we may endure its trials, and having done so, emerge with a greater knowledge of ourselves. This phenomenon—this Sifting of Satan—is never more apparent than when a soul seeks to liberate itself from egoic identity, for it is then that phenomenal storms will arise like never before. Satan is portrayed as sitting on the Divine Council of God in order to illustrate that there is really no such thing as a rogue element in creation; if something exists, it exists either due to the direct will of God, or because He is allowing it for some higher purpose.

Therefore, as you come to abide as the Spirit that you truly are, you should expect to meet extreme resistance from your egoic identity in a variety of ways. All things that exist work towards fostering remembrance within the souls that are living our their experience of individuality, and it is not just that this is also true of Satan and the egoic desires that he personifies—it is especially true of Satan and the egoic desires that he personifies. Without them, Peter could not have been tested in the way that he was, and nor could he have ultimately repented as he did, becoming a wiser disciple of Yeshua than he was before, and one that (according to tradition) ultimately did die in his name. Sifting is, after all, a process of refinement.

I have explained all of the above so that you may face your

139

Sifting, and indeed any trial, with the wisest disposition, recognising that no matter how detrimental they may seem to be to your experience of reality, they are ultimately serving you, for as with everything else in existence, they necessarily function under the direct sanction of God. Therefore, the wisest souls will not merely grudgingly accept suffering as a student tolerates an unpleasant teacher, but will instead be just as grateful for their suffering as they are for everything else.

Blinding Expectations

> As it is written, "What no eye has seen, nor ear heard, nor the heart of man imagined, what God has prepared for those who love Him." These things God has revealed to us through the Spirit, for the Spirit searches everything, even the depths of God.

> - The Apostle Paul, The First Epistle to the Corinthians
> 2:9,10

A very common issue faced by souls undergoing remembrance is a sense of disappointment that their experiences are not matching the expectations that they had of what it would mean to lead "a spiritual life". This causes them to grow disheartened and may even cause them to abandon their focus on remembrance altogether, reasoning that it cannot be the way to truth because it does not seem like truth to them.

This is actually a more subtle form of the mental counterfeit spirituality that I have already expounded upon—you have ideas within your mind that you expect the spiritual to conform to, and if it does not then you will deem it unworthy of further attention. This is to place yourself—which is to say, your egoic identity—as the arbiter of what spiritual truth is. You are waiting for the idols of your mind to manifest before you instead of receiving whatever God graciously bestows you with through the Spirit.

Be clear on this matter: when you come to experience your own

140

spiritual essence, whether it is in a momentary epiphany or through complete transcendence, you will be in absolutely no doubt whatsoever about it, and all of your former ideas about what the spiritual should be like will be revealed as silly and misguided. All of your focus from that point forth will be upon returning to that direct experience and upon testifying of it to others. This is why overt acts of grace such as my own spiritual awakening are such a gift, for there is nothing that will instil a greater desire for God within a soul as much as a glimpse of heaven. Therefore, do not imagine that you might experience the truth that you are and not find it to your liking. I laughed to myself at the very idea as I wrote that last sentence, and there will come a time when you will understand just how laughable the idea is. How can you be dissatisfied with perfection?

Yet your very expectations will prove to be a barrier to an experience of the Spirit. If you fully anticipate that the spiritual will manifest in ways that conform to your expectations then your focus is misdirected and you will miss the sublimely subtle experience that is your spiritual essence. Ironically, in many cases those expectations will have been informed by sacred texts such as those that I have employed throughout the course of this book due to the way that their terminology is so greatly misunderstood, and so even ideas informed by such highly respected sources must be abandoned.

As a consequence of whatever expectations a soul might have within their mind, they unwittingly invest their time not in being, but in waiting, and if you allow your mind to set expectations for your experience of reality then be assured that it will do so forever. You must surrender your expectations to silence just as you surrender all notions of identity to silence. Indeed, your perception would not be so clouded by expectations if you were not still invested in a form of egoic identity to some degree, for only an ego expects. But this need not trouble you: simply surrender all of these things to silence and focus upon reality as it unfolds before you within the Eternal Moment.

Expectation can also hinder a soul when it comes to their conduct. It may be that, having begun to engage in experiential spirituality, and perhaps also having experienced an increasing sense of liberation, one momentarily slips in terms of behaviour, acting in a way that causes their conscience to condemn them. Such a slip can easily cause a soul to become disheartened and disillusioned with themselves.

Perhaps you lash out in anger at another soul in front of many others and afterwards you begin to fear that you have actually made no true spiritual progress whatsoever. Not only that, but you know that you have shamed yourself before others that must surely recognise just as you do that you are at best misguided and at worst a fraud. At that point, it seems that there is nothing left to do but wallow in defeat, for what soul can possibly take you seriously after having fallen so publicly?

But what are you that can feel so defeated? It can only be some form of egoic identity—some idea of what you are that you are retaining. In this case, you would be holding onto an idea of yourself as a spiritual seeker, which is to say, a human being that is endeavouring to attain to some spiritual state. Any errors in conduct will therefore be understood as the human being having failed in their task, and so a sense of shame and defeat are inevitable. But the reality is that you are Spirit and can never be anything else; no matter what phenomenon arises before you, and no matter what your mind tells you about that phenomenon, you will eternally remain that transcendent Spirit. To truly accept this is to experientially recognise it.

Therefore, for you there can be no defeat because your true essence always remains as the Spirit which is undefeatable. Defeat and deficiency can only be felt when you experience certain phenomenon that your mind interprets in erroneous ways that you then accept without question due to your attachment to some form of egoic identity, even forgetting all that you may have already experienced of the Spirit. But that phenomenon and those interpretations themselves are nothing, for they rise and fall before the transcendent Spirit that you are. However, if you bestow them with your focus and believe them, it is then that they become something, and your experience will be brought low as a result. I have not addressed the problem of being a prisoner of the opinions of other souls, for I assume that anyone that would read a book of this nature would have progressed beyond that infantile stage of development. Needless to say, the way that other souls react to you is itself another form of phenomenon and should be treated as such. Whether another soul regards you as an ascended master or as a foolish cretin is going to make no difference whatsoever to the reality of your state of being unless you allow it to.

Momentary lapses in behaviour are nothing more than residues of the conditioning that you have spent the vast majority of your mortal life living under. They are not reflective of the Spirit that you truly are, but rather reflective of the behaviour and thought patterns of the egoic identity that you are now letting go of. Without your investment through identification, such patterns of behaviour will inevitably wind down and cease altogether. Allow this to occur as it will. You are the transcendent Spirit beyond all form and beyond all corruption. Accept that, surrender all else to silence, and then see what is ultimately capable of leaving you feeling deficient and defeated.

Detachment and Alienation

"If the world hates you, know that it has hated me before it hated you. If you were of the world, the world would love you as its own, but because you are not of the world, but I chose you out of the world, therefore the world hates you. Remember the word that I said to you: 'A servant is not greater than his master.' If they persecuted me, they will also persecute you. If they kept my word, they will also keep yours."

- Yeshua, The Gospel According to John 15:18-20

For as long as you exist within mortal form your personhood will be relevant to you because it informs you of the place of your mortal form in the world and because it reflects the way that most other souls will always understand you.

If, having transcended all forms of egoic identity, you encounter a familiar soul that does not share these understandings, they will greet you as nothing more than the human being they have always taken you to be. You should not correct them, but rather, match their expectations; you will simply not be able to function in this world without speaking and acting according to your personhood, because human society has naturally been built based upon anthropocentric assumptions.

There is nothing to be feared in this—egoic identity was not a mistake, but something that is necessary for the human world that souls sought to experience to be able to function. This is why the goal was never to destroy all egoic identity, nor to deny that it exists, but rather to simply recognise its proper place beneath the Spirit that you actually are, and to directly experience that spiritual reality. Having transcended egoic identity in this way, not only do you not have to fear any form of egoic identity, but you are also best placed to employ it because you are employing it without operating under the delusion that it represents the totality of what you are. In this way you can see how even that which binds souls to the material realm becomes as a plaything to the soul that has become unbound through direct experience of the Spirit.

You are not being dishonest with other souls by matching their expectations, for your mortal form and the personhood that is informed by it are actually you—it is just that they are a lesser and temporary extension of what you fundamentally are as immortal Spirit. Therefore, when interacting with other souls, you are not deceiving them by talking according to personhood, you are merely being sensitive to how they understand you, and wise regarding when it is appropriate to evoke mystic truths—those times are typically not when you are eating at a family dinner or engaging in some manner of business transaction.

You should always interact with souls that are receptive to mystic truth in a way that resonates with their level of understanding. This is the true meaning behind the apostle Paul's much misunderstood statement in 1 Corinthians 9:19-22 where he wrote, "Though I am free from all, I have made myself a servant to all, that I might win more of them. To the Jews I became as a Jew, in order to win Jews. To those under the law I became as one under the law (though not being myself under the law) that I might win those under the law. To those outside the law I became as one outside the law (not being outside the law of God but under the law of Mashiach) that I might win those outside the law. To the weak I became weak, that I might win the weak. I have become all things to all people, that by all means I might save some."

The understandings that you have acquired by reading this book have often been regarded as secret truths, not so that those that know them can indulge their ego, feel more important than every other soul, and form a secret society that no-one else is allowed access to, but because the world and most souls in it are simply not ready for these understandings and they will become deeply confused and distraught if you speak in accordance with them. You are only obliged to bestow understanding upon those that are both ready and willing to receive it.

It is something of a cliché to understand a mystic as being a recluse, but isolation is strongly associated with spiritual development for a very good reason: as you become aware of your transcendent nature, it is inevitable that you will become increasingly detached from the souls around you, and in the beginning this can be disconcerting or even distressing for those that undergo the experience. Yet the reason that this must happen is very straightforward and is well summarised by the words of Yeshua that opened this section.

It has been said that "like attracts like", and this unwittingly refers to the fact that souls of similar levels of remembrance desire to associate with one another more than they do with anyone else. This is quite naturally the case, since every soul feels that they can be more free and open around those souls that they resonate with. Indeed, the much romanticised term "soul mate" refers to a soul that one resonates deeply with due to being at a similar level of remembrance, and this may or may not be within the context of a romantic relationship.

It is also commonly said that "opposites attract", and this is also true. It seems contradictory to the former observation only because, like that former observation, it is typically made in a throwaway fashion and is not at all examined. Souls may resonate tremendously with those that differ with them in superficial ways—which is to say, on the level of egoic identity—because details of egoic identity so often say nothing about a soul's level of remembrance. Therefore, a soul may indeed feel a profound connection with those that differ with them religiously, politically, and in many other unimportant areas, but they will never feel a deep connection with one that is of a drastically different level of remembrance, regardless of how similar they are in terms of egoic identity. But because it is the level of remembrance that fundamentally determines to what degree souls will resonate with one another, the nature of a relationship will never change more radically than when one soul involved in that relationship is endeavouring to recall its own transcendent nature, for that process necessarily involves an increasing level of remembrance.

This is why, having made a commitment to know God through the process of remembrance, you should fully expect old relationships to wither and die. It has always been this way, and this phenomenon is nothing more than souls mutually recognising how different they are in terms of their level of remembrance. But because this recognition is usually unconscious, when souls begin to sense a former connection waning, they can become confused and frustrated, and this often results in artificial, interpersonal melodramas as each soul tries to justify its inexplicable feelings to itself. You may also find that former friends come to actively resent you, and this is because they naturally sense that you are walking a path that they also must, but are not yet ready to—the Spirit that they are recognises your progress, and this recognition, filtered through the mind and interpreted by an egoic identity, is so often translated into resentment.

The opposite is also true: as relationships with those that you no longer share a similar level of remembrance with wither and die, new relationships with those that share your new level of remembrance will be seeded and flourish. However, because high levels of remembrance are exceptionally rare, the higher your level of remembrance, the fewer the souls that you will resonate with. This is why the great spiritual masters always ended up with only a few loyal followers, the others having fallen away, and it is why you may go from being surrounded by friends to having only one or two, or perhaps none at all.

I remember when I was reading through the Bible for the very first time, understanding little about what any of its texts were trying to convey. Reading the gospels, I came across Yeshua's well known statement in Matthew 13:57 where he said, "A prophet is honoured everywhere except in his home town and among his family." Upon reading that, I thought to myself, "well, that is because they knew him before he was a prophet." I did not take my own interpretation seriously —it was merely the first thought that arose within my mind. But what I would later realise is that my initial understanding of Yeshua's statement was completely correct. Indeed, the kind of adversity that a soul will face from those familiar with them having transcended egoic identity is something that is frequently addressed within the biblical texts, and it is something that Yeshua himself had to endure on several occasions throughout his ministry.

The primary narrative of the canonical gospels begins when Yeshua was anointed by the Spirit in the River Jordan and was recognised by God as a son—a recognition that he had entered into the rest that Christians would describe as "salvation". It is after that event that Yeshua was led into the wilderness by the Spirit of God to endure various temptations from Satan before returning to civilization in order to begin his ministry. But those that had known Yeshua prior to his remembrance could not reconcile the man that they once knew with the one that now taught among them. More than once, those in the crowds that thronged about Yeshua questioned his new status as a spiritual teacher. In Matthew 13:54-56, someone asked, "Where did this man get this wisdom and these mighty works? Is this not the carpenter's son? Is not his mother called Mary? And are not his brothers James and Joseph and Simon and Judas? And are not his sisters with us? Where did this man get all these things?"

Nobody thinks that they know a soul better than their family and friends, and this is why your spiritual transformation is likely to be resisted more fiercely by those closest to you than by anyone else— Yeshua's own mother and brothers initially believed him to have gone mad. Yet such resistance will not come purely from an inability to understand your radical transformation. In fact, it will primarily come from the concern that they have for the person that they always took you to be; your transformation makes them feel that they are at risk of losing, or have already lost, a person that they care deeply for.

There is nothing to be done about this, for until those souls understand all that I have already taught you, they will not understand the reason for such a transformation, or that it is ultimately a positive change that they, in this lifetime or another, will also have to undergo. Fortunately, genuine love for another does not require that you like or understand their state of being, but only that you are willing to accept their freedom to develop as they will, and it is as important for you to remember that as it is for anyone else. Be wary of any soul or collective that would seek to exploit this feeling of detachment in order to separate you from your family and friends, for this is a form of manipulation practised by many sects, and even within certain denominations of major religions in more subtle ways. It may be that it would be beneficial for you to distance yourself from certain souls, but never cede such responsibilities to other souls; cede them to God.

There will inevitably be those souls that react to your new state of being and whatever they know of your understandings from a place of hostility. All such hostility is born of a level of egoic ignorance that it is simply not worth engaging with. When a soul asks me a question in a mocking fashion or otherwise expresses contempt for the mystic way, I often simply turn around and walk away without saying a word, thereby leaving them with the very silence that would be their salvation if only they had the humility to seek understanding.

Yeshua often spoke to the crowds that gathered around him in parables that he knew perfectly well that they would not understand, the reason being that it was not yet time for them to understand. For different reasons I will likewise often make statements that I know perfectly well will be misunderstood. For example, I might say that "God tells me what to do from moment to moment", knowing that most secular souls will assume me to be insane. I do this despite knowing that if I were to instead say, "I live according to my conscience and intuition", then my words would be far more acceptable to them. If a soul genuinely seeks understanding then they will inquire further about statements that are confusing to them instead of responding with ridicule, and so I deliberately make statements that, while true, I know will sound bizarre to the majority of souls in order to determine which of them are open to greater understanding. This naturally leads to most souls thinking of me as strange (at best), but if I was concerned about how the world perceives me then I would have no business writing a book of this nature.

The one that knows God knows that they are never alone and they are therefore never lonely. I am an introvert and a loner in my own personhood, and so I have never at any time in my mortal life felt that I needed the company of others. But the egoic identities of most souls are not so inclined, and most of you will feel uncomfortable with the period of isolation that comes about during remembrance. Yet this isolation is just one manifestation of a process of detachment, and like so much phenomenon that seems abhorrent, it is a positive development.

You must understand that the intent to know your true nature is not something that could ever arise from a human being—your motivations are literally not human. Not only are they not human, they are anti-human, in the sense that they involve becoming detached from the very personhood upon which identity as a human being depends. The process of recognising your transcendent state will ultimately take you beyond motivation altogether, and therefore you cannot be surprised that most others souls will be increasingly unable to relate to you.

You will come to know the Spirit that is your true essence, and that Spirit is perfect. It is therefore inevitable that you will become disinterested in and detached from the material and mental matters that most other souls are enamoured with because it is through such matters that they consciously and unconsciously seek to alleviate their sense of deficiency. Their hopes will no longer be your hopes and their fears will no longer be your fears. The world that most take to be the totality of reality will begin to feel distinctly unreal as you come to know the Spirit that alone is real, and you will increasingly feel as though you are slowly but surely awakening from a dream, for so you are.

I can remember even the changes that I had fully anticipated manifesting in ways that I did not anticipate. There came a point where physical death was no longer a concern for me—my own and that of others. This is something that anyone that embarks upon the spiritual path might foresee—after all, to face God necessarily involves facing death, but I was surprised to find that my comfort with death made it impossible for me to get invested in so much entertainment, since the drama in that entertainment so often comes from characters being at risk of physical death; since I no longer saw physical death as being consequential, I could not take the predicament of those characters seriously, and therefore such entertainment was no longer capable of gripping me. That was most unexpected.

But it will not take long at all for you to become accustomed to your new perspective on reality, and that is because it is not a new perspective at all, but rather your most natural perspective remembered. Indeed, you will very quickly forget what it is like to be immersed in egoic identity. One consequence of this is that you fail to perceive just how strange your existence is to the vast majority of souls. Yet have no fear of that, for there are plenty of them that will be more than happy to remind you. The fact that most other souls can no longer relate to you will typically result in them growing cold towards you, or perhaps even resentful, as stated. But you will not grow cold towards them, because accompanying your increasing remembrance there will inevitably be a growing compassion for all life, but this compassion is general and not personal, just as the Spirit that you are is impersonal and not personal, and it will manifest as such.

The way that you perceive your enemies will also inevitably change, even if they remain unworthy of these understandings. There may be a soul that you once would have described yourself as having hated, and perhaps even now as you undergo remembrance there yet remains some feelings of animosity towards them, and maybe even some desire for retribution over past wrongs. Recognise that those that hate you as you openly make a conscious effort to know the Spirit that you are can only do so because they exist in some form of hell, and you do not need to defeat someone that languishes in hell, for they are already defeated in the most profound sense and have much suffering to endure before they receive their calling to remembrance. This is why the apostle Paul, quoting the Hebrew Bible in Romans 12:19, wrote, "Beloved, never avenge yourselves, but leave it to the wrath of God, for it is written, 'Vengeance is mine, I will repay, says the Lord.'"

A sense of detachment and alienation is a sure sign of progress towards rest, and it will only be experienced as a form of suffering while you are still invested in some form of egoic identity. The end result of this is not some cold detachment from physical, mental, and aethereal reality, but an unshakeable equanimity. A good way to gauge how invested you still are in something of the world is to ask yourself if you would be troubled if your mortal form were to die before you got to experience it again. If you would, then you are still attached to some degree. Yet there is no reason to force this process of detachment, and nor can you; abide in the awareness of your transcendent status and enjoy what you will while you still feel inclined to do so.

Ideological Opposition

> When Mary came to where Yeshua was and saw him, she fell at his feet, saying to him, "Lord, if you had been here, my brother would not have died."
>
> When Yeshua saw her weeping, and the Jews who had come with her also weeping, he was deeply moved in his Spirit and greatly troubled, and he said, "Where have you laid him?"
>
> They said to him, "Lord, come and see."
>
> Yeshua wept.

> - The Gospel According to John 11:32-35

Despite what some may believe, mystics have never been soft and sentimental in their approach to anything. In fact, more often than not they are perceived as being harsh, and as you will come to see, not only was this also true of Yeshua, it was especially true of Yeshua, contrary to how he is understood and portrayed within popular culture.

Besides anger, the only emotion that Yeshua conveyed within the canonical gospels was sorrow, most notably in the excerpt from the Gospel of John that opened this section. I have always found the events surrounding that particular incident highly insightful regarding Yeshua's disposition towards others, and therefore very informative as to how we should find ourselves behaving in the Spirit, even when another soul challenges those truths that have transformed our experience of reality. The narrative from which that excerpt from the Gospel of John is taken began when Yeshua announced to his disciples that their friend Lazarus had died. This knowledge was clearly obtained through supernatural means, since there was otherwise no way for Yeshua to have known about it. But this is typical of the Gospel of John where, unlike in the synoptic gospels, Yeshua is portrayed as knowing everything from the very beginning.

It should be noted that when Yeshua told the disciples of the death of Lazarus, he expressed no sorrow whatsoever. And why would he? If any one of us can learn not to mourn for those humans that have

151

died, we should naturally expect the same of Yeshua who was one with God and who knew exactly what the fate of souls was to be. Besides that, he fully intended to raise Lazarus physically from the dead, and so having informed his disciples of the death of Lazarus, he told them that they must go to him. Since Yeshua did not tell his disciples that he intended to resurrect Lazarus, they presumably thought that they were merely going to attend his funeral. When Yeshua does express emotion concerning the death of Lazarus, it is for the reason conveyed within the excerpt that I cited, namely that he witnessed the grief of the family and friends of Lazarus. In other words, although he had no cause to grieve for Lazarus himself, knowing God as he did and fully intending to resurrect the deceased, he was nonetheless still saddened by the grief of others, because they were simply not in a position to know what he knew. They mourned in ignorance—they suffered due to ignorance, and Yeshua was sorrowful at the fruit of their ignorant state.

While a period of detachment is inevitable as you come into a recognition of your transcendent state, there is a danger that, during this period, you may become desensitised to the concerns of those that are still bound in personhood. This happens because, just as you very quickly become used to your transcendent state because it is your most natural state, so too will you very quickly forget what it was like to be so enamoured by egoic identity because it was so unnatural to you, and therefore it becomes as a dream that quickly escapes your memory to be entirely forgotten.

This is a very positive development as far as your experience of reality is concerned, for those things that once troubled you no longer will, and while you must never indulge the inherent pettiness of concerns based around egoic identity, if you are to maintain any compassion at all as Yeshua did, you must always be conscious of what it is like to be bound by egoic identity, and this is especially necessary when you find yourself being opposed by ideologues with a perspective contrary to that of the mystic way.

You will find that ideological opposition comes most commonly in the form of different religionist perspectives, and yet religionists being religionists, they will have nothing to oppose you with except for raw assertions about reality based upon their interpretation of sacred texts or

152

based upon their tradition. These cannot even begin to contend with a soul's daily experience of the Spirit, and so they are not something that will ever challenge you when you have come to know that experience.

However, there has a arisen a more modern argument against mystic thought, and it is one that is worth elaborating upon. It is rather difficult to put a name to this particular argument, but I will call it "the escapist argument". It is an argument that may come from any source, but it most often comes from those that have a focus on psychology, though they will not necessarily have any worldly qualifications in that area. Indeed, anyone that is actually qualified in that area is less likely to be as belligerent as the souls in question can be. Quite simply, the escapist argument posits that the experience of that which many would call "enlightenment" as I have explained it throughout this book is in fact nothing more than a way for souls to avoid having to face past traumas or other unpleasant aspects of their mental body. Curiously, many such souls do not deny that enlightenment is a reality, only that it is not what teachers like myself say that it is.

The way that I have explained the journey to enlightenment throughout this book is entirely consistent with what every great mystic has ever said on the subject, not least Siddhartha Gautama himself whose title "the Buddha" is practically synonymous with the concept of enlightenment. Yet many of those that employ the escapist argument feel no hesitation in condemning the message of even the great mystics, in the case of Siddhartha himself, often pointing out that he abandoned his wife and child to seek enlightenment, thus seemingly demonstrating their point that what this all really amounts to is a refusal to face one's problems. While they are factually correct regarding the story of Siddhartha's early life, their interpretation of it is unusual, to say the least. But what it is important to recognise immediately is that souls that make the escapist argument are suggesting that others reject three millennia of mystic wisdom in favour of psychological understandings that have emerged within the last century, a position that can generously be described as "brave". Yet it would not be right to dismiss the escapist argument on that basis alone, for the accusation that this is all a form of psychological avoidance is worth answering seriously, even if only to quell any doubts that exist within your own mind on the issue.

The escapist argument is based on a misunderstanding of what mysticism involves, for it supposes that the ultimate goal of the mystic is the erasure or denial of the egoic identity and its deficiencies. Now, to be completely fair, I have witnessed some souls carelessly throw words like "illusory" around without due explanation of what exactly they mean (assuming that such souls even know what they mean). If you tell most souls that the material realm and the mind are "illusory" without clarification, then they will just assume you to be stupid, for from their perspective the material realm and the mind are the most obvious realities. They would also not be entirely wrong to think you stupid if your intent is to bring understanding and yet you just casually denounce plainly observable realities as "unreal", because that is quite a foolish approach. Now, if your true motivation in adopting such an approach is merely to come across as mysterious to other souls, then you have bigger, egoic problems. I can see why misunderstandings such as the one under discussion here would arise as a consequence of such folly.

I can only account for my own teachings, and I have been explicit in saying that our egoic identities—whatever form they take—are a reality in that we experience them, and that for as long as we live in mortal form, we always will. The mystic way fully acknowledges the reality of a soul's physical, mental, and aethereal state of being and places the responsibility for that state of being squarely on that soul itself. The mystic does not ask how they might erase the egoic identity or deny its existence, but rather they ask whether or not it is the sum total of what we are, and if not, how we might come to know what we truly are. If you have understood all that I have written and have put my recommendations into practice then you already know that you are something far beyond your mental body and the egoic identity around which it centres. The certainty that comes with this experiential knowing is simultaneously that which immediately vanquishes all intellectual arguments against it, and that which makes it difficult to respond to critics in a way that will satisfy them, for being limited to the mind, they will require intellectual explanations for that which lies beyond the intellect.

In order to be truly satisfied that mysticism has manifested around the world throughout history because it is genuine spirituality itself and the true means of liberation from all suffering, one must be willing to walk the mystic path and experientially verify it, but I have yet to encounter a single critic of the mystic perspective that is willing to even entertain doing so. Nor have I ever heard an explanation from those that allude to an alternative understanding of enlightenment as to what that alternative understanding is and where it originates.

My intuition tells me that I will never receive such an answer because there really is no such answer; it tells me that such souls merely pretend to give the concept of enlightenment credence so that their psychological focus will appeal more to those that do take the idea of enlightenment seriously, and that their motivation, conscious or not, is not to know truth, but to maintain an excuse to indulge their egoic desires. After all, if our egoic identities are truly representative of all that we are, then we can do little else.

When a child reaches adolescence, that phase within which they have a firmly established sense of self, but one that is not yet well defined and not at all refined, they can behave in ways that are highly irritating to the adults about them. They expect things that any adult knows are unreasonable and they will throw tantrums over matters that any adult would perceive as incredibly minor. Yet if any of those adults were to grow callous or even contemptuous of the feelings of such a child, they would be regarded as dysfunctional, for it is accepted that adulthood comes with the responsibility to be concerned for the physical, mental, and emotional welfare of even the most annoying child.

In the same way, the one that comes to remember their true nature immediately assumes a responsibility over those that yet languish in forgetfulness, for as Yeshua said in Luke 12:48, "Everyone to whom much was given, of him much will be required." There has been many a mystic that desired to live in complete isolation, never again seeing another soul in mortal form, yet there have been almost none that did, for in the Spirit they are aware of their obligation to other souls. Mystics will invariably lead reclusive lives, but they will also make themselves available to those that are willing and ready to receive the insights that they have to share. In this way they will live apart from the world and yet still fulfil the function of the mystic, which is to help others into the rest of God through the remembrance of their true, transcendent state.

As with so much else, this desire will arise naturally as you

155

abide in the experience of your true essence, but if you want an example of how mystics typically conduct themselves, I would encourage you to examine the behaviour of Yeshua and the apostle Paul; they made their message available in order to gather all of those that were ready to hear it, they were generous and patient with those that desired to transform their understanding and experience of reality, and yet they did not tolerate fools and were firm in their condemnation of those that sought to oppose their message for egoic reasons.

The ancient Gnostics were famously not evangelistic in the way that their proto-orthodox counterparts could be, and it is because they perceived the wisdom in the approach of Yeshua and the apostle Paul, both of whom they loved. Religionists betray their own worldly disposition through their emphasis on converting other souls to their tradition and upon expanding that tradition with worldly edifices. They talk as though, were their religion to be destroyed, the Kingdom of Heaven itself would be overthrown. This is because they are not truly working for the Kingdom of Heaven, but rather they are constructing their own substitute for that kingdom here in the world. If every soul currently alive within mortal form were to renounce all spirituality tomorrow, it would not make one iota of difference to the Kingdom of Heaven as it truly exists. There is therefore no need for me to attempt to convince any soul of the legitimacy of experiential spirituality; a soul is either ready to make use of it or they are not, and it makes no difference to me either way, just as it makes no difference to the Spirit itself.

When the time comes, you will be ready to explain mysticism, and especially to testify of your experiences of the Spirit, but while there is nothing wrong with telling a soul why they are wrong on a certain issue (especially for the benefit of others that may be witnessing the exchange), you should not attempt to convince any soul that is not immediately receptive to your message, and nor should you participate in debates with those that oppose the mystic message. So many debates are had for egoic reasons, and that is certainly not something that any soul undergoing remembrance should participate in. But more than that, you only debate that which is debatable; your direct experience of the Spirit is not debatable. Your understandings may be, but believe me, when you come to abide in rest it will not matter one iota to you if someone disagrees with the way that you interpret some passage of a sacred text or the way that you view some historical event. Of course, those that know nothing beyond the mind will often interpret your refusal to debate as fear on your part (or they will at least pretend to interpret it that way) and they may openly accuse you of being unable to defend your position. But since this is an obvious attempt to provoke your ego, it is something that you will be best placed to endure with good humour.

What is most important is that if you are ever tempted to be dismissive of the suffering of those that are still besieged by the phenomenon that no longer concerns you, even if they are challenging mystic thought and taunting you on a personal level, just take some time to contemplate the responsibility that is now yours when it comes to other souls, and to remember the occasion upon which Yeshua wept, and why he did so.

Chapter Nine: Virtue

To be virtuous is to demonstrate a high standard of moral conduct, and yet different souls have very different ideas about what it means to behave in a morally upright manner. This is especially true among religious collectives, the theistic of which have always had an emphasis on moral conduct due to the belief that God desires souls to live in a certain way. While such collectives might agree on the most major issues concerning moral conduct, such as the belief that murder is wrong, the morality of religious collectives often goes beyond such issues and into areas relating to the proper manner of worship, dietary practices, and other matters that a great many souls would consider insignificant. As a consequence, souls often become deeply confused regarding how they should live in the world. However, God is already telling those souls how they should live, but they are ignoring His guidance while they search for a worldly substitute.

The Folly of Moral Codes

> "When they bring you before the synagogues and the rulers and the authorities, do not be anxious about how you should defend yourself or what you should say, for the Holy Spirit will teach you in that very hour what you ought to say."
>
> - Yeshua, The Gospel According to Luke 12:11,12

Morality is a subject that is so closely tied with spirituality that the two are often seen as synonymous. This is understandable, since souls that accept the reality of the spiritual usually suppose that there is a correct way in which they should live in the world. But while behaviour is obviously important, I do not advocate any kind of moral code, and in this section I will use the subject of warfare to illustrate why.

158

Warfare is inevitable on any material world upon which the survival of its inhabitants is dependent upon them competing with one another for limited resources. Warfare is in fact one of the many consequences of the deficiency inherent within matter itself. The question of how involved a soul on the spiritual path should be in conflicts of any kind is one that I hear often. For most souls, the confusion on this issue stems from the fact that the world's sacred texts seem to give contradictory admonitions on the subject. If one looks to the Bible, one will see that although the Old Testament is full of warfare (much of which was enacted at the behest of God), the New Testament (being centred around the teachings of Yeshua) seems to demand pacifism even if it results in the death of one's mortal form. Let me be clear that Yeshua did indeed teach pacifism. It is necessary that I emphasise this because there are those Christian religionists that, in seeking to justify their own desire to engage in violence, will misconstrue the words of Yeshua on the subject and put forth arguments that can be shown to be flawed upon even a cursory examination.

The best example of such an argument involves Luke 22:36 in which Yeshua told his disciples, "But now let the one who has a moneybag take it, and likewise a knapsack. And let the one who has no sword sell his cloak and buy one." Some will claim that this verse makes it clear that Yeshua desired that his followers be armed for their own protection. If anyone ever makes this argument, then know that they are either woefully ignorant of the New Testament or dishonest, for in the very next verse Yeshua revealed the reason for his instruction: "For I tell you that this scripture must be fulfilled in me: 'And he was numbered with the transgressors.' For what was written about me has its fulfilment." In other words, Yeshua told his followers to buy swords not to use them in combat, but to fulfil an Old Testament prophecy, specifically a prophecy from Isaiah 53:12. This is why, in Luke 22:38, the disciples are revealed to have bought only two swords, which Yeshua deemed to be sufficient, despite two swords obviously being insufficient for the protection of their group.

Besides that, if Yeshua really had instructed his followers to buy swords in order to inflict violence, he would have been contradicting every other teaching that he had ever given on the subject. When Peter actually did attempt to use his newly acquired sword at the point of

Yeshua's arrest, Yeshua rebuked him for it, for Yeshua knew that it was the will of God that he be crucified. The Christian martyrs of the first three centuries clearly understood all of this perfectly well. It was only when Christianity became wedded to state power in the Roman Empire that Yeshua's plain teachings on the matter of violence began to be gradually undermined for the sake of that state.

Yet while those souls that restrict themselves to the Christian tradition are highly likely to take Yeshua's plain teachings to be the final authority on this or any other matter, those that heed the teachings of the great mystics of other traditions will encounter much confusion, for there are those sacred texts in which mystics and even God Himself are portrayed as having given licence to the use of violence.

One of the most obvious examples of this is to be found within the Hindu Bhagavad Gita, which is part of the Mahabharata epic, the details of which are far too vast to even summarise here. The narrative of the Bhagavad Gita begins as a prince by the name of Arjuna, atop his chariot, prepared to lead his army against his foes in war. However, upon learning that many of his own kin were on the opposing side, he began to despair, ultimately reasoning that it would be better for him to die than to engage in such a conflict. It is at that point that his charioteer, who is revealed to be none other than Krishna Himself as the Supreme Manifestation of the Godhead, began to instruct Arjuna concerning his plight. All of the Bhagavad Gita's seven hundred verses consist of that teaching upon the eve of battle, yet the narrative concerns not only the rightness of war, but also details the nature of reality and the ways in which the spiritual soul can best live in the world. It is the vast scope, deep insight, and yet relative brevity of the Bhagavad Gita that makes it a beloved text of so many.

Concerning war, Krishna explained that Arjuna's concerns were ultimately foolish, and that it was a minor thing to engage in a battle the likes of which Arjuna faced, for, "Neither he who thinks the living entity the slayer, nor he who thinks it is slain has knowledge. For the self slays not, nor is it slain. For the soul there is neither birth nor death at any time. He has not come into being, does not come into being, and will not come into being. He is unborn, eternal, ever-existing, and primeval. He is not slain when the body is slain."

160

Just as I have done throughout this book, Krishna emphasises the distinction between the mortal form that acts within the world and the soul that is behind it, ultimately reasoning that there is no need to refrain from battle because only mortal forms are killing and dying, while the souls behind them remain ever immortal. Not only did Krishna give licence to Arjuna to slay his foes in battle, He told him that he would be neglecting his earthly duty if he did not. Such a teaching coming from one held to be a manifestation of God may surprise those of you that are primarily familiar with the Christian tradition, but its sentiment is one that Yeshua himself would have shared, despite his own pacifistic teachings, for the Hebrew Bible (the Old Testament that contains those writings that were his own sacred texts) contains much warfare that was regarded as righteous and many statements concerning the ultimate insignificance of mortal life when the spiritual is in view. Yeshua himself made similar assertions concerning mortal life, as did his apostles within their New Testament writings; you would be utterly wrong to assume that because Yeshua taught pacifism that he therefore held to a modern, humanist view of humanity.

I can assure you as someone that lives among many of them that there are some souls in this world that, being especially ignorant, understand and respect nothing but violence. When such souls become aggressors, the humbling that comes from a solid punch to the face would do far more to elevate their thinking than a ten hour exposition on mystic wisdom would, information of a kind that they are nowhere near spiritually developed enough to make use of. It is easy to esteem an approach like pacifism, but unless you are prepared to have your mortal form destroyed for the sake of it, reality will at some point force you to reconsider. The reason for the contradictory teachings of the great mystics of the past on the subject of violence is perfectly simple: those teachings were given to souls in radically different times, places, and circumstances; Yeshua was speaking to a small flock of helpless followers that were opposed by the powerful Jewish religionists and even more powerful Roman authorities that existed at the time. More than that, it was the will of God that Yeshua be crucified. Krishna, conversely, was speaking to a prince that had command of a vast army and that had a God ordained purpose to engage in warfare.

There is a contemporary spiritual teacher (the name of whom I will not share out of respect) that used to teach his followers to practise pacifism. However, those followers began to be routinely assaulted by religionists in the local area that took exception to the spiritual teacher and his students. In the end, that spiritual teacher, distraught at seeing his followers treated in such ways, altered his teaching and told them that if any soul assaulted them, they should respond with violence. The problem is that all that spiritual teacher did is shift from one moral absolute to another, and moral absolutes will inevitably prove to be insufficient.

To assume that there are infallible moral absolutes for every situation is a great error. Moral absolutes can almost always be shown to be utterly unworkable; for every moral absolute that you might insist upon, another can imagine a dozen hypothetical scenarios, however absurd and unlikely, that demonstrate the folly of them. As previously stated, this is why no code of conduct can ever be as perfect a moral guide as your conscience, which is to say, the Spirit of God, for the Spirit of God, unlike any code of conduct, is living and responds dynamically.

Codes of moral conduct, including those devised by religious collectives, are very necessary for civilizations to prosper because the vast majority of souls in any generation will not look to the Spirit of God for moral guidance and will therefore require a substitute more appropriate for their level of development; moral codes are like the religions that emphasise them in that they are for souls at a relatively infantile state of spiritual development. I am writing for the benefit of those that are ready to advance beyond that stage.

Something else that served to distinguish the ancient Christian Gnostics from their proto-orthodox counterparts was their identification of ignorance as being the core problem afflicting mankind, as opposed to sin. This is because they recognised that to focus on immorality was to focus on a symptom of the core problem, which was that souls are ignorant of their true nature. If a soul could be brought to remembrance of their true nature through gnosis, then the erroneous behaviours resulting from their ignorance would simply dissipate. In that, those ancient Gnostics were correct, and it is for the same reason that I am not ever interested in bestowing any kind of moral instruction except when that instruction has a direct bearing upon the process of remembrance.

The Spirit that you truly are needs no moral instruction and therefore recognition of yourself as that Spirit will liberate you from misdeeds in a way that moral codes never can. It was around this very issue that the New Testament tension between the Mosaic Law of the Old Covenant and the Spirit of the New Covenant centred, something that the Gnostics (unlike most Christians even today) fully understood. It was again for this reason that the apostle Paul wrote in 2 Corinthians 3:5,6 that, "It is not that we are sufficient in ourselves to claim anything as coming from us, but our sufficiency is from God who has made us to be ministers of a new covenant, not of the letter, but of the Spirit. For the letter kills, but the Spirit gives life."

There is nothing wrong with deriving wisdom from the words attributed to mystics within sacred texts and other works—I have been doing that very thing within this book—but you err if you pretend to be one of their immediate followers when you are not. Remember the way that Yeshua chastised his disciples for heeding the words of dead men over his living presence within saying fifty-two of the Gospel of Thomas; if you can know God and receive guidance through the Spirit, then why would you ever need to engage your intellect to work out which moral code you should adhere to? Unless, of course, you lack faith that God really is willing or able to guide you in such a way.

If someone challenges my claims, then I might ignore them, or I might refute their arguments. If someone shouts a curse at me from a short distance away, then I might shrug it off, or I might rebuke them. If someone physically confronts me, then I might turn the other cheek, or I might punch them on the jaw. I am not inclined to do any one of those things, and it is ultimately not up to me—I have surrendered all intent to silence, and so whatever I do, I do according to the Spirit. Therefore, whatever I do, I do in good conscience, and I will not allow my mind to trouble me over it for even a second, regardless of how much any soul or any human law might likewise object. This is why the apostle Paul wrote in 1 Corinthians 2:15 that "the spiritual person judges all things, but is himself to be judged by nobody." It was for the same reason that in 1 Corinthians 4:3, he wrote, "It is a very small thing that I should be judged by you or by any human court. In fact, I do not even judge myself."

Not only does the Spirit liberate you from the delusion that you can ever rely on any set of moral absolutes, it also liberates you from the hypocrisy that so often accompanies them. To be a hypocrite means to practise the very thing that you teach against, or to fail to practise the very thing that you advocate. By eschewing all codes of conduct, you give hypocrisy no opportunity. The apostle Paul went even further on this matter when comparing the Mosaic Law to the perfection of the Spirit, such as in Romans 7:7-9 where he explained that it was that very law that had made him aware of what it means to do wrong in the first place: "If it had not been for the law, I would not have known sin. For I would not have known what it is to covet if the law had not said 'you shall not covet'. But sin, seizing an opportunity through the commandment, produced in me all kinds of covetousness. For apart from the law, sin lies dead. I was once alive apart from the law, but when the commandment came, sin came alive and I died."

If you have truly surrendered your egoic identity and intent to silence then you will act as you are led to. Because of this, the mystic can never truly be civilized. It is not the place of any words in any book to give you moral instruction, not even those words that are attributed to the great mystics. To believe otherwise is to entirely undermine the notion that there is a Spirit from which you receive direct guidance. If you strive to adhere to a moral code then you will become rigid in your behaviour and will inevitably err. But if, as you come to experience the Spirit, you heed the voice of God that comes through your conscience and intuition, then you will behave in the world as the Spirit—in a way that is fluid, dynamic, and never predictable.

Do not let your mind trouble you concerning activities that your conscience and intuition are silent on. The apostle Paul addressed such activities when he wrote in 1 Corinthians 6:12 that "All things are lawful for me, but not all things are helpful. All things are lawful for me, but I will not be ruled by anything." If you want to engage in sexual activity, eat unhealthy food, drink alcohol, enjoy tobacco, or whatever it may be, then you do that—we are in this world to enjoy it while we still feel inclined to. If such activities become a moral problem within your life, then your conscience will make you aware of it.

True Faith

> Now that faith has come, we are no longer under a
> guardian, for in Mashiach Yeshua you are all sons of God
> through faith. For as many of you as were baptised into
> Mashiach have put on Mashiach. There is neither Jew nor
> Greek, there is neither slave nor free, there is no male and
> female, for you are all one in Mashiach Yeshua.

> - The Apostle Paul, The Epistle to the Galatians 3:25-28

Despite being one of the most widely exalted virtues, there are few
virtues that are as abused and as misunderstood as that of faith. In order
to understand what faith is, you must first recognise the way in which it
is almost always presented in our world in order to understand what it
absolutely is not.

The lowest understanding of faith is that most often maintained
by philosophical materialists, which is that faith is nothing more than
believing something to be true for no reason at all. There are many
religionists that, being ignorant themselves, give this understanding of
faith legitimacy. Indeed, for many of them it is precisely the lack of
reasons to accept an idea that makes that idea so appealing, for the
fewer the reasons that they have to accept an idea, the more "faith" that
they require to do so, and therefore the more virtuous they believe
themselves to be in accepting that idea to be true. This is what some
would call "blind faith", but that term is an oxymoron, for "blind faith"
is no faith at all.

Serious religionists understand that faith is trust and that trust
requires something to trust in, but being religionists, they invariably
misidentify what the object of that trust should be. They confuse their
ideas, beliefs, and theologies concerning truth with truth itself, and
therefore the object of their faith becomes not the Spirit of God, but
their books, doctrines, and creeds about the Spirit of God. This is
especially true when it comes to the Bible, because as explained within
chapter six the Bible is widely known as "the Word of God", even
though in the New Testament that is a title that belongs to Yeshua. As a

165

result of this confusion, there are statements made about Yeshua within the New Testament that most Christians assume to be about the Bible itself, something that, as I have explained, is utterly impossible given that the authors of those statements had no idea that their work would one day end up within a compilation of texts called "the Bible".

The best example of this by far comes in Hebrews 4:12 where the author of Hebrews wrote, "For the Word of God is living and active, sharper than any two-edged sword, piercing to the division of soul and of spirit, of joints and of marrow, and discerning the thoughts and intentions of the heart." It is little wonder that Christians view the Bible as being infallible when statements like that are read passionately aloud by preachers as though they are about the Bible. But if anyone were to read just two more verses, they would see the problem with that notion: "Nothing is hidden from his sight, but all are naked and exposed to the eyes of him to whom we must give account. Since then we have a great High Priest who has passed through the heavens, Yeshua, the Son of God, let us hold fast our confession." The "Word of God" that is the subject of Hebrews 4:12 is Yeshua—not the Bible. You may wonder how it is that so many souls that make themselves out to be serious Christians miss this when it is stated so plainly, but as I have said, most religious adherents do not read their own sacred texts and instead rely upon isolated verses, and believe it or not, this is just as true of those that are in positions of authority within those religions, which is why even they will reinforce such pitiful errors.

It is such misunderstandings that lead Christian religionists to place their faith in not just a book, but in their interpretation of a book, instead of placing their faith in the experiential knowledge of the Spirit that Yeshua as the Word of God truly represents. The consequences of this are obvious: notice that when a Christian religionist tells you that you must have "faith" in "Jesus Christ", they are not talking about a soul, a spiritual force, or even a person that they can direct you to experience—they are actually talking about their own biblically derived doctrines concerning "Jesus Christ"; if you were to deviate from their ideas about "Jesus Christ" then they would simply not recognise your "faith" as being legitimate.

Such religionists will often encourage others to have faith even in worldly matters. To give just one example, it is not uncommon for

166

Christian apologists to present arguments to support the idea that Yeshua really did rise from the dead three days after his crucifixion. Many souls have told me that they once adopted a particular tradition due to the strength of such historical argumentation. In such cases, faith is being placed in a mere historical hypothesis. Since souls within religious spheres so often misdirect their faith in these ways, and since it therefore goes unrewarded, they gradually come to believe that faith is something that is only sometimes rewarded, even when their own sacred texts state that faith is always rewarded.

It is because of this error that many souls turn away from the spiritual altogether, for they were misguided into trusting in that which by nature is not trustworthy. If a soul has faith in a book such as the Bible, then what happens to that faith if it is demonstrated that the texts of the Bible often contradict one another or are shown to be in error? If a soul has faith in doctrines, then what happens to that faith if that doctrine is undermined? If a soul has faith in the historicity of an event, then what happens to that faith if the historicity of that event is overturned by new discoveries?

When souls describe their faith as being "tested", what they really mean is that the deficiencies of something that they erroneously placed their faith in are now becoming apparent. Many are they that, having misplaced their trust in such ways, walk away from the spiritual path entirely disillusioned, never coming to understand their error. It is most unfortunate that most religious adherents do not read their own sacred texts, for many of them clearly convey what faith is, and none more clearly than the Bible.

Throughout the canonical gospels, Yeshua frequently chastised his disciples for their lack of faith in him. Was that because he expected them to accept that he was the Son of God despite having no real reason to do so? Not at all. In fact the opposite is true: the disciples had every reason to accept that Yeshua was what he claimed to be, for they had heard his teachings and they had witnessed his miracles, and that was the problem—despite all that they had seen, they still would not trust in him; they were called "faithless" precisely because they had every reason to trust in Yeshua and yet still did not. You will not find a single instance in any sacred text where a soul is expected to exercise faith in deity or the divine based upon nothing whatsoever. That is because genuine faith is putting your trust in that which you know of deity or of the divine through direct experience.

Yet through this understanding you will have discovered the very reason that religionists are forced to misdirect their faith and to encourage others to do likewise: while a religionist may well have had some manner of transcendent experience, being a religionist they do not consistently experience the reality of Spirit. Therefore, in the absence of a direct experience of the Spirit, they must instead place their faith in the testimony of books, doctrines, and creeds, and then encourage others to do likewise, being incapable of leading those others into a state of being of which they themselves are ignorant. If you have been engaging in experiential spirituality as I have been encouraging you to throughout this book then you may already have tasted of the sublime silence of the Spirit and you may already have perceived something of its infinite grandeur. This alone is worthy of your faith, for this alone is eternal and unshakable. What force then, could compel you to have faith in anything less? What voice could be so seductive that it could lure you into trusting in its ideas? What system of theology could be so intricate that you would rather trust in its conclusions?

But now that you know what you should trust in, be aware of the end to which you are trusting it. Faith in God is not trust that all of your petty egoic desires will be fulfilled, but trust that, no matter what happens and no matter how much you may dislike it on the level of personhood, it is ultimately for the greatest of ends. You may not know what those ends are and the path that will lead there, but knowing the perfection of the Spirit, you will be content and you will be able to bear any experience. It is in this way that your faith is supremely rewarded by a peace that cannot possibly be surpassed and by an ever increasing experiential knowledge of the glory of God.

Prayer

"When you pray, you must not be like the hypocrites, for they love to stand and pray in the synagogues and at the street corners, so that they might be seen by others. Truly, I say to you, they have received their reward. But when you pray, go into your room and shut the door and pray to your Father who is in secret. Your Father who sees in secret will reward you."

- Yeshua, The Gospel According to Matthew 6:5,6

It is very common to hear a philosophical materialist assert that prayer changes nothing and is therefore a pointless exercise. If a religionist responds, they will typically insist that prayer can actually be effectual, and they may cite one or more dubious studies in a desperate bid to give the practice some credibility. Yet in such a situation, both souls are operating based on an erroneous assumption, namely the assumption that engaging in prayer is tantamount to making a wish.

Prayer is the act of communing with deity or with the divine, however any given soul understands those things. That communion may or may not involve a soul making requests, but making requests is not the primary purpose of prayer. This is not something that would immediately occur to the soul that is bound in egoic identity, be they philosophical materialist or religionist, because such a soul is inherently selfish in the truest sense of the word and will therefore expect material benefits from even spiritual activities. Praying for the sole purpose of asking things of God is where most begin, and it is certainly better to pray in such a short-sighted manner than to not pray at all, but you will need to advance beyond that stage.

Some will say that asking something of an all-knowing being makes no sense, since any all-knowing being would already know what any soul was going to ask them, which would make asking pointless. This objection is often raised as though the objector is being terribly clever, but it actually demonstrates a pitiful ignorance not just of spirituality, but of even the material history of spiritual thought. This is

169

doubly true when Christian religionists cannot answer the objection, because the synoptic gospels record Yeshua as having raised this very issue two thousand years ago in nothing less than the famous "Sermon on the Mount". Immediately before he gave "the Lord's Prayer" in that sermon, Yeshua said to his disciples in Matthew 6:7,8, "And when you pray, do not heap up empty phrases as the unbelievers do, for they think that they will be heard for their many words. Do not be like them, for your Father knows what you need before you ask Him."

It is a testimony to the sheer hubris of so many philosophical materialists that they so often raise such painfully obvious objections to spiritual understandings, honestly believing that they had never once occurred to anyone before the modern era. But such is the contempt with which they so often view those with an active spirituality. It is also a condemnation of those Christians that are taken by surprise by this objection in particular, such Christians apparently not having taken the time to even read the most famous sermon in one of the most important texts contained within the very book that they assert is "the Word of God".

Of course God knows everything, including anything that you might say to Him in prayer. Therefore, God obviously does not need you to convey that information. Indeed, God does not need anything from us at all because He is by definition perfect. Therefore, if we are required to do something on behalf of God, then you can be assured that it is for our benefit and not for His.

The very act of prayer—the very act of communing with deity or the divine, benefits us. It benefits us because it experientially bridges the gap between us as souls undergoing an experience of individuality and God. This is why you will feel empowered having engaged in prayer, even if all that you did was tell God about all that has been transpiring in your mortal life and how you feel about it on a personal level. Of course God knows those things, but the mere sharing raises your level of awareness. This is why it was that, in 1 Thessalonians 5:17, the apostle Paul recommended that souls pray without ceasing, meaning that they be ever mindful of God, and thankful to Him.

While most souls understand prayer as nothing but the means by which one asks things of God, the best thing that you can actually do in prayer is to convey your gratitude for all that you have already been given. My own prayers have consisted of almost nothing but thanksgiving for many years now, for having the utmost faith in the destiny God has laid out for me, I feel little need to ask anything from Him, unless I am led to believe that He desires me to do so. Praise is also a powerful thing to give in prayer, praise being an articulation of the greatness of deity or of the divine. The more selfless that you are in the expression of your prayers, the more that you will benefit from them. The soul that does nothing but complain and make demands of God in prayer may benefit, but scarcely.

The same principle regarding selflessness applies even when you do ask things of God: it is always best to ask on behalf of others, and when you ask for yourself, it is best if you ask for that which will serve to benefit others. In every case it is superior to ask for spiritual gifts—patience, forgiveness, tolerance, and so forth. You may ask for divine insight and supernatural knowledge, but be prepared to receive what you ask for, as such requests can be honoured very powerfully. Petitions for material luxuries are the lowest form of request that you can make in prayer, and while you may well have made such requests in the past, you should no longer do so. Petition in prayer plays its part in cause and effect just as much as any physical action that you might take within the material realm, and it is often the case that, for the sake of your own spiritual development, God will not grant you something unless you specifically ask for it in prayer, no matter how much effort you make towards it in other ways.

The practices of prayer and meditation are rarely both practised within the same tradition, and when they are, they are rarely called by those terms. In fact, there are many Christian denominations in the west that not only scoff at the idea of meditation, but even suspect it or even outright accuse it of leaving a soul open to "demonic influence", just as they do with yoga and many other practices of which they are entirely ignorant. But in truth, prayer and meditation are inseparable. I like to say that prayer is speaking to God while meditation is listening to God; I would not make a statement to another soul in mortal form and then walk away before listening to their response, and nor do I pray to God without sitting in silence for a period of time significantly longer than that which I spent speaking. You cannot rule anything out in matters pertaining to God, but generally speaking, any response that you receive will be within your deepest being, for as established, God speaks in the silence of our shared Spirit, and you will know when God has spoken without doubt.

The Active Love

> "A new commandment I give to you, that you love one another. Just as I have loved you, you also are to love one another. By this all people will know that you are my disciples, if you have love for one another."

> - Yeshua, The Gospel According to John 13:34,35

It may have occurred to some of you that the word "love" has been almost entirely absent from this book until now. It is undoubtedly noticeable because so many discourses on spiritual matters are littered with it. But its absence in this book is due to the fact that some words have become so misunderstood that it is unwise to use them without first explaining their proper meaning, and "love" is certainly one of those words.

We live in an age within which emotionalism is exalted, and like so much else, love has come to be understood as being nothing but an emotion by many souls. This is not only disastrous in practical terms, but it also results in some severe misunderstandings. If a soul were to read the canonical gospels for the first time, expecting to see the emotive and gregarious Yeshua of popular culture, one would be very surprised to instead discover a Yeshua that is very reserved, aside from occasionally being angry. In all likelihood, such a soul would conclude that Yeshua was not loving in the slightest.

But love is an act before it is anything else. Indeed, love can only make a difference if it is an act. If a soul believes themselves to feel a deep love towards another and yet does not behave in a loving fashion towards them, then their alleged emotional disposition is useless

172

to everyone but themselves. Many are they that claim to love another on the basis of how they feel, while clear hatred is manifested through their actions towards them. Yet emoting over others is certainly far easier than actually doing something practically beneficial for others, and that is why this misunderstanding of what love is has become so prevalent. If a soul were to judge the biblical Yeshua as having been unloving based upon his cold demeanour, then that soul would be judging him according to this superficial understanding of love as being nothing but an emotion, instead of judging him according to his actions. Remember what Yeshua said in John 7:24: "Do not judge by appearances, but judge with right judgement." Most mystics have come across as indifferent due to their equanimity, but that does not mean that they are unloving.

Without understanding that love is an act before it is anything else, you simply cannot make sense of so much that is said on the subject of love within the sacred texts of the world. I have spoken to many souls that are confused about Yeshua's commands to "love your neighbour as yourself" and to "love your enemies", especially in light of how harsh Yeshua and his apostles often were in their dealings with others. This confusion stems from misconstruing love to be nothing but an emotion, for it leaves those souls with the impression that Yeshua insisted that his disciples have a positive emotional disposition towards everyone, even though it is clearly impossible to change your feelings towards another by sheer force of will. However, when you understand that love is an act, then you can see that Yeshua only insisted that his disciples treated others well regardless of how they felt about them. If love is understood as being only an emotion, then the application of love is fundamentally beyond your control, but since love is primarily an act, it is never beyond your control, for it is a nothing more than a choice to behave in a benevolent fashion towards even those that you feel animosity for, and as Yeshua rhetorically asked in Matthew 5:46, "If you love only those who love you, what reward do you have?"

Very rarely do occurrences of the word "love" within sacred texts refer only to an emotion; when you understand that they almost always refer to an act, such occurrences are transformed and made all the more illuminating. For example, it is commonly asserted that "God is love". This is a biblically based assertion that comes primarily from the First Epistle of John, such as in 1 John 4:8 where the apostle John wrote that "Anyone who does not love does not know God, because God is love." Since most souls understand love to be nothing but an emotion, they will invariably interpret such verses to be portraying God as a supernatural maelstrom of emotion, when what such verses really mean is that God is infinitely benevolent towards His creation.

Because of all that I have explained, love, properly understood and put into practice, becomes another means by which we die to self, for it requires us to be benevolent towards those that we would not be if we were living according to personhood, and what it means to be loving is no mystery—none of you need me to tell you how to be kind.

But in case there is any doubt, always remember "the Golden Rule" as given by Yeshua in Matthew 7:12: "Whatever you wish that others would do to you, do also to them." Although that rule is associated almost exclusively with Yeshua, he himself derived it from his own Hebrew sacred texts, and the same sentiment can be found in even older sources from around the world. But while you do not need anyone to tell you how to be loving to others, I will tell you to be mindful of ways of being unloving that many souls overlook, and such ways all involve abusing one's superiority over another in some manner.

Let us say that you enter into a dispute with another soul on a matter regarding which you are highly knowledgeable. That other soul is asserting things that you know to be flatly false, and is doing so in an arrogant and demeaning fashion. Since that soul can be proven to be in error very easily, and since they are not particularly intelligent or articulate in conveying their point of view, you know that you can win the dispute soundly. Because of your opponent's lack of grace, the prospect of utterly humiliating them may feel good, and you may even justify doing so to yourself by reasoning that it will be a humbling experience for them and therefore ultimately for their own benefit. Even souls that consciously determine to be more loving in the practical fashion that I have described within this section can find themselves tempted in such ways.

Yet the purpose of the repeated biblical assertion that vengeance belongs to God is to remind you that it is not your place to intentionally humble other souls or to otherwise bring about your idea of justice. As established, there is a tremendous difference between acting as you are led to act by the Spirit of God, and consciously behaving according to your own idea of righteousness. Be assured that your justifications for doing so are rooted in ego and that no matter how convinced of them you may be, demeaning and humiliating another soul is not a loving act and is therefore not appropriate for the one that seeks to recognise their true, transcendent nature. If you feel that it is important to correct the soul in question, then the superior way is to correct them in a straightforward and matter of fact fashion, and then leave it there. Besides the folly that becoming embroiled in lengthy disputes can lead you into, you cannot possibly hope to correct the whole world, and attempting to do so is not a worthy investment of your time.

There is a similar temptation that you should be aware of, and it is one that is particular to those undergoing remembrance. As with the above example, this temptation relates to having an advantage over others, the advantage in this case being the fact that you no longer suffer abrasive phenomenon as most other souls do. As you break free of the influence of material, mental, and aethereal phenomenon, you will come to understand the true nature of this phenomenon and you will come to see just how much power you once allowed it to have over you, and just how much power most other souls still allow it to have over them. This puts you in a position to be able to exploit this weakness in others and will enable you to very easily manipulate them for your own gain. You must not scumble to such temptations, for they are no accident, but rather a test to see whether you truly are pure of heart, or whether you are really still driven by egoic impulses.

I have written all of this not to give you definitive moral instruction on how to be loving, for as I explained within the first section of this chapter, the Spirit itself will guide you when you come to know it; I have written all that I have here for the benefit of those that do not yet know the Spirit, and to settle any confusion that might have existed within your mind concerning the nature of love.

Chapter Ten: Aether

In the very first chapter I stated that reality is composed of matter, mind, aether, and Spirit, but while the categories of "matter", "mind", and "Spirit" will be immediately recognisable even to those who have no interest in spiritual matters whatsoever, the category of "aether" will require considerable explanation. There was no need for me to expound upon aether to any great extent before now because most souls are only exposed to it in the form of their emotions and impulses throughout the course of their mortal lives, but now that you know what it means to surrender to God through silence, what follows on the subject of aether will become increasingly relevant as you do so.

The Nature of Aether

> Yeshua said, "When you see your likeness, you rejoice. But when you see your images which came into being before you, and which neither die nor become manifest, how much will you have to bear?"
>
> - The Gospel of Thomas, Saying 84

"Aether" is my chosen term for a category that is necessary in order to place phenomenon composed of that which others might call a "ghostly", "phantom", or "astral" substance. Since such phenomenon (however any soul might understand it) is undoubtedly a part of our reality, any spiritual framework must acknowledge it. This is especially true in the case of my framework, which is based upon my own direct experience, an experience that involves encounters with the aethereal.

The words "aether" and "aethereal" are merely archaic forms of the more widely employed terms "ether" and "ethereal". My usage has very little to do with the philosophical speculations of ancient thinkers, medieval alchemists, or certain scientists from the 20th century that likewise spoke of "aether". As is always the case within experiential spirituality, what matters is not the term that is used (except as far as its effectiveness is concerned), but the phenomenon that the term refers to. Most souls will carelessly refer to aethereal phenomenon as "spiritual phenomenon", but remember that Spirit cannot be perceived by the senses because it is that as which we perceive. Utilising the category of "aether" enables me to be far more specific than assigning all non-material and non-mental phenomenon to the category of "spiritual", a category typically understood in an extremely vague fashion.

In modern parlance it is common for someone to describe something as having been sent "into the ether", meaning that it has been released only to be lost to an unknown place. Aether is intangible and permeates the world around us. It is not subject to change and therefore time in the strict way that matter is, and nor is it consistently perceived by the physical senses as matter is. Only under certain conditions can aether be perceived by our physical senses, and it is usually not directly; inexplicable and consistent sounds, strange smells, dips in temperature, and a subtle distortion in how you are hearing audible phenomenon are all indicators that the aethereal realm is manifesting within the material realm about you to some extent. To outright see or hear something of the aether while in mortal form is far rarer.

Just as you have a material body that enables you to traverse the material realm, so too do you have an aethereal body that enables you to traverse the aether and its realms, but do not confuse your aethereal body with your soul as so many do—your aethereal body is not the soul that you are any more than your material body is the soul that you are. Your soul is Spirit and therefore, unlike aether, it can never be perceived by the senses. Whereas physical sex is an attribute exclusive to matter, gender is an attribute of aether, and so while your aethereal form is neither male nor female, it is either masculine or feminine. The sex of the mortal forms that souls incarnate within will generally correspond to the gender of their aethereal forms, but not always.

I would again point to the story of Adam and Eve within the Garden of Eden—they were recognised as masculine and feminine even within the garden, but it was only when they were cast out of the garden that they began to experience that which comes naturally to male and female (such as pain in childbirth), because it was only at that point that they were incarnated into the material realm where physical sex and all that comes with it is a reality.

You have almost certainly heard many accounts of aethereal beings and of aethereal realms throughout your life, primarily in the form of ghost stories. Some of you may even have had some manner of aethereal encounter yourself, and many of you will know other souls that claim to have had such an encounter. I have had several such encounters, two of which I will testify of later on within this chapter as a means of illustrating the nature of the aethereal further.

I have also known other souls that claimed to have had such an encounter. One such soul was a former colleague who suddenly developed a brain tumour. On one occasion when I was in his home following his diagnosis, he described to me how a few nights earlier he had watched as phantoms had come through the walls of his living room, something that he seemed more fascinated than perturbed by as he described them. When I later saw that man for the last time before his death, he was unconscious, and it was obvious to me that his true essence had long since departed his mortal form, even though that form was still breathing. I am confident that upon leaving his body he found himself among the very phantoms that he had previously seen, before being guided to a heavenly aethereal realm. Of course, such accounts are easy for sceptics to dismiss. In this case, they would immediately say that because the man who witnessed the aethereal phenomenon had a terminal brain tumour, it would be ridiculous to take his testimony seriously, because what he saw was so obviously a hallucination brought about by his condition. But in supposing that only commonly shared experiences are to be taken seriously, such souls demonstrate a fundamental misunderstanding concerning the nature of reality.

A soul might well mistake material phenomenon or mental phenomenon for aethereal phenomenon, but when souls unambiguously witness aethereal phenomenon, that phenomenon is necessarily real in that it constitutes a part of our shared reality, even if it is only witnessed by a single soul. The fact that such phenomenon is so rarely witnessed because witnessing it is dependent upon very specific conditions is irrelevant. My former colleague saw phantoms coming through the walls of his home, and therefore those phantoms are a part of reality, even though only he was able to see them due to the deterioration of his brain. Attempting to subject aethereal or spiritual forces to the standards of material science is deeply misguided on the face of it, for the terms "aethereal", "spiritual", and all equivalent terms were created for the very purpose of categorising that which is not material in nature.

Yet I am not at all interested in lowly debates on this subject, since anyone's scepticism is irrelevant to me. What matters is that since I myself have had multiple encounters of an aethereal nature, I have useful information to share with those of you that will inevitably experience such phenomenon yourselves, besides the emotions and impulses that you experience each day, emotions and impulses that you feel on the level of your aethereal body in the same way that you feel physical sensations on the level of your material body.

Emotions and impulses have proven to be phenomenon that are difficult to place within spiritual frameworks, especially when those frameworks only acknowledge matter, mind, and Spirit, for in which of those categories would you place emotions and impulses? One could argue that they are felt physically, and yet they can clearly also be provoked by mental phenomenon. The reality is that unless you acknowledge the existence of our aethereal forms then you will never be able to place or understand emotions and impulses adequately, and this is just one more reason that the category of aether (by whatever name it might be called) is so essential.

It is because emotions are felt on the level of our aethereal forms that we will feel them even during transcendent experiences that take us outside of our material forms and render our minds incapable of thought. Not only are emotions still felt in such circumstances, they are felt more powerfully than ever, for reasons that will be explained within the next chapter. It is also the reason that there are souls that, although they might have expertly mastered their physical body and although they might have acquired profound insights concerning the mind, are nonetheless still subject to emotional chaos, the equanimity of the mystic being far from them.

It is only as one comes to know the Spirit that emotions are mastered just as the mind is. This is why mastery over emotion eludes those that focus exclusively upon the body or upon the mind. The indulgence of emotions is particularly prevalent at the current time given that we live in an age in which emotions are highly esteemed to the extent that they are often understood as being an acceptable substitute for (or even more valuable than) reasoned thought. Immature souls that stew within their emotional states will go in whatever direction their emotions pull them, regardless of how contrary to sound reasoning and even the guidance of the Spirit their course of action is.

The most obvious counterfeit spirituality of aether follows from such indulgence: it is the mistaking of high emotional states to be experiences of the Spirit. This is understandable from a certain perspective, since emotional states can be very powerful—a feeling of euphoria, when contrasted with a soul's common experience of life, could easily be mistaken for some manner of transcendent experience by one that has never had a transcendent experience. An experience of the Spirit will often be accompanied by extreme emotion, but extreme emotion alone does not constitute an experience of the Spirit. As with all forms of counterfeit spirituality, such emotional highs will leave you exactly as you were before they arrived and they do not bestow you with any great spiritual insights.

Pleasant emotional states are to be received with gratitude and enjoyed, but do not mistake them for the spiritual and therefore take them to be that which is to be pursued on your spiritual journey. There are many that do this very thing, and within Christianity there are entire denominations the worship of which centres around all manner of dramatic emotional displays, but for the reasons stated, you will not find the members of such denominations to have any more insight to share as a result of them. Such a focus is nothing more than the indulgence of aethereal phenomenon in the guise of spirituality.

Artificial Afterlives

"Let not your hearts be troubled. Believe in God. Believe also in me. In my Father's house are many rooms. If it were not so, would I have told you that I go to prepare a place for you? And if I go and prepare a place for you, I will come again and will take you to myself, that where I am, you may be also."

- Yeshua, The Gospel According to John 14:1-3

Aethereal realms are places that we visit in transcendent experiences and that we will enter into after the death of our mortal forms. The "afterlife" paradise that most would call "heaven" is an aethereal realm, but most aethereal realms, unlike heaven, are highly subjective both in terms of how we experience them and their form. Aether exists beyond time, permeating material creation, and the way that it manifests can be massively informed by the state of the souls that experience it.

Dreams and nightmares make for a good comparison to the heavenly and hellish aethereal realms because they are experiences in which time and space mean little and that are massively informed by our material and mental states. It is because our dreams are so informed by our state of being that the pleasure or horror that they bring can be the most obvious indicator of the manner of aethereal realm that we will enter into upon the death of our mortal form unless changes are made. While heaven and hell are experiential realities that we enter into while still in mortal form, dreams and nightmares can serve as a vision of how we will experience those realities after the death of those forms.

An uncommon example of sojourns to aethereal realms (though not as rare as some would suppose) are the Near Death Experiences mentioned previously, wherein a soul will undergo some manner of heavenly or hellish experience during a time when their mortal form is close to death. If you have heeded testimonies of such experiences then you will already know that they too are highly subjective—a Christian will invariably encounter "Jesus", and even philosophical materialists will experience aethereal phenomenon informed by religious ideas from

181

the cultural background that informs their egoic identity, even though they consciously rejected such ideas.

Aether often manifests in a way that is appropriate for the soul witnessing it, and because of this the aethereal realms are made up of a myriad of heavens and hells. These are the "many rooms" that Yeshua spoke of in the excerpt from the Gospel of John that opened this section. When the ancient Gnostics claimed that the "psychics"—the form of soul above the hylics, but beneath the pneumatics (mystics)—might be able to obtain a form of "lower heaven", it was the aethereal realms that they referred to. These are places fitting for those that, still clinging to their egoic identity, retain a very rigid notion of the way in which spiritual realms and their inhabitants would manifest. Therefore, religionists and other dogmatic souls are bound for them.

The aethereal realms at once meet the expectations of those that enter into them, and yet also bestow a soul with the experience that it will need in order to develop spiritually. Therefore, a Christian religionist may encounter "Jesus" in accordance with their firmly held convictions, but they may also be chastised by him and made to understand the nature of their wrongdoings.

Those aethereal realms that would be described as "hellish" are obviously nightmarish in their manifestation. Such realms expose a soul to the wrongs they have committed against their own conscience, even though they may have grown deaf to that conscience during their most recent mortal lifetime. But remember that the conscience is nothing other than the voice of God speaking through our shared Spirit, and so, souls very much face their own idea of who and what they are and their misdeeds in comparison to the reality of their true nature as Spirit, and such a comparison can be a torturous experience. Souls are not made to endure this as some form of punishment, but rather correction, so that they may be better prepared for their next mortal incarnation, for such subjective aethereal realms, whether they be heavenly or hellish, are only ever temporary abodes. The hellish aethereal realms are vaguely recognised within the traditional Catholic understanding of what they call "purgatory".

The popular notion of an eternal torment arises from a gross misunderstanding of the terminology, idioms, and hyperbole of the New

Testament texts. To give just one example, English translations of the New Testament texts make several mentions of "eternal destruction", which English speakers naturally interpret to be referring to a process of destruction that goes on forever. Actually, it refers to destruction that is eternal in its finality, not its duration. A very important distinction.

And so, for example, in the New Testament text, the Epistle of Jude, Jude wrote in Jude 1:7 that the cities of Sodom and Gomorrah were "destroyed by fire and serve as a warning of the eternal fire of God's judgement." Jude and those that received his letter knew perfectly well that the cities of Sodom and Gomorrah were not still on fire in their day; when Jude wrote of "the eternal fire of God's judgement", he was not referring to its duration, but to its finality, and even then he was speaking of the destruction of the material, and not the aethereal or the spiritual. This is a particularly definitive example, because in that excerpt, Jude explicitly wrote that the cities of Sodom and Gomorrah were "destroyed" before citing them as an example of "the eternal fire of God's judgement", necessarily meaning that he understood "eternal fire" to be permanent destruction and not unending burning. If you re-examine any of the New Testament texts in light of even this simple recognition, you will see very clearly that such references to a negative "eternal" fate are not at all suggesting what most souls would immediately understand them to be suggesting.

"But," some of you may say, "Yeshua clearly described 'souls' as being subject to destruction." Yes he did. That is because the biblical terms being translated into English as "soul" are "nephesh" in the case of the Hebrew of the Old Testament and "psyche" in the case of the Greek of the New Testament. Those terms do not refer to an immortal soul, but rather they refer to a living creature of flesh and blood that also has a mind. The word "soul" in such a context is very similar to the word "entity" in the way in which we use it, which is why Yeshua makes mention of both body and "soul" being in hell (and I have already explained the relevance of hell to one in mortal form). Indeed, when Yeshua uses the word "hell", it is being translated from the word "Gehenna", and there is good reason to believe that this was a direct reference to a physical location in which the local population would incinerate garbage, thus explaining the fiery imagery that so often colours Yeshua's descriptions of it. Those that heard Yeshua speak would have been very familiar with this location, and so would have understood that Yeshua was using it as a comparison to the wretched state of those souls that turned away from God. It is because the word "soul" within a biblical context is so often referring to the flesh that the Hebrew Bible makes reference to "dead souls", something that would be an oxymoron if its authors had been referring to the immortal soul that I and most others so naturally refer to. When the Hebrew Bible uses the term "dead souls" it is referring to nothing more than physical corpses—mortal forms from which the Spirit of God that made them alive has departed.

You must be very careful when attempting to understand texts written thousands of years ago by authors that belonged to entirely different cultures, the paradigms of which were entirely different from that of your own. You cannot afford to take translations of such texts at face value and just assume that the English terms that translators chose to employ successfully convey the author's intended meaning to the mind of the modern reader. Many religionists would desperately want you to believe otherwise, but which souls do you think are doing the translating in most cases? If you assume that they are above attempting to lead readers along particular lines of thinking through the use of odd word choice, grammar, and punctuation in their translations, then you will be disappointed should you ever examine the issue—entirely new translations of the Bible have been crafted explicitly for the purpose of better supporting a particular theology. This is just one more of the many manifestations of "the lying pen of the scribes" that the prophet Jeremiah warned of in ancient times, and it is why Yeshua condemned "the scribes" alongside the Pharisees and Sadducees of his day.

I have only written as much as I have on this issue because I know that it is subject that deeply concerns many souls, but it can only concern those souls that have never so much as glimpsed the reality of Spirit, because to even suggest that God would torture souls forever in some fashion is just about the most ignorant and blasphemous notion that I can think of. Since I am writing this book so that you might come to know the Spirit through remembrance, any notion of God torturing souls will be recognised as the foolishness that it is when you do so, and so as with so much else, there is little need for me to spend too long refuting such erroneous ideas on a logical, historical, or scriptural basis;

experiential spirituality resolves such issues definitively in a way that no other approach can, because engaging in experiential spirituality necessarily involves coming to know the realities in view, not merely knowing *about* them.

However, do not mistake me to be saying that there is never any value in encouraging a fear of God. As Solomon wrote in Proverbs 9:10, "Fear of the Lord is the beginning of wisdom, and the knowledge of the Holy One is insight." Fear of God is the beginning of wisdom because it is so often fear that motivates souls to begin inquiring into the great spiritual mysteries, and from a human perspective there is indeed much to fear. But fear should be inspired by that which is true and not that which is untrue—there is no eternal torment to fear, but there are temporary sojourns to countless hellish aethereal realms to fear. However, fear is only experienced by a soul until it comes to know the perfect nature of God and then surrenders to it through silence. It is then that such a soul can truly understand the apostle John's words in 1 John 4:18: "There is no fear in love, but perfect love casts out fear. For fear has to do with punishment, and whoever fears has not yet been perfected in love." The words contained within Proverbs 9:10 and those contained within 1 John 4:18 are not contradictory, but rather they are insights concerning souls at vastly different levels of remembrance.

In chapter three I stated that the Garden of Eden as described within the biblical Book of Genesis is in fact an aethereal realm. Are we then to understand that particular narrative to be giving us an accurate portrayal of the true heaven? Not at all, for to do so would be to fall into the same trap that most souls do by having a rigid idea of what God is and what He has prepared for us.

Souls that are entirely unfamiliar with the biblical texts tend to understandably assume that they are rich in descriptions of what heaven is like, but that is not the case. The few biblical accounts that could be understood as visions of heaven come in the form of utterly bizarre descriptions, such as those written by the prophet Ezekiel and the John that wrote the Book of Revelation. The biblical authors are otherwise utterly silent when it comes to descriptions of heaven. The account of the Garden of Eden contains the closest thing that there is to such a description, and even that is a simplistic allegory that was intended to convey truth concerning the origin of the soul, the aethereal form, and its descent into stark duality—it was never meant to be taken as a literal portrayal of anything.

This silence on the subject of heaven is of course intentional, for a soul with any significant insight knows that it is futile to attempt to express in language that which cannot be expressed in language. Besides that, far more important than knowing what it is like to be in the presence of God is knowing the way to get there and being aware of those things that will prevent you from doing so. Therefore, the biblical authors primarily concern themselves with informing the reader as to the ways that they might come to know the Spirit of God and with warning them against those things that will experientially alienate them from it. Though always remember that the biblical authors wrote to the personhood of the souls reading their works, as opposed to writing to them as souls in human form in the way that I have been writing to you.

If you are to know the true heaven, then you must surrender your conceptions of it to silence, just as you surrender conceptions of your identity to silence, for just as conceptions of identity will ensnare you experientially, so too will conceptions of the "afterlife". Recall again the words of the apostle Paul when, quoting the Hebrew Bible, he wrote in 1 Corinthians 2:9, "As it is written, 'What no eye has seen, nor ear heard, nor the heart of man imagined, what God has prepared for those who love him.'" If you attempt to define what heaven will look like within your mind, then you are building your own idea of heaven, and should you become enamoured with that idea, it will manifest in the form of an aethereal realm and you will not experience the glory that God would have you experience until you learn the appropriate lessons within future mortal incarnations.

When Yeshua told his disciples that there were many rooms in his Father's house, he did not attempt to describe any of them, and nor did he encourage his disciples to imagine them or to work out what they might be like. He simply asked that they believe in God and that they believe in him. You likewise need do nothing other than have faith in God, surrender all such speculation to silence, and remain with reality as it is currently manifesting before you within the Eternal Moment.

Aethereal Beings

As to the eating of food offered to idols, we know that "an idol has no real existence," and that "there is no God but one." For although there may be many so-called gods in heaven or on earth—as indeed there are many "gods" and many "lords"—yet for us there is one God, the Father, from whom are all things and for whom we exist, and one Lord, Yeshua Hamashiach, through whom are all things and through whom we exist.

- The Apostle Paul, The First Epistle to the Corinthians
8:4-6

The aether could easily be called "the realm of gods and ghosts", for the aethereal beings that exist within it are beyond number. While some of them are formed or at least show themselves in accordance with the imagination of the beholder, others are beyond imagination. Although aether is not normally tangible, certain aethereal beings can nonetheless manifest in a tangible way and interact with the material realm using their aethereal forms. Yeshua resurrected in aethereal form after his crucifixion before ascending to an aethereal realm, and this is why, although matter was no longer an impediment to him, he could nonetheless still interact with it, such as in Luke 24:43 where he ate a piece of broiled fish given to him by the disciples.

Recalling the distinction between deity (that which is God) and the divine (that which is of heavenly origin), you should know that positive aethereal forces are divine, whereas negative aethereal forces are dreadful ("dreadful" being as good an antonym for "divine" as any). Because gender is an attribute of aether, there is such a thing as "the divine masculine" and "the divine feminine", just as there is such a thing as "the dreadful masculine" and "the dreadful feminine". You undoubtedly already know of many divine beings that were held to be either masculine and feminine, and advanced Gnosticism involved a belief in a feminine divine being called "Sophia" that was central to its creation myth. The most widely recognised form of aethereal beings are those commonly known as "ghosts" or "phantoms", but then there are those sentient entities that are held to have either a benevolent or malevolent disposition towards souls in mortal form, the most obvious examples being those entities called "angels" and "demons".

"Angels" are actually souls that have attained rest, whether they are embodied or disembodied. This is why Gnostic groups like the Valentinians and the Manichaeans held that every soul had an angelic "divine twin" that they would inevitably be consciously reunited with; the "divine twin" is nothing other than our aethereal form—Adam and Eve were created as angels. Demons, on the other hand, are souls that are lost in hell, whether embodied here in the world or disembodied within a hellish aethereal realm. And so, the terms "angel" and "demon" refer not to a unique form of entity, but to the status of souls such as ourselves. Demons are often known as "fallen angels" precisely because such souls have fallen from the state in which God originally created them. Until we enter into the rest of God and so experientially return to Him, we are all fallen angels to lesser and greater degrees, and we are made such by enslavement to Satan, which is to say, enslavement to egoic impulses. The one that is "demonically possessed" is therefore possessed by such impulses and is themselves functionally a demon; to truly exorcise another soul is to liberate them from that ensnarement. The word "angel" literally means "messenger", and those with angelic status exercise precisely that function on behalf of God, bringing understanding of Him to yet wayward souls. Those accounts of angels appearing as beings of bright light are accounts of the aethereal forms of those souls that exist in an angelic state.

There are those that would argue that angels and demons are merely metaphors for positive and negative internal phenomenon, in the same way that I explained Satan to be a personification of egoic desires. Disembodied angels and demons can certainly influence our thoughts and emotions, but they are not mere metaphors for such phenomenon, and I would suggest that those that believe them to be simply lack the experience to know better. Besides that, such a view does not account for so many statements on the subject that are to be found within sacred texts. For example, the author of the Epistle to the Hebrews wrote in Hebrews 13:2, "Do not neglect to show hospitality to strangers, for thereby some have entertained angels unawares." That verse is either referring to souls in mortal form that have attained rest, or disembodied souls that have attained rest visiting the material realm in the guise of human beings; in no way can such statements be adequately explained while maintaining that angels and demons are merely metaphors for internal phenomenon.

Regardless, have you ever found it odd that ghosts and other such entities, while held to be entirely unhindered by the boundaries of the earth, are nonetheless spoken of as though they only exist within its confines? For a long time there has been an idea that if life were to be discovered elsewhere in the universe it would present a problem for the Abrahamic religions, which seem to posit life on this planet as being wholly unique. The truth is that the universe is teeming with life, and yet humanity is indeed unique, for the life that may be found across the universe is aethereal in substance; those planets that seem dead and devoid of life are not so, and nor is the space between them. It is not for no reason that the ancients associated the planetary bodies with lesser deities of various kinds and sought to determine the nature and degree of influence that they had upon the earth. I hope that you recognise what I just wrote to be the raw assertion that it is and that, knowing that you cannot yet verify such a thing yourself, you do not simply accept that assertion as fact. I have no interest in abusing whatever trust I may have earned by asking you to accept anything on my mere say so—I wrote what I did merely to appropriately expand your vision regarding the aethereal.

The aethereal forms that most are concerned with are those of departed souls that were formerly their friends and family according to the flesh. There is a great demand to know the fate of such souls, and often to communicate with them. Whether a departed soul may choose to remain within the material realm in aethereal form for a time or even to return to watch over a soul still incarnated here will depend upon whether or not they were liberated from the grasp of their egoic identity while they were still alive in mortal form. If they were not, they would have been guided or taken to the appropriate aethereal realm upon the death of their mortal form. This is why the disembodied souls that were thought to have watched over another that was still alive in mortal form were always known for their wisdom and love during their mortal lives.

Frankly, the fate of souls after the death of their mortal form is not your concern and any focus upon it is either egoic attachment to a human that you once knew, or a desire for understanding that has been misdirected. Either way, you will need to surrender such concerns to silence. But I will certainly tell you this much: while it is possible to communicate with those souls that remain close to this world in aethereal form, nobody that has become so aware as to have that ability would ever take money for doing so.

There is a phenomenon here in Britain called "Big Cat Sightings", whereby many souls claim to have witnessed unusually large felines prowling the countryside. There have even been confirmed cases of such animals roaming free having escaped from captivity. Even so, the phenomenon remains mostly a mysterious and unexplained one, with many doubting that witnesses actually saw what they believed they did. There have even been such sightings up here in the northern Highlands of Scotland, and certain farmers just a few miles west of where I am now have attributed the nightly slaughter of livestock to such felines.

    I once had a friend that lived on a farm about five miles outside of my home town. Myself and some other friends would often visit him, making the journey to his home in the afternoon by following the country roads, and then returning to town in the early hours of the morning, often travelling in a straight line across the countryside rather than following the roads again. On one such occasion in my early twenties, I was with one other friend, and having spent the evening at the farm, we decided to walk back into town in the early hours of the morning, taking our "shortcut" across the fields and wilderness. It was dark, but the moon was full in the sky, and it cast a generous amount of its white light across the landscape. At one point in our journey, having just climbed over yet another fence, we both froze at the sight of an enormous feline striding casually past us no more than six feet away in the darkness. We remained still for several moments, each of us trying to process what we had just seen, before we turned to look at one another, wordlessly confirming that it was a shared sight.

    It could be that what my friend and I saw was in fact a form of the aforementioned "blind ghosts"—phantom animals being another phenomenon testified of for centuries. You may recall that in the first chapter I explained that this county, Caithness, is named in part because cats are strongly associated with it. It is known that lynx once roamed these lands, and while such a species is unlikely to have been able to persist into the modern day undetected, in the right circumstances it is possible to see their aethereal forms, just as a soul might witness a human "ghost" behaving as it did in the past. These forms are not sentient and are therefore in no way "trapped souls" as some might describe them—they are what you might call "aethereal echoes", traces of souls that once existed within mortal form imprinted upon time. Though this does not account for the slaughter of livestock; that is a phenomenon that I would have to investigate before drawing any conclusions, but stray dogs could easily be responsible for such killings —such incidents are a relatively common occurrence.

The second of the testimonies that I will share concerning my interactions with aethereal beings is actually ongoing. There is a certain mountain here in the Highlands of Scotland by the name of Ben Macdui. It is the second highest mountain in all of the British Isles and its summit is said to be haunted by a terrifying entity known in Scottish Gaelic as Am Fear Liath Mòr ("the Big Grey Man" in English). It has been reported to stalk visitors to the mountain, instilling within them a dread strong enough to compel them to flee, potentially to their death. It is certainly the best known cryptid of the Highlands, second only to the Loch Ness Monster, which is another story altogether.

I do not know exactly what manner of entity the Grey Man is, but I certainly know that it is not a "brocken spectre" or any other form of visual illusion, and nor is it a humanoid cryptid comparable to creatures such as the Sasquatch. The Grey Man is definitely some form of disembodied aethereal being, for although I have never been to Ben Macdui, the entity has been calling me there for several years now. The thought of being at the summit of the mountain is both alluring and yet dreadful to me, and if I close my eyes and consider the matter, my breath quickens and my palms begin to sweat. I feel the urge to sit alone on its summit out in the open overnight, something that is only possible in the summer, for I would certainly freeze to death during the winter. I desire to confront the Grey Man in this way, and I feel that if I can resist what I know will be overwhelming dread then I will have defeated it, permanently banishing it from Ben Macdui. Yet there are times when I am certain that I will die on that mountain, and oddly enough, I cannot think of a place that I would rather die.

Of course, I am above being compelled by such a maelstrom of mental and emotional phenomenon. Even so, I find the experience to be deeply fascinating, for of all the mental and aethereal phenomenon that I have experienced, this stands as the most powerful to come from something other than the Spirit itself. Mountains have always been portrayed as places of great power within spiritual traditions from around the world—Moses received the ten commandments from God atop Mount Sinai, Yeshua underwent his transfiguration and delivered his most famous sermon upon mountains, and the Prophet Muhammed received his first revelation from the angel Gabriel in a cave within Mount Hira, to give just three Abrahamic examples. But it would seem that such power is not always positive. I have no idea why the Grey Man holds such power over Ben Macdui or why he calls to me specifically, but in my personhood I very much desire to meet this entity face to face. Whether I will venture to Ben Macdui to do so, I do not yet know—that is up to God.

A book on mysticism that did not contain a chapter addressing aethereal phenomenon would be lacking, just as how that chapter would be lacking if it did not elaborate upon the subject of aethereal beings. Yet having just given such an elaboration, I must warn you not to become distracted by and enamoured with the aethereal.

This subject matter can very easily excite the mind and cause souls to lose sight of their immediate reality as they engage in useless speculation and allow their imagination to waste their time. There are many souls in this world that obsess over ghosts, angels, and other forms of aether, imagining that they represent the ultimate manifestation of reality. You must appreciate the irony of them understanding aethereal manifestations in this way, all the while perceiving them as the Spirit which is in fact the ultimate manifestation of reality. This is yet another example of how subject matter that excites the mind so often causes souls to overlook the obvious.

All that I have written and all that I will write within this book is based upon my own direct experience, and as is always the case when I am expounding upon experiential spirituality, the challenge for me is to take what I have learned through direct experience, structure an explanation of it that will be understandable to as many souls as possible, and to then explain the ways in which it is or will be relevant to their direct experience of reality. You should not become fixated upon the aforementioned structure, but rather you should bear all that I have written in mind, remembering to remain grounded in your own direct experience. Nothing that I have elaborated upon within this chapter will yet be a reality for most of you, but when it becomes one, you will have an advantage having read my words.

Believe me, those of you that have had no major encounters with disembodied aethereal entities would not be so eager to experience one if you had. This is not to say that you have anything to fear from the aethereal—if you understand and follow my instructions throughout this book then you do not, as will be made explicit within the following section—only that there is no wisdom in seeking to hasten experiences that you may not yet be truly ready for. You will inevitably experience the aethereal in a major way, whether during your current mortal lifetime or after it, but until then, let your focus be set upon reality as it currently manifests before you.

Aethereal Evil

> I am convinced that neither death nor life, nor angels nor rulers, nor things present nor things to come, nor powers, nor height nor depth, nor anything else in all creation, will be able to separate us from the love of God in Yeshua Hamashiach our Lord.

> - The Apostle Paul, The Epistle to the Romans 8:38,39

There is little that needs to be said of divine beings because all aethereal manifestations carry powerful auras with them, and should you ever encounter a disembodied divine being while you still live within mortal form, you will need no instruction. Indeed, having been confronted with such a one, you will not desire anything except the continuation of that

193

experience. But there is much that can be said about those disembodied aethereal beings that, due to their hellish existence, carry with them an aura of dread.

The one that recognises their true transcendent nature will have no fear of human beings or the destruction of their mortal form, but this is not such an astounding thing, for even souls still bound within egoic identity can develop mental bodies that render them immune to the effects of fear. However, aethereal evil carries with it such an aura of dread that it seems to threaten the very fabric of your being. Against such forces there are few that can stand. Religionists will invariably proscribe exactly the wrong approach in order to rid oneself of such phenomenon. Their first mistake is always to portray it as a grave threat, perhaps even to the very existence of the soul. Their second mistake is to engage in all kinds of ritualistic practice derived from their tradition in a bid to banish the aethereal evil. But all any of that does is build the evil up in the mind of the one that is tormented by it, thereby rendering them even more experientially vulnerable to it. The soul that desires to preserve their mortal form has far more to fear from those fanatics that obsess over aethereal phenomenon than from the aethereal phenomenon itself.

You are Spirit and are therefore greater than all that you are capable of perceiving. Yes, greater than even the most glorious angel or the most wretched demon. As explained, such manifestations are themselves the aethereal forms of other souls in different states of being. The dread aura and often terrifying visage of aethereal entities can seem to pose an existential threat, but this is illusory, for regardless of their ontology, such entities can only threaten your idea of who or what you are; they cannot harm the perfect Spirit that you truly are. Do not allow the visceral presence of such entities to blind you to the truth that you have already experientially come to know, if indeed you have experientially come to know it.

Whereas most souls will cower in the presence of aethereal evil, there are some that, for various reasons, will show defiance in the face of it, often as a consequence of the so-called "fight or flight" impulse. Although there is no risk in doing this, aethereal entities feed off of negative emotions, and so raging at them can only prolong their presence. There are those that have recommended merely laughing at them, but mockery is also a negative expression and so will have the same effect as raging. The superior way is to do nothing at all: be as the equanimous, unchanging, and formless Spirit that you are, and allow the aethereal phenomenon before you to pass, as all phenomenon must. Let even the most terrifying manifestations be for you as nothing but interesting anecdotes that you can later testify of.

Many occultists have sought to make contact with aethereal beings, something that I would not recommend if only because there is no need to do so. However, some entities may communicate with you regardless. Sometimes they will merely abuse and demean you, but the more clever among them will attempt to manipulate you, claiming to be able to bestow insight concerning your life or future events that they claim will transpire upon the earth. This is the kind of psychological manipulation that many souls in mortal form have attempted throughout history; when a local man or woman was understood to be a witch or sorcerer, even the most vague of their mutterings could incite hysteria and paranoia in those around them. But it was the ability to incite such hysteria and paranoia that alone was their power, and so they could only maintain a hold over other souls for as long as those souls took them seriously and believed in their abilities.

The same is true of malevolent disembodied aethereal entities, the difference being that their dread aura makes it difficult for a soul to doubt that they have great power. But the reality is that they do not for as long as you do not heed their words. Notice that such malevolent aethereal beings communicate with you either audibly or telepathically; they do not speak from your innermost being as God necessarily does, and they do not because they cannot.

It could be that you encounter aethereal evil within the dream world where you may seem to be at its mercy due to the unique and seemingly random rules of the dream world, rules that may well render you unable to recall the very understandings that would help you. But I can assure you that this will only be so early on in your journey of remembrance.

I suffered from that which is called "sleep paralysis" from my youth, which is an experience wherein you seem to wake from sleep only to find yourself unable to move. This experience is almost always accompanied by fear, and entities may be witnessed in the environment about you, sometimes appearing human, sometimes not, but almost always malevolent, some to the extent that they even inflict physical violence. My own experiences were never as extreme as that; I would wake unable to move, and I would feel an evil presence in the room and a dread certainty that if I did not somehow force myself to wake up then I would simply die in my sleep. I experienced this frequently across fifteen years to the extent that I was often afraid to go to sleep. I must have tried everything that I could think of to try and break free of the grip of whatever was holding me in those states. It was only as I was undergoing the process of remembrance that I was able to permanently rid myself of those experiences.

One night, I had a particularly bizarre nightmare within which I underwent sleep paralysis as I lay on my couch where, in the waking world, I had become accustomed to falling asleep. In the nightmare I would experience the paralysis, encounter some strange entity, and then find myself in that state of paralysis once again as though the nightmare had reset itself. This occurred three times within the nightmare.

The first time that I freed myself from paralysis within the nightmare, I walked through to my kitchen, convinced that I was in the waking world. However, the blinds in the kitchen were open, and since I always close them at night, I knew that I was still in the nightmare. In that instant I found myself lying upon my couch and paralysed within the nightmare again.

The second time that I freed myself from that paralysis, I stood up from my couch, again convinced that I was actually awake, and I walked to my hallway only to see some manner of apelike humanoid standing there. It stood upright to a height of around seven feet, had reddish-brown fur, and stared at me with a blank expression and what seemed like very human eyes. And then suddenly I once again found myself lying down upon my couch and paralysed within the nightmare.

On this third occasion, I did not succeed in freeing myself from the paralysis, and as I lay upon my couch, I felt the presence of an entity standing behind the top of my head where I could not see it, and I felt its fingers running across my face. Although I could not see those fingers, I somehow knew that they were elongated and grey. What I considered strange at the time was that the sense of dread that I had previously felt was gone; I did not feel threatened by whatever it was that was touching me. In fact I felt certain that it was doing so from either affection or curiosity. I lived alone, as I still do, and so this was not some sensory experience in the waking world making its way into my nightmare. But as I lay there helpless before this being that was scrutinising me, I suddenly recalled the process of remembrance and all of the understandings that came with it, and I remembered that I was not the one that was lying there paralysed and helpless, but rather the transcendent Spirit, and in an instant I woke up from the nightmare and I never again had even a mild experience of sleep paralysis. I had engaged so consistently in the practices that I have recommended to you throughout this book that remembrance of them made its way into my nightmare and liberated me from such experiences permanently.

That was many years ago, and whatever state I find myself in now, I carry with me an awareness of the Spirit that I am and with it the knowledge that I am invincible. When I dream, I am able to watch my dream-self from a distance as though I was watching an actor upon a stage, and I retain full awareness and control, enabling me to assess all that is unfolding. This is an example of just how thoroughly the fruits of experiential spirituality will come to permeate your existence.

Chapter Eleven: Spirit

Remembrance is a journey of no distance that begins when you seek to become aware of the Spirit that you are. You already know all that you need to know in order to venture into the depths of that Spirit, and so now it is appropriate for me to elaborate upon all that I have learned of that Spirit through my own explorations in order to try and help you make sense of all that you will come to experience. There is no subject greater than that of God and His Spirit, but while much of what I will go on to describe will remain unfamiliar to you until you have begun to practise experiential spirituality yourself, as with so much else that I have elaborated upon, these matters are not as far removed from your day to day experience of life as you might initially suppose.

God

> "God is Spirit, and those who worship Him must worship in Spirit and truth."

> - Yeshua, The Gospel According to John 4:24

Souls have conceived of God in thousands of different ways throughout recorded history. To the religionist that accepts one of those conceptions at face value, it seems obvious that their chief concern should be to exalt that conception above all others. To the philosophical materialist, this great diversity of conceptions is confirmation that they are all the products of man's imagination. Both of those views are in error and for the same reason: they take those conceptions of God literally in a way that mystics never have. Humans have always understood God in a manner befitting the time and place in which they lived; to suppose that the mere existence of such contrary understandings presents a dilemma is simply false.

Those known as the ancient Israelites were an Iron Age, tribal

198

culture that engaged in near constant warfare with their neighbours. Therefore, their conception of God (as recorded in the Hebrew Bible) was as the patriarchal and warlike deity, Yahweh, from whom Moses received the ten commandments upon Mount Sinai. The disparity between the warlike Yahweh that is presented as God within the Old Testament and the all loving "Father" that Yeshua presented as God within the pages of the New Testament is something that has troubled souls from the birth of Christianity. The 2nd century proto-Gnostic, Marcion, he who was the first to devise a New Testament canon, felt that the disparity was so great that it could only be explained if the Yahweh that Moses had communed with and the Father of Yeshua were in fact two different beings, with the latter being the true God and the former being a petty usurper.

Yet Yeshua affirmed on many occasions that the Yahweh worshipped by his Jewish ancestors was indeed the very Father that he taught of. However, Yeshua came with a greater revelation of Yahweh than his people had ever known. The reason for the disparity between Yahweh and the Father of Yeshua is not that they were different beings, but rather that Yeshua revealed more about the true nature of Yahweh than had been known previously, for as the apostle John wrote in John 1:17,18: "The law came through Moses; grace and truth came through Yeshua Hamashiach. Nobody has ever seen God. The only Son, who is at the Father's side, he has made Him known."

This comparison of the portrayal of Yahweh within the Hebrew Bible to the Father as portrayed by Yeshua within the New Testament serves as a perfect example of how easy it is to interpret testimonies of the same entity as being testimonies of two entirely separate entities. Understanding how this can happen within the same culture and within a relatively short period of time, you can easily understand how the experiential accounts of mystics that come from vastly different cultures spread across far greater periods of time can, at face value, seem to be describing something entirely different when they are not.

The function of the mystic is to make Spirit known to those ready to undergo that experience, but they must always explain their understandings in a way that their culture will resonate with. There is always wisdom and insight to be derived from the teachings of even the most ancient mystics, but to cling rigidly to ancient conceptions of God as though they perfectly encapsulate the nature of God is a mistake that has only ever created division and strife.

As I have previously stated, when the terms "person" and "personhood" are used in reference to deity, they are describing a singular intelligence with a particular character and not a human centred egoic identity. This distinction is vital, for to say "God is a person" without clarification is to invite the kind of anthropomorphising that souls have engaged in for thousands of years, attributing all manner of petty traits to deity. It is precisely because such souls know nothing of their own transcendent nature that they reduce even God down to their own level of awareness, remaking Him in their own image and according to their own lowly understandings.

Conversely, there has been a habit among those influenced by eastern thought to suppose that the kind of personal God conceived of by the Abrahamic faiths is merely a crude and erroneous understanding of the impersonal force associated with the Dharmic traditions. It would surprise such souls to learn that, within the Bhagavad Gita, Krishna confirmed the supremacy of a personal intelligence many times, such as when he said, "Unintelligent men, who do not know Me perfectly, think that I, the Supreme Personality of Godhead, Krishna, was impersonal before and have now assumed this personality. Due to their little knowledge they do not know My higher nature, which is imperishable and supreme." Contrary to what many would assume, the Bhagavad Gita consistently portrays devotion to a personal God as being superior to introspection in acknowledgement of an impersonal force.

It is very easy to understand how God can be perceived as a personal intelligence with a particular character based upon direct experience of the Spirit. I have explained that your conscience is the voice of God speaking through your shared Spirit; if you discovered that your conscience consistently warned you against being cruel, it would not be unreasonable for you to conclude that God hates cruelty, and in doing so you will have assigned at least two personal traits to God, namely that of being capable of hate and that of hating cruelty. I suspect that the author of the Bhagavad Gita argued so strongly for the supremacy of a personal deity because so many in that period had come to understand the highest manifestation of reality as an impersonal force

200

that was entirely indifferent to the behaviours that souls engaged in, an idea that could obviously be very dangerous.

However, there is a big difference between acknowledging that the highest manifestation of reality is a personal force with a particular nature, and anthropomorphising that highest manifestation of reality down to the petty level of the human based upon cultural assumptions and the wishful thinking of your own mind. If every soul that currently exists in mortal form were to attempt to understand the personality of God through only the kind of direct experience that this book centres around, then they would all testify of the exact same deity. But if they were to instead attempt to understand the nature of God according to their cultural influences, their own interpretation of various sacred texts, and their own mental and emotional inclinations, then we would have a world in which souls posited the existence of thousands of different deities, a great many of whom would go by the same name. And that is exactly what we have.

God as a personal intelligence and His impersonal Spirit have a particular nature that we draw close to by acting in accordance with, and that we become distant from by acting in opposition to. It is the recognition of this that has traditionally led even mystics to depict God as a person with certain likes and dislikes. Remember that as souls we are of the impersonal Spirit of God; when we construct an egoic identity for ourselves, we are creating a substitute for the very person of God that we must be submitted to through obedience to our conscience if we are to come to know Him once more.

God is the personal, intelligent, and forever transcendent aspect of the impersonal Spirit that is both His being, and our own. Therefore, the one that is devoted to God is rightly devoted to God, and the one that is introspective is rightly introspective. Those that engage in both devotion and introspection, understanding why they do so, are even greater. Yet, I have been daring in attempting to explain even this much about God, and I did so only to bring clarity to your understanding, for the highest understanding of God is no understanding at all.

The most common approach employed when a soul seeks to illustrate the nature of God is known as "cataphatic theology", or more simply, "positive theology", which means that the soul is attempting to explain

201

God using positive statements such as "God is love", "God is infinite", and so on. But there is a much lesser known approach called "apophatic theology", or more simply, "negative theology", whereby God is only described in negative statements such as "God is not hate", "God is not finite", and so on.

The reasoning behind the approach of negative theology is that negative statements concerning the nature of God are always going to be more accurate than positive statements; one may say that "God is love", but what does our lowly conception of love really tell us about the infinite love of God? It is therefore far more accurate to say that "God is not hate". Negative theology is something that can be found around the world and throughout history in a variety of forms, and it is strongly associated with mystic thought. There is much wisdom in such an approach, for what those that employ negative theology are doing is deferring to silence in their attempts to illustrate the nature of God. Yet only partially, for while a negative statement concerning the nature of God certainly leaves much more to silence than a positive statement, it is still nonetheless a statement.

I am writing this book in order to help you to recognise your true spiritual nature through which you will necessarily come to know God. I have no interest in attempting to shape your understanding beyond that, for at that point you will be conscious of God's guidance in your life. And so, I will not tell you how you should seek to understand God or if you should even seek to at all—that is between you and God. I will simply say that if you have experienced the benefits of deferring to silence in all of the ways that I have recommended since chapter seven then you should also consider the possibility that the wisest approach might be to defer all questions concerning the nature of God to that same silence. Regardless, it is enough for you testify of whatever insights you gain through experiential spirituality and then leave others to make of those insights what they will. Attempting to turn such insights into dogmas is folly of the highest order, and when you come to know the Spirit you will fully understand that, for such experiences inevitably convey just how utterly beyond such intellectual constructs the Spirit of God truly is.

Every transcendent experience that I have ever had involved being overwhelmed by the inexpressible majesty of Spirit, but there is one such experience in particular that impressed the ineffability of God upon me: I was sitting in contemplation when I suddenly felt myself fall, yet I did not fall physically, but rather my aethereal body fell through my mortal form and into a dark sea, into which I began to sink. That may sound like a terrifying experience, and yet I felt nothing but peace as I sank into the depths of that sea, the water of which glittered with gold, for I knew it to be the very Spirit of God, and I knew that I could spend an eternity swimming through those waters in perfect joy as I came to understand the great mysteries that were somehow innate to the water itself.

I cannot say how long that experience lasted in human time, but when I fully returned to my mortal form, I could not help but recall the words of the apostle Paul as recorded in Romans 11:33: "Oh, the depth of the riches and wisdom and knowledge of God. How unsearchable are His judgements and how inscrutable His ways." I had read that verse hundreds of times, but it was only after having had that experience that I had any real notion of what the apostle Paul was futilely attempting to convey in words. Of course, the Spirit of God is not truly a dark and glittering sea—the aforementioned scene was merely the way that my mind interpreted the experience that I was undergoing. The only way to fully appreciate the profundity of such experiences is to undergo them yourself, as indeed you may. When attempting to explain them to others, you will find yourself in the same dilemma as every mystic before you.

My advice would be to engage in devotion to God as you see fit and to persist in the introspective practices that I have recommended. Major experiences of the Spirit will come, and when they do, you should testify of them to others. But do so without being dogmatic, knowing that your words and the concepts that they are evoking within the minds of those listening are utterly failing to approach the grandeur of the experience and the glory of God.

The Divine Attributes

"The fruit of the Spirit is love, joy, peace, patience, kindness, goodness, faithfulness, gentleness, self-control; against such things there is no law."

- The Apostle Paul, The Epistle to the Galatians 5:22,23

While religionists, theologians, philosophers, and those that likewise attempt to understand deity through intellect alone have made many contradictory statements concerning the nature of the Spirit of God as a consequence of the nature of their inquiries, the verdict of those mystics that have had direct experience of the Spirit is unanimous.

All mystics testify that the nature of God and therefore of the Spirit—as far as our minds are capable of grasping it—is that of pure goodness. Some have simply said that the words "peace", "love", and "truth" are enough to convey the nature of Spirit to our minds, whereas others have gone further and listed many more attributes. But however many attributes one might perceive as being innate to Spirit, I call such attributes "the Divine Attributes", for although there is a difference between that which is deity and that which is divine in terms of status, they necessarily share the exact same attributes, for the divine is an expression of deity made comprehensible; the very reason that God uses divine messengers is so that those that languish in forgetfulness might remember Him through the lesser expression of those messengers. To put it simply, the divine translates deity to the rest of His creation.

As we live out our mortal lives here in the material realm we naturally distinguish between one Divine Attribute and another because we perceive them as being distinct. And so, for example, we understand love to be distinct from beauty, even while recognising that they are both Divine Attributes. The divine also conveys those attributes as though they were distinct, because that is how most souls understand them. But the closer that one experientially gets to deity, the more that the distinction between the Divine Attributes fades; I may speak of "truth", "love", "peace", "beauty", "grace", and a host of other Divine Attributes, but if you had experienced the Spirit as I have, I would be

204

able to simply say, "it is God", or "it is Spirit", and those statements would evoke every Divine Attribute within your mind.

The Spirit is pure positivity, and within that pure positivity are all of the positive attributes that humankind can conceive of, but in the Spirit those attributes are one in a sublime way that is utterly impossible for the mind to grasp. As with ingredients placed into a bowl and thoroughly mixed together, you cannot separate one of the Divine Attributes from another, and the closer that one comes to Spirit, the more the sublime oneness of those attributes is experienced. Therefore, as the soul comes to know their true spiritual nature, they likewise come to know peace, beauty, love, and every other attribute that is present within the Spirit. That the Divine Attributes are actually inseparable is a very important recognition, for it means that when you draw close to any of the Divine Attributes, you ultimately draw close to all of them, and therefore to the Spirit from which they come forth. Conversely, to shun one is to ultimately shun them all, and if there is something that is undoubtedly true of every aethereal hell, it is that the attributes that take a soul there are the inverse of the Divine Attributes.

When souls forget their true spiritual nature and therefore God through the process of conditioning having been incarnated within mortal form, they are also forgetting the source from which the Divine Attributes emanate. Having come to identify with a personhood that is necessarily deficient in the way that all egoic identity is, they come to experience that deficiency as though it is innate to them and they fully believe it to be so. As a consequence, in seeking love, happiness, truth, or any other Divine Attribute, they will invariably do so by looking outwards into the external world, attempting to find those things within relationships, careers, and so much else that, due to its transitory nature, can never bestow them indefinitely. It is a journey that is invariably ones of highs and lows as the Divine Attribute that they sought is found, and then inevitably lost. Few such souls in any generation will come to recognise that those attributes can be found within their own Spirit, a Spirit obscured by their egoic identity.

When a soul expresses love, forgiveness, joy, or anything else that we would identify as one of the Divine Attributes, they are literally expressing the nature of the Spirit that they are, for which their human form serves as a conduit. All that is good comes from Spirit and there is no alternative source from which the Divine Attributes might come. Because you are also Spirit, the Divine Attributes are innate to your very being, and you would be incapable of expressing them if it were otherwise. I once received a lengthy correspondence from a soul lamenting that although all of his practical needs were met, he could not feel the love of God, and he asked me what he could do to experience that love. Yet that soul lived in an environment surrounded by loving family members, and so I told him that I could help him to know the Spirit, but that he should first recognise that God was already bestowing His love upon him through the very souls closest to him. Besides that, the best way to experience the love of God is to have love for others, for love only comes from God. Therefore, when you express the love that can only come from the Spirit of God, you will know the love of God.

All good things come down to us from God, but souls living in mortal form are usually ignorant of that fact and therefore fail to perceive the goodness of God where they should. We must always distinguish between the material, the mental, the aethereal, and the spiritual, but the Divine Attributes can actually be found within all of those substances for reasons that I will explain within the next section.

It is important that I elaborate upon one Divine Attribute in particular, namely that of forgiveness, especially in light of all that you now know concerning the way in which souls are brought to remembrance through repeated mortal incarnations and repeated stays within numerous aethereal realms of various kinds. Since most souls understandably assume God's forgiveness to be unconditional, they often ask why it is that any soul would ever be kept from an experience of His presence.

Christian notions of God withholding forgiveness from souls are especially strange given that Yeshua himself repeatedly emphasised the necessity to be endlessly forgiving. In Matthew 18:21, Peter asked Yeshua, "Lord, how often will my brother sin against me, and I forgive him? As many as seven times?" To this, Yeshua responded within the following verse by saying to Peter, "I do not say to you seven times, but seventy-seven times." In other words, Yeshua told Peter that he must forgive his brother as many times as that brother asked it. Many have rightly observed that Yeshua therefore required his disciples to be far more forgiving than most Christians portray God Himself as being—

206

Yeshua wanted his followers to forgive those that wronged them indefinitely, but the very God that he called "Father" will apparently condemn you to eternal torment for the slightest deviation from His laws, laws that you have no good reason to believe actually come from Him in the first place. Only a soul hopelessly imprisoned by ideology could strive to maintain such an obviously ludicrous view.

The Parable of the Prodigal Son that Yeshua related within the Gospel of Luke can help to greatly illuminate the truth of this matter: in the story, there is a son that demands his inheritance from his father, and that, having received it, left for a distant country to indulge himself with his newly acquired wealth. However, in time there arose a famine within that country, and having squandered all of his money, the son was forced to work feeding pigs; he was in such an impoverished state that he found himself wishing that he could be fed as well as those pigs were, and it occurred to him that even his father's servants were well fed. Therefore, he determined that he would return to his father, humbly admit his wrongdoing, and agree to live as one of his servants from that point forth. The son did return home, but his father, rather than holding his wrongdoing against him and reducing him to a servant, said to his servants, "Bring quickly the best robe, and put it on him, and put a ring on his hand, and shoes on his feet. And bring the fattened calf and kill it, and let us eat and celebrate. For this my son was dead, and is alive again; he was lost, and is found."

You now know enough to be able to recognise that the Parable of the Prodigal Son is an allegory for the journey of the soul: the soul leaves the Father's abode and ventures into the material realm in order to seek out new experiences and inevitably disgraces itself while there. But when that soul has suffered enough, it will remember the home from whence it came and seek to return there. Having done so, it will find that not only will God the Father not hold its wrongdoing against it, He will rejoice in its return and acknowledge that soul as His child.

You see, the dilemma for wayward souls is not that God will ever withhold forgiveness from them, but rather that repentance is a prerequisite of forgiveness. The Father is always willing to forgive the son, but the son must first recognise his folly and return to the Father to receive that forgiveness; one cannot return to God until one has shed all false identity, and with it, all inclination towards wrongdoing. Every

207

mortal lifetime that we endure and every aethereal realm that we find ourselves within is a direct result of our insistence upon heeding our imaginary idea of ourselves instead of heeding our Father in the ways that I have already elaborated upon.

There is one final detail within the Parable of the Prodigal Son that is worth expounding upon, namely that the son that is the protagonist of the story has an older brother that remained obedient to their father. When the prodigal son returns and the father rejoices, the older son is resentful, pointing out that he himself had never received such lavish treatment despite his obedience. To this the father replied, "Son, you are always with me, and all that is mine is yours. It was fitting to celebrate and be glad, for this your brother was dead, and is alive; he was lost, and is found."

This older brother is a reference to the souls that never departed heaven in order to experience mortal incarnation within the material realm and so remained in the same state as Adam and Eve prior to their descent. And so while Yeshua focusses upon the younger brother for the majority of the Parable of the Prodigal Son's narrative, at the very end he turns his attention to the elder brother as a warning that, regardless of our spiritual status, for as long as we have the capacity to think and act independently of God, we still have the potential to fall from grace.

Interestingly, certain groups within Christianity and Islam have believed that the fallen angel that they call "Satan" fell from paradise because he was envious of humanity. It could be that this notion has its origin in a particular understanding of the Parable of the Prodigal Son, though I have no way of verifying that.

Creation

> "And He made from one man every nation of mankind to live on all the face of the earth, having determined allotted periods and the boundaries of their dwelling place, that they should seek God and perhaps feel their way toward Him and find Him. Yet He is actually not far from each one of us, for 'in Him we live move and have our being'; as even some of your own poets have said, 'for we are indeed His offspring.'"

> - The Apostle Paul, The Acts of the Apostles 17:26-28

God created, yet He could not create within the fullness of His Spirit, for creation requires duality—one thing existing in relation to another—whereas the Spirit of God is perfectly unified. Therefore, God created a boundary within His own Spirit within which He increasingly restrained His own presence, thereby introducing greater and greater degrees of deficiency. It is God's Spirit in its varying degrees of deficiency that is creation as we commonly observe it.

Aether, mind, and matter are Spirit manifesting with increasing degrees of deficiency. A useful comparison is that of water, snow, slush, and ice: we have unique terms for water, snow, slush, and ice because they are distinct enough from one another to warrant them. Yet we still know that snow, slush, and ice are ultimately just water manifesting in different forms. In the same way, although I will emphasise again that one must never mistake aether, mind, or matter for Spirit because they are distinct, that distinction exists due to the deficiency inherent within aether, mind, and matter. Ultimately, aether, mind, and matter are lesser manifestations of Spirit, and therefore of God. This is why, while insisting that there is one Spirit, the authors of the New Testament nonetheless make reference to seemingly lesser spirits like "the spirit of the world"—it is the same Spirit manifesting with different degrees of deficiency. Therefore, all is Spirit—all is consciousness.

This explanation of God's relationship to His creation would be categorised (by those that care for such categories) as "panentheism", and one must distinguish between panentheism and the more widely

209

known pantheism. The difference between pantheism and panentheism is that in a pantheistic belief system, creation is understood as being ontologically identical to deity and therefore the highest expression of It; in a panentheistic view, such as the one that I have just conveyed, creation is understood as being a manifestation of deity, but not the highest manifestation.

It is the deficiency within matter, mind, and aether—that which causes the nature of their substance—that gives rise to all phenomenon that human beings perceive as negative. But note that, since deficiency is merely the dearth of something, that negative phenomenon is not inherent to the nature of Spirit, and has no independent existence of its own. Consider a beam of light projected into a dark room. Were you to follow that beam into the room, you would see it gradually fade as darkness became increasingly mixed with its light; the darkness is not projected from any source in the way that the beam is, but rather exists as a deficiency of the light, and as such, depends upon the light to exist, even though it does not originate within it. The Spirit of God is as that beam of light at its most powerful, whereas aether, mind, and matter come about as the beam weakens and becomes deficient. But in the case of a beam of light, deficiency comes about because the source of the beam is of finite power and so cannot project that beam in its fullness for an unlimited distance; God's power is not finite, and therefore any deficiency in His light is necessarily intentional. This is why different spiritual traditions speak of aether, mind, and matter as being fallen or ultimately illusory—those manifestations that we call aether, mind, and matter can exist only when God introduces deficiency into His own spiritual being to allow their existence, and unlike the pure Spirit from which they come, they are impermanent. Due to the perfect unity that is innate to God's Spirit, without that deficiency being introduced, creation could not exist.

It is because all of creation is Spirit manifesting with different degrees of deficiency that there was much validity in the animistic, pantheistic, and polytheistic traditions of the ancient world, for they rightly perceived the Spirit as permeating all of creation and therefore personified the phenomenon of that creation in numerous ways. Things have not changed as much as some might suppose, for even in the modern age souls assign names to natural phenomenon such as storms and hurricanes, thereby personifying them. The main difference is that they do not usually take such personifications as literally as most ancients peoples would have. And so, while there are higher and lower manifestations of God and His Spirit, no soul has ever worshipped their god or gods in vain, for they are relating to the same source in different ways in accordance with their understandings.

God knows well our insights and our ignorance, and any sincere effort made towards worshipping the supreme reality, however a soul might understand it, is acknowledged and rewarded. There was many a Pictish warrior that met his ancestors in the great halls after the death of their mortal form, just as there were many Viking warriors that drank with Odin in the halls of Valhalla. These were, of course, the aethereal realms appropriate for them to reside in before being reborn within the material realm once more.

Although this book has been ordered in such a way as to suggest that aether came into being prior to the mind, they actually came into being simultaneously, for both attributes are necessary for Spirit to experience duality in the form of souls—aether to provide souls with a distinct being, and minds to enable souls to think independently and to deviate from the will of God.

An aethereal realm was created for these newly independent souls to inhabit, that written of in allegories such as the biblical Garden of Eden. Although the souls in that aethereal realm had a sense of independence from the Spirit from which they emanated and from one another (having distinct aethereal forms and their own minds) they still nonetheless retained a conscious awareness of God that prevented the development of egoic identities that would bring about the illusion of separation from Him. Therefore those souls lived in harmony with God as distinct beings. But they could not remain within that aethereal paradise, for God manifested as souls so that He might experience different modes of being through them. It was for this reason that most of those souls ventured beyond that paradise aethereal realm, eventually finding themselves within bodies of flesh here in the material realm. God's "motivation" is one that anyone could understand, for souls themselves have striven for thousands of years to create the means by which they might experience realities beyond their own, and such realities often involve the imposition of greater limitations, for as souls we love to experience reality within different confines.

Yet however far from God souls may sojourn, that journey is only experiential. Although most models and illustrations that seek to explain creation (including that which I have used here) speak in spacial terms, this is only so because it is easier for the mind to grasp. In truth, we never left the bosom of God—we never left His being. We can never be apart from that Spirit because we are that Spirit. We only forget that reality, and in doing so, undergo innumerable experiences as though we were completely distinct from God. Yet the truth of our oneness with the Spirit of God is eternally so, and the implications of that are of the utmost importance. In their despair, souls so often ask, "where is God throughout my suffering?" The answer is that He is experiencing that suffering with you. God is with each and every one of us as the Spirit that He is and that we are.

To merely believe that is one thing, and such a belief may bring comfort in difficult times, but to know it absolutely through a direct experience of the Spirit is to be free of all internal suffering. Wherever you may sojourn, and whatever experiences you might undergo, God is with you. It is just a question of whether or not you have come to experientially know it.

Understanding that matter, mind, and aether are just Spirit manifesting in deficient forms, you can understand why the Divine Attributes can be perceived throughout all of creation. But when the Divine Attributes are present within the deficient substances of matter, mind, and aether, they are naturally found in a degenerated form, and the more deficient the substance the more degenerated a form the Divine Attributes manifested through it will be found in.

Souls that undergo Near Death Experiences report a wide array of phenomenon, but there are certain elements that almost all such accounts share in common, two of which are directly relevant to the subject at hand. The first is a vision of the well known "tunnel of light" or a being of light, and the second is that which souls tend to describe as "heightened senses". Both of those phenomenon come about quite simply because in a Near Death Experience a soul is being exposed to Spirit and its Divine Attributes in a less deficient form that they have

212

been throughout the course of their mortal lives, namely the aethereal form. The perception of deity or the divine as a bright, yet not blinding light comes about because that is how the mind typically interprets the fullness that the soul is perceiving. The "heightening of senses" is not a heightening of senses at all, but an experience of the Divine Attributes in a less deficient state. Therefore, those souls that return to the mortal world to testify of such experiences will say things like, "the love and beauty that I felt in that place was so overwhelming that nothing that we count as lovely and beautiful here in the world can compare to it."

Yet one need not hope for such a dramatic experience in order to experientially confirm all that I have said here while you still live in mortal form. Because all of creation is Spirit, and because the Divine Attributes therefore also manifest throughout it, one can utilise even the deficient forms of those attributes in order to remember one's higher essence. This is the reason that souls testify of having transcendent experiences when visiting places of exceptional beauty like cathedrals —such places convey Divine Attributes in such a powerful way that it experientially uplifts the souls that witness them. Nature itself abounds with similar opportunities: concentrating upon the beauty of a flower can have as profound an effect as any marvel of architecture or work of art created by souls in human form. It is only because the Divine Attributes are to be found throughout creation that contemplation upon positive forms—such as the contemplation upon positive thoughts that I recommended within chapter five—is at all effective in helping souls reconnect with the divine, and therefore with deity.

This is the reason that it has often been said that mystics are able to perceive beauty in anything. Even when mystics did not develop a specific framework in order to explain these matters as I have, and so would not have articulated themselves as I do, they nonetheless came to be intuitively and profoundly connected with the world about them as a consequence of their remembrance. I have repeatedly emphasised the need to recognise that matter, mind, and aether are not the highest manifestation of reality, and some may fear that such an insistence might encourage souls to become contemptuous of those lesser realities, but actually the opposite is the truth—it is precisely when you come to know the superiority of Spirit and the way in which it manifests as all of creation that matter, mind, and aether become truly alive to you.

The natural world quickly becomes mundane to most souls, and that feeling of mundanity can reinforce their sense of alienation from God. Therefore, I would encourage all of you to be mindful of all that you now know of the Divine Attributes and their presence within every manifestation of creation. Make a point of seeking the Divine Attributes as they manifest in the world around you as you go about your day to day activities, and make time to sit and reflect upon them, for the one that does so is never far from a glimpse of the Spirit.

Yeshua Hamashiach

> Yeshua said to his disciples, "Compare me to someone and tell me what I am like."
>
> Simon Peter said to him, "You are like a righteous angel."
>
> Matthew said to him, "You are like a wise philosopher."
>
> Thomas said to him, "Master, my mouth is utterly incapable of saying what you are like."
>
> Yeshua said, "I am not your master, because you have drunk and have become intoxicated from the bubbling spring that I have given out." And he took him, withdrew, and told him three words.
>
> When Thomas returned to his companions, they asked him, "What did Yeshua say to you?"
>
> Thomas said to them, "If I tell you one of the words which he told me, you will pick up stones and throw them at me, and then a fire will come out of the stones and consume you."
>
> - The Gospel of Thomas, Saying 13

An entire book could be written about Yeshua Hamashiach, he who is more widely known as "Jesus Christ", though I feel that it would be misguided to write such a book for reasons that will soon be explained. However, given the confusion that surrounds this figure, it is necessary for me to address certain misunderstandings. The most destructive of these, I feel, is the notion that Yeshua presented himself, and therefore Christianity, as the only way to know God, necessarily meaning that souls are damned without them.

There is no New Testament verse that is used to reinforce this notion more than John 14:6 in which Yeshua said, "I am the way, the truth, and the life. Nobody comes to the Father except through me." It is a statement that seems very unambiguous, and yet as is the case with so many biblical statements, examining its context casts a different light upon it altogether. In context, Yeshua had just told his disciples that he would soon be leaving them, and that they knew the way to where he was going. This confuses the disciples who believed that they did not know the way, and so in John 14:5, Thomas said to Yeshua, "Lord, we do not know where you are going. How can we know the way?" And it is in response to that question that Yeshua said, "I am the way, the truth, and the life. Nobody comes to the Father except through me." In other words, that statement was made to comfort the disciples; Yeshua was letting them know that they could not somehow lose him as they feared, for anyone that goes to God will do so through him.

Nonetheless, Yeshua's words still state that anyone that goes to God must go through him, and this is a reference to Yeshua's function as "the Word of God", something that the Gospel of John, alone among the canonical gospels, heavily emphasises. Remember that "the Word" is "the Logos", that held to be the "divine reason" through which man might know God. The Word of God came to many souls throughout the Hebrew Bible, but what made Yeshua unique in the history of Israel was that, having attained rest, he himself became the Word of God—a personification of Truth. More specifically, he became the Word of God to the Jewish people at that time, and therefore the only one through whom they could know God. You must again be mindful of the fact that Yeshua was not speaking to you when he made the statements that are recorded within sacred texts, and nor was he speaking to any soul alive in mortal form today; he was speaking to Jewish disciples in the Middle East two thousand years ago, souls that almost certainly knew nothing of events transpiring outside of their homeland. Statements such as that in John 14:6 have nothing whatsoever to do with Hindus that lived thousands of years earlier or those of us that live two thousand years later. If you want unambiguous statements from Yeshua that really do mean what they seem to, then I would suggest that you heed those such as that within Matthew 15:24 where Yeshua said, "I was sent only to the lost sheep of the house of Israel".

Yeshua made perfectly clear that his ministry was only to the Jews that were alive within the 1st century. It was the apostle Paul that determined to bring Yeshua's teachings to the non-Jewish world, but he was likewise clear that they were directly relevant only to those souls that lived in that generation, since Yeshua would be returning within their lifetimes, as I explained within chapter six. My point here is not that Yeshua no longer has any relevance whatsoever—my own spiritual awakening and my constant reference to his teachings plainly indicate that I believe otherwise—my point is that Yeshua's earthly ministry was to the Jewish people of the 1st century, and that while we can still derive immeasurable insight and wisdom from his words, they were not directed at us, and that pretending that they were is deeply misguided and has been the source of much needless havoc throughout history.

God raised Yeshua up for the Jews of the 1st century, just as He had raised up and would continue to raise up many different messengers for many different peoples around the world. Yeshua's mission was not to found a new religion called "Christianity", for he himself was a Jew that sought to free the Jewish tradition from the corruption brought about by religionists. The term "Christian" merely referred to one that followed Yeshua, but his message was only for those within the 1st century, and so they are the only souls that have ever called themselves "Christians" legitimately. To be a Christian within the 1st century meant being directly anointed by the Spirit; in the present day it means nothing more than to belong to one of the many collectives that call themselves "Christian". This is the reason that modern day Christians do not routinely perform miracles in the way that the New Testament records those in the 1st century as having done. None of this is to say that those that call themselves "Christian" now cannot have a fruitful spirituality —of course they can, and the significance of the crucifixion and resurrection are as relevant as ever, but as always, we must be willing to accept the truth, and the truth in this case explains why modern day

"Christianity" bears only a superficial resemblance to the Christianity testified of within the pages of the New Testament.

Neither that which calls itself "Christianity" today nor any other religious collective has any ownership of Yeshua whatsoever—nobody can claim a messenger of God in such ways, for their message, whoever it was originally delivered to, is the inheritance of all souls that come to be incarnated within mortal form.

But how are we to understand the nature of Yeshua? In saying thirteen from the Gospel of Thomas—the saying that opened this section—Yeshua asked three of his disciples, Simon Peter, Matthew, and Thomas, to compare him to something in order to illustrate his nature. Simon Peter and Matthew did not hesitate to give their answers, believing that they had come to understand Yeshua.

The history of Christianity (and of many other religions) is full of such confident statements concerning the true nature of Yeshua. Trinitarians might say, "Yeshua is deity, God the Son, second person of the trinity, and co-equal and co-eternal with the Father and the Holy Spirit." Biblical Unitarians might say, "Yeshua was a human being who was adopted as the Son of God at his baptism in the River Jordan." Muslims might say, "Yeshua was a prophet of Allah just like Moses before him and like the Prophet Muhammed—peace be upon him—after him." Philosophical materialists might say, "Yeshua was a wise moral teacher of his time." Entire books can and have been written just elaborating upon the sheer number of ways in which Yeshua has been understood throughout history.

Although the Gospel of John calls Yeshua "the Word of God", something that I have elaborated upon enough, he is more widely known as being "the Son of God", the meaning of which is laid out plainly within the New Testament. The scriptures therein state that Yeshua was the firstborn Son of God amongst the Jewish people, and the apostle John wrote of Yeshua in John 1:12,13 that, "to all who received him, who believed in his name, he gave the right to become Children of God, who were born, not of blood nor of the will of the flesh nor the will of man, but of God." When the New Testament speaks of "the Children of God", it is speaking of mystics—those that have attained rest through remembrance of the Spirit. It is for this reason that

217

in Romans 8:14, the apostle Paul wrote, "all who are led by the Spirit of God are Sons of God."

The Gospel of Thomas is vague in its statements concerning the true nature of Yeshua, although it is clear that he is held in the highest regard. The most unambiguous statement concerning the nature of Yeshua comes in saying seventy-seven in which Yeshua is recorded as having said, "It is I who am the light which is above them all. It is I who am the All. From me did the All come forth and unto me did the All extend. Split a piece of wood. I am there. Lift up a stone, and you will find me there." The term "the All" is one that the Gnostics frequently used to reference the whole of reality, and so that saying is bestowing Yeshua with the highest possible status, and you would do well to contemplate it in light of all that I have written concerning the way that the Spirit of God is to be found throughout all of creation.

There are so very many understandings of Yeshua and of his relationship to God that souls have dedicated entire mortal lifetimes to studying and expounding upon the subject. Rarely is anyone reserved when it comes to offering an opinion on the matter. This is because most souls wrongly believe as they do with God Himself that Yeshua can be encapsulated within beliefs and expressed within doctrines. But in saying thirteen from the Gospel of Thomas, Thomas himself admitted that he was incapable of comparing Yeshua to anything else in all of creation. It was because Thomas answered in this way that Yeshua stated that he was no longer the master of Thomas due to the disciple's insight, and it was then that Yeshua took Thomas aside to tell him three secret words.

Who or what Yeshua was during his mortal life, I have no idea whatsoever. I have no way of verifying whether or not he even existed within mortal form; concerning his mortal life, I can only go by the testimonies of sacred texts, which by themselves are proof of nothing. Such statements are an offence to many souls, and yet in what way are they not true? Do you have some way of knowing that Yeshua definitely lived within mortal form? If so, then you should share it with the world. Let me tell you what I do know of Yeshua with certainty: I know that my spiritual awakening left me with the impression that he was the cause of it. I know that both the canonical and non-canonical Christian sacred texts attribute words to him from which I derive great insight and the spiritual merits of which I have verified through direct experience. I know that when I commune with Yeshua in prayer, something powerful happens. And I know that even as I write these words, I feel the presence of Yeshua, and he is pleased with me. I am more than content for Yeshua to remain as mysterious to me as God Himself, and I would not exchange my direct experiences with him for any number of ideas, theologies, doctrines, apologetics, or historical arguments concerning him. You are welcome to keep such things, if you desire to rob yourself.

Saying thirteen of the Gospel of Thomas places Simon Peter and Matthew as the religionists of its narrative; they are all too eager to assert their ideas concerning the nature of Yeshua, for their egos will not allow them to admit that they are ignorant on the subject. The humility of Thomas allows him to learn from Yeshua in secret, but what he learns would not conform to the beliefs of Simon Peter and Matthew, and therefore, hearing Thomas state such things would enrage them to the point of murder, for which they would endure judgement. Such is the history of the relationship between mystics and religionists.

I can assure you that if you stand with Thomas in saying to Yeshua, "Master, my mouth is utterly incapable of saying what you are like", then you will lose nothing but delusion. When you make this confession having previously held very strong beliefs on the nature of Yeshua, you will feel a tingling around your shoulders and great relief as though a heavy weight had been lifted from them. You may even find yourself smiling at the sensation. That is a physical manifestation of the liberation that honouring truth brings. If Yeshua is ever going to reveal something of himself to you, it will only be after such an admission and not before.

Chapter Twelve: Oneness

The Spirit of God permeates all of creation and that creation is therefore united by it. Now that I have given you a framework through which to understand how that is so, and now that I have explained the means by which you might experientially verify the truth of it, I will conclude this book by elaborating upon those subjects that it is not possible to fully comprehend without a recognition of that oneness.

Free Will and Destiny

> "Men of Israel, hear these words: Yeshua of Nazareth, a man attested to you by God with mighty works and wonders and signs that God did through him in your midst, as you yourselves know. This Yeshua, delivered up according to the definite plan and foreknowledge of God, you crucified and killed by the hands of lawless men. Yet God raised him up, loosing the pangs of death, because it was not possible for him to be held by it."

> - The Apostle Peter, The Acts of the Apostles 2:22-24

The supposed dilemma of "free will" is usually presented as a tension between the will of God and the will of human beings, with the issue centring around the question of where the former ends and the latter begins: do we enact a destiny that God has already predetermined? Are we completely free to forge our own destiny in a way that may please or displease God? Or does the truth lie somewhere in the middle? The question of moral culpability is strongly tied to this issue, for in the case that all of our actions are predestined by God, it would seem that we could not be either fairly rewarded or fairly punished for having carried them out, since we ourselves had no choice in the matter.

While the issue of free will has always featured heavily within the thought of the Abrahamic traditions, it is almost never raised within the context of the Dharmic traditions. Most sacred texts do not raise the issue and are written with the seeming assumption that souls have the free choice to do as they will. The biblical texts are no exception to this, yet there are certain statements within them that could be construed as suggesting otherwise, and those statements have been enough to allow theologians to derive all kinds of conclusions on the matter.

Many mystics have been reluctant to speak on the issue of free will at all, despite it being one of the most commonly inquired about matters. This is understandable, since souls tend to be very emotionally invested in the issue: there are those that despise the idea that we have no free will, and then there are those that insist that you cannot make sense of anything until you acknowledge that we do not. Until a soul comes to know the truth of the matter through experiential spirituality, they are unlikely to be fully at ease holding any position on the subject. I have already said that when you surrender all identity and all intent to silence, contrary to you doing nothing at all, you actually act more efficiently in the world than ever. The reason for that is directly related to the question of free will, and so despite how understandable the reluctance of others to speak on the issue is, I myself am not reluctant, for it is necessary that I expound upon the subject.

However, of all of the great issues that I have touched upon throughout this book, there are few that are as potentially complicated to explain as that of free will. Discussion surrounding the subject has become so utterly convoluted that it would be unwise for me to even begin to elaborate upon the history of thought concerning it, something that I do not consider worthy of your focus in any case. Therefore, rather than referencing a host of historical thought on the subject of free will, I will expound upon the issue in a more direct and straightforward fashion.

Debates concerning free will in light of the existence of God are almost always misguided from the beginning because they assume that if souls have a will then it must be distinct from the will of God. This is false. The only will that exists is God's will. This is why it is not possible to understand this issue without first knowing of the oneness of all creation, and I suspect that this is also the reason that this supposed dilemma does not often arise within the Dharmic traditions, since they are far more likely to recognise the innate unity of creation.

There is only God's will, but since, as souls, we are portions of the Spirit of God living out experiences of individuality, we carry with us that capacity of will. Because we forget our true spiritual nature and our unity with God through conditioning within the material realm, we inevitably come to believe that this capacity of will is uniquely ours. When we surrender to God through silence, we come to recognise the true source of that capacity and so naturally fall back into alignment with God's intent, and our lives play out according to that intent. If, conversely, we seek to forge our own destiny, then we misuse that portion of will that we carry with us to the end of fulfilling our egoic desires. But such a misdirection of will is ultimately illusory, because it can only last for as long as a soul's investment in egoic identity does, and such investment can never be permanent.

This is why the New Testament texts present a binary choice between being children and servants of God through Yeshua, or being slaves to the flesh. Because every soul forgets their unity with God through the process of conditioning, every soul becomes lost within egoic identity and misuses their will for a time. But while God allows souls to stray for as long as is necessary for the appropriate lessons to be learned, there is still a greater plan for creation that cannot be undone by such wayward souls. Indeed, God uses the corrupt intent of souls bound in egoic identity to achieve His own will.

Consider Judas Iscariot, the man who betrayed Yeshua to the Jewish religionists that sought his death, handing over a Son of God for a mere thirty pieces of silver. Even within popular culture the name "Judas" is synonymous with betrayal of the worst kind. Yet without Judas betraying Yeshua to the Jewish religionists, they could never have handed him over to the Romans to then be crucified, and without the crucifixion there could not have been the resurrection upon which all of Christianity depended; without Judas, the greatest symbol of what it means to die to self in order to be raised into spiritual life could never have been. It is for such reasons that, in the Gnostic Gospel of Judas, far from being portrayed as an antagonist in the life of Yeshua, Judas is portrayed as the most important of all of the disciples, and the one of whom the others are envious. In the gospel's narrative, Yeshua tells Judas that he has the most important role to play in future events, and that it is a role that he will ultimately be despised for. The Gospel of Judas is rather typical of the kind of thought experiment that the Gnostics loved to engage in within their writings, much to the horror of their proto-orthodox counterparts.

If it had not been the will of God that Yeshua be crucified, then Judas would have simply been prevented from betraying him. But since it was the will of God that Yeshua be crucified, Judas was allowed to misuse the one will and act as he did. In this way, Judas was used to fulfil what God had predestined, and yet can still be rightly regarded as morally culpable for freely indulging his personhood as he did.

Another clear biblical example of the way in which God uses the misdirected will of wayward souls for His own ends comes from the story of Joseph as contained within the Book of Genesis within the Hebrew Bible. Joseph is sold into slavery in Egypt by his envious brothers who wished to be rid of him, but across the course of a lengthy narrative, Joseph rose to become the rich and powerful vizier of Egypt and worked to the benefit of many other souls. At the conclusion of the narrative, when Joseph had been reunited with his brothers and all that had transpired was known, he said to them in Genesis 50:19-21, "Do not fear, for am I in the place of God? As for you, you meant evil against me, but God meant it for good, to ensure that many people would be kept alive as they are today. So do not fear, I will provide for you and your little ones." Note that Joseph first assured his brothers that they need not be afraid of retribution, for he was well aware that vengeance belongs to God alone. He then drew a distinction between their evil intent and the good intent of God—it was the will of both his brothers and of God that Joseph be sold into slavery, but for different reasons; if it had not been the will of God that Joseph be sold into slavery, then his brothers would simply have been prevented from selling him into slavery. Finally, being in alignment with the benevolent intent of God, Joseph told his brothers that despite their evil acts he would provide for them and for their children.

Let there be absolutely no confusion on this matter: as Spirit, you carry with you the power of God's will, and you use it no matter how ignorant you may be of your true nature. If you employ that will to become fully invested in your egoic identity, then you will have empowered that egoic identity and its lower inclinations and you will behave according to them, though that behaviour will be restrained by God if it would threaten what He has predestined. If, conversely, you have surrendered yourself to God and thereby died to all egoic identity, you fall back into alignment with God's intent. Therefore, there is no such thing as a will that stands in opposition to God's will—there is only a single will that is temporarily being subverted by wayward souls. An important distinction.

The excerpt from the Acts of the Apostles that opened this section is confusing for many souls, for in it, the apostle Peter declared that the crucifixion was predestined by God, and yet also clearly held

223

the Jewish authorities to be morally culpable for it. Now that you understand the ways in which God uses the freely chosen behaviour of souls to enact His ends, you will understand how the apostle Peter could have asserted such seemingly contradictory things.

I would invite you to compare what I have asserted about the nature of our freedom of will to what any sacred text says on the subject; you will quickly find that this matter is nowhere near as complicated as many souls have made it. Yet do not lose sight of what is most important— verifying such truths through direct experience.

How you might go about verifying what I have said concerning God's will and the way that souls misuse it may not be immediately obvious, but as you die to all forms of egoic identity, you will find that whereas you once felt that you had to fight to impose your will upon reality, you will discover that God has already laid a superior path for you, and that walking that path is a simple matter of surrender to His will. As stated within chapter seven, contrary to you doing nothing at all, you will act in the world more efficiently than ever before. More than that, life itself seems to unfold in your favour, as if reality is conspiring to help you, when previously you may have suspected that it was doing the opposite—there is rarely a day that goes by that I do not marvel at the potential obstacles that God removes from my path. You will experience such things because, having ceased usurping God's will for your own ends through investment in egoic identity, you are now allowing your experience to unfold according to God's intent. There is nothing that can thwart God's purpose for our lives except for ourselves.

Therefore, there is such a thing as destiny, in that there is a particular end towards which you are always moving—either towards God's end or the end of an egoic identity. Great mystics such as Yeshua taught with the urgency that they did because it is only during our time here in the material realm that we have the opportunity to choose the alternative path. Failure to do so will result in a soul residing in an appropriate aethereal realm for a time after the death of their mortal form, before they are once again reborn into the material realm in a new physical body, as previously explained.

God lives our experiences with us, for as souls we are portions of His Spirit living out different experiences of individuality. In doing so, we have the freedom to utilise the will that is innate to us within limitations that God enforces so that we may not prevent what He has predestined to happen.

Divination

> The apostles put two men forward, Joseph called Barsabbas and who was also called Justus, and Matthias. And they prayed and said, "You, Lord, know the hearts of all, show which one of these two you have chosen to take the place in this ministry and apostleship from which Judas turned aside to go to his own place." And they cast lots for them, and the lot fell on Matthias, and he was numbered with the eleven apostles.
>
> - The Acts of the Apostles 1:23-26

To divine something is to acquire knowledge of it through supernatural means, usually knowledge of the future. Therefore, while the term "divination" is usually associated with the use of specific tools said to foretell the future, it would also apply to the receipt of any prophecies, including those that are to be found within spiritual traditions.

The best known of the aforementioned tools of divination are the tarot, the casting of runes, and the reading of tea leaves. Divination by means of the tarot or other cards (including regular playing cards) is called "cartomancy", whereas the casting of runes and the reading of tea leaves is form of divination called "cleromancy", whereby something is displayed in a seemingly random fashion which the diviner then derives significance from. Even the simple casting of dice has been used for the purposes of cleromancy.

Divination is broadly shunned within most religious circles on the basis of it being condemned within many sacred texts, and yet in the case of the Christian tradition, things are more complicated than they may initially seem. There are certainly some forms of divination that are clearly forbidden within the biblical texts, such as necromancy, which is divination through communion with the dead, yet cleromancy is employed throughout the Bible in what it describes as "the casting of lots", which could be the use of dice, sticks, or many other objects for the purposes of divination. The best known instance of this comes when, after the crucifixion, resurrection, and ascension of Yeshua, the remaining apostles cast lots in order to determine whether Barsabbas or Matthias should take the place of Judas.

However, the more sophisticated Christian religionists will rightly point out that whenever cleromancy is employed within the Bible, there is always the explicit intent on the part of the practitioner to receive an answer from God through the chosen medium, and even the most amateur dabbler in the occult should know better than to open some manner of aethereal gateway and invite anything to speak or enter through it. Therefore, while most Christian religionists will always condemn any form of divination in the strongest terms, any soul that has taken the time to study or engage in even a cursory reading of the biblical texts that those religionists bestow with so much authority will know that such a strong stance cannot be maintained of one is to be honest about what those texts say, for they present a nuanced view on the subject of divination.

Absolutely anything could be strewn in a random fashion and then used for the purposes of cleromancy. Novice cleromancers will typically interpret the resultant pattern strictly according to an established system of interpretation, whereas more advanced cleromancers will merely use that underlying system as a loose guide and rely more upon what their own intuition is telling them about the resultant pattern.

You could devise your own system by which to interpret the pattern of particular lots when cast, but that would be no small project if your system was to provide interpretations of any great insight, and so it is simpler to use a tool with an already established system. Yet in many cases those systems themselves can provide far more insight on their own than they can when being employed for the purposes of divination. The tarot cards and the Chinese book the I Ching (the Book of Changes) are the greatest examples of this, but I will speak of the tarot specifically, for it is the system that I am the most familiar with.

The tarot deck is traditionally composed of seventy-eight cards: the twenty-two Major Arcana (the Greater Secrets) and the fifty-six Minor Arcana (the Lesser Secrets). The Minor Arcana are composed of four suits including court cards just as in a regular deck, and they are usually named "Wands", "Cups", "Swords", and "Pentacles"; these correspond to the elements of fire, water, air, and earth, respectively.

While most souls understand the tarot only as a means of divination, the cards of the Major Arcana tell the story of a soul's journey in mortal form, while the minor arcana portray different states of being and circumstances, and much insight can be derived by just studying the meaning of their cards and the relationship between those cards. The most well known card of the Major Arcana is the Death card, which is almost always used in entertainment as though it signifies physical death, though in actuality it almost never does. Rather, the death it refers to is the death of an egoic identity, which can sometimes be due to an unexpected and sudden trauma. But as the Major Arcana acknowledge, such a death for most souls will merely mean the assumption of a new egoic identity, rather than remembrance and rest.

What I have described to you thus far is the tarot as it is traditionally found in decks such as the Rider-Waite deck, which is easily the most popular deck. However, in the modern day there are many different tarot decks available, and while most of them are based upon the Rider-Waite deck and differ only in theme, some of them fundamentally alter the system of the tarot.

The most famous example of this is Aleister Crowley's Thoth Deck. The much misunderstood Crowley was one of many ancient souls incarnated within the 19th century to bring about a revival of interest in occult matters. Other such souls include Helena Petrovna Blavatsky, Rudolf Steiner, and Edgar Cayce. My mention of such figures is not to be taken as an endorsement of their teachings—I am merely seeking to inform. Crowley altered the order of the Major Arcana and even changed the significance of certain cards therein. It takes a brave or presumptuous soul to make such alterations, and yet if any soul had sufficient occult knowledge to justify doing so, it would certainly have been Crowley. But while Crowley's deck, painted as it was by the artist Lady Frieda Harris (allegedly under the influence of hallucinogens), is the most striking and beautiful of all decks to me, his changes to the tarot cannot be understood without a full comprehension of his entire system of "magick". He wrote a book called *The Book of Thoth* to accompany the deck, but without prior understanding of his "magick" system and the kind of obscure knowledge that Crowley himself had no shortage of, it is utterly incomprehensible. For that reason, I would recommend only the Rider-Waite deck or those decks that are explicitly based upon it.

There was a time when I was obsessed with the tarot and would contemplate the significance of each card and commit to memory the symbology of different decks. On one occasion, while contemplating the significance of the Wands suite within the Thoth Deck and its relationship to the element of fire, I suddenly saw the world about me as fire—everything within my sight that my mind could associate with fire became as a burning flame, yet a flame that did not consume anything.

For all of these reasons, whenever I encounter a soul that employs the tarot and yet talks of it as though it is nothing but a set of cards by which they might foretell the future, I know that they have not yet begun to truly understand the nature and power of the tool.

Because it is on the level of the Spirit that we are united with God and with all creation, it is the Spirit that makes divination possible. When occultists refer to "the Akashic Records" (an alleged supernatural suppository of all knowledge), it is the Spirit that they are referring to, knowingly or not. Tools of divination only work because all is Spirit, regardless of how deficient its substance may be, and therefore what is known by the Spirit can be conveyed through such physical tools.

Those that engage in divination will usually speak of the importance of intuition, but remember that what souls call "intuition" is nothing other than the guidance of God; tools of divination merely aid a soul in hearing the voice of God more clearly. You cannot understand the mechanics of divination without experientially knowing the utter unity of all reality, for it is that unity that makes divination possible. It is also possible for souls to unconsciously draw from the knowledge of Spirit and convey it within their creative works, which is why such works looked at in hindsight can seem to have anticipated an event that unfolded after their creation. However, the vast majority of souls that claim to be able to foresee the future cannot. Some are deliberately dishonest, while others are merely misguided. Yet identifying those that are false is no difficult matter: since divination is possible only through the Spirit, a soul must have come to be aware of themselves as Spirit, and having done so, their conduct will be blameless. You cannot wield spiritual power unless you have died to all egoic identity. This is what you might call a "cosmic fail-safe". Contrary to what much fiction would suggest, there cannot ever be a malevolent soul with supernatural knowledge of the future, for their very alienation from God keeps them from such knowledge.

Yet the one that has died to all egoic identity rarely has any need to seek knowledge of the future or to pry into matters that life does not present them with. Such desires stem from the sense of deficiency caused by identification with egoic identity; the one that has died to all egoic identity knows that they cannot improve themselves through such knowledge. The only reason that such a soul would ever utilise spiritual foresight is for the benefit of others. It may be that a soul is called upon to prophecy to an individual or even a multitude just as the prophets of

228

ancient Israel were. The soul still bound up in personhood conceives of this as a great thing, imagining the wonder and admiration of those to which they would prophecy. But such a responsibility is actually a tremendous burden, for the ways of the Spirit are not the ways of the world, and as those Israelite prophets discovered, telling worldly souls that they must change or face destruction does not foster fondness.

In the modern day, if you tell souls of something destructive that will come to pass, they will resent you for doing so as though you yourself had caused the event by the mere foretelling of it. Having contemplated this phenomenon, I have concluded that it has come about as a consequence of the materialism that is now so prevalent; many do not accept any reality beyond the material, and as a consequence most souls are simply unable to face their own physical mortality or the idea that there might be anything beyond the material reality that they know. The one that can foretell death and destruction therefore becomes a manifestation of their worst fear—that there is a spiritual dimension to reality and that they will die one day and have to face that reality having neglected it for all of their mortal lives. Such a fear motivates many seemingly inexplicable attitudes and behaviours.

If you feel drawn to some form of divination, then let the unity of creation that allows for it ever be your focus. Most importantly, do not allow divination or systems of interpretation to become a distraction from remembrance, for the mind will certainly attempt to use them as such. The importance of divination lies not in the fact that it works, but in the reason that it works. Always remember that no matter how insightful any tool of divination may be, and no matter how accurate the information that they convey is, all such things are as nothing compared to the Spirit from which everything comes, and that Spirit is known only in the Eternal Moment. May your focus be fixed upon that above all else.

Overcoming the World

"Behold, the hour is coming, indeed it has come, when you will all be scattered, each of you to your own home, and you will leave me all alone. Yet I am not really alone, for the Father is with me. I have said all of these things so that by being united with me you may have peace. The world will make you suffer, but be brave, I have overcome the world."

- Yeshua, The Gospel According to John 16:32,33

Despite all of the supernatural accounts contained within the canonical gospels, the above statement from Yeshua could well be the most unbelievable thing contained within their narratives from a human perspective. To understand why, you must understand the context within which the statement was made.

Yeshua was speaking immediately before delivering his "High Priestly Prayer", after which he and his disciples went to the gardens where Yeshua was arrested by the Jewish authorities that had been led there by Judas Iscariot. In other words, Yeshua made that statement at the end of his ministry, at which time he had no material possessions, no worldly power, had been abandoned by everyone including all but eleven of his disciples, and at a point when he knew perfectly well that he was about to endure one of the most painful deaths possible within that period of history. He was either thirty-three or thirty-five years old, depending upon the source that one uses to determine his age, and he had almost certainly never once in his short life ever left the territory into which he had been born. Even so, he said, "I have overcome the world." What soul, in such circumstances, could say such a thing?

Only one for which possessions have become as nothing due to their wealth in Spirit. Only one for which worldly power has become as nothing due to their knowledge of the infinite power of God. Only one for which personal companionship has become as nothing due to their conscious unity with all creation. And only one for which all possible sufferings inflicted upon their material, mental, and aethereal forms have become as nothing due to the knowledge that they are enacting the will of God in suffering them. Such a one has transcended all egoic identity and forever reigns over all reality in perfect oneness with God through His Spirit.

It was because Yeshua was such a one that he went gladly to the cross so that the world might have an example of what it means to die to self to be made alive in the Spirit as he was. Therefore, Yeshua said in John 17:19-24 during his High Priestly Prayer to God, "For their sake I sanctify myself, that they may also be sanctified in truth. I do not ask on behalf of these disciples only, but also for those who will believe in me through their word, that they may all be one, just as you, Father, are in me, and I in you, that they also may be in us, so that the world will believe that you sent me. The glory that you have given to me, I have given to them, that they may be one even as we are one—I in them and you in me—that they may be perfectly one, so that the world will know that you sent me, and that you love them even as you love me. Father, I desire that they may be with me where I am, to see the glory that you gave me, for you loved me before the world was made." That was the destiny that Yeshua prayed to God for on behalf of his immediate disciples two thousand years ago, and as mystics throughout history have testified of in their own unique ways, it is a destiny that any soul may choose for themselves by surrendering everything to God.

The title of this book is *Experiential Spirituality: The Mystic Answer to Everything*, and I knew that most would interpret the subtitle to be hyperbole. Yet while no book can directly answer every question, I have presented enough information to at least indirectly answer every question. However, the title can also be interpreted to mean that all questions will be answered by a single mystic response, and there is indeed a single mystic answer that is an appropriate response to every question: experiential spirituality itself is the mystic answer to every question, for it is experiential spirituality alone that brings a soul into a recognition of its perfect spiritual nature, and into a recognition that it therefore needs nothing else. It need simply be.

I have repeatedly stated that as Spirit you transcend all phenomenon, whether it comes in the form of matter, mind, or aether, and I have endeavoured to guide you into an experiential recognition of that fact. Whatever sense of deficiency drives you to act is illusory, because it emerges from an erroneous idea concerning who and what you are.

Living in mortal form, you are confronted with all manner of negative phenomenon day after day, and so what? What is that to you? You are the Spirit that is above all such phenomenon and only your own empowerment of that phenomenon will allow it to be detrimental to your experience of reality. You want the truth, but you are the truth; you want happiness, but you are happiness; you want companionship, but within you resides every soul that ever was, for through the Spirit we are eternally united; you want consolation, but in the Spirit you are one with the ultimate Consoler. As Spirit, you are, in any case, beyond the need for anything.

You might suppose that such assertions are useless to you until you have spent time practising all that I have recommended throughout this book, but actually, just being conscious of them as you are adjusting to those practices can be enough to trigger a dramatic moment of remembrance. But coming into an experiential recognition of such power is only the beginning of coming to know just how infinitely powerful you truly are; there is no end to this discovery, because understanding the power innate to you necessarily involves becoming increasingly aware of the infinite depths of the Spirit that you are. In seeking to awaken you to your true nature as Spirit, I have expounded upon practices, sacred texts, and traditions, but all of these are as signposts upon your journey of remembrance—you are greater than all of them and have no need for any of them once recognition of your innate supremacy is yours. Even great mystics like Yeshua are only ever greater than you due to their superior awareness of the Spirit, but there comes a time beyond time when even that is not true any more; you cannot be one with Yeshua in the way that he described within his High Priestly Prayer if you are always to understand yourself as beneath him. So it is with every spiritual master.

This is why, in saying thirteen of the Gospel of Thomas (which I elaborated upon within the previous chapter) Yeshua told Thomas that he was no longer his master. Similarly, in John 15:15, Yeshua said to all of his remaining disciples, "No longer do I call you servants, for servants do not know what their master is doing. Now I have called you friends, for all that I have heard from my Father I have made known to you." Yeshua became even more explicit in emphasising that the power that had once been unique to him in that time and place was now available to the disciples: in John 20:22,23, verses that you will almost never hear repeated from a pulpit, Yeshua said to his disciples, "Receive the Holy Spirit. If you forgive others their sins, they are forgiven. If you do not forgive them, they are not forgiven." In this way Yeshua declared that those disciples, now being experientially united with the Spirit, had the same divine authority that he himself had exercised.

I have no hesitation in saying that I am a Son of God because I am of the Spirit of God, and that living in conscious recognition of that fact, I do the will of God in my life. Therefore, any soul that opposes me as I endeavour to expound upon mystic truth opposes God and will incur suffering for doing so. I have previously warned against foolhardy proclamations and emphasised the importance of remaining grounded in your immediate experience of reality, but there comes a time to cast aside all timidity and to openly acknowledge all of the power and all of the authority that is innate to you as the Spirit, and that time is when you have come to experientially know the Spirit that you are and can therefore sincerely declare as Yeshua did, "I have overcome the world."

Rest

Yeshua said, "He who seeks should continue seeking until he finds. When he finds, he will be troubled. When he becomes troubled, he will be amazed. He will reign, and reigning, he will find rest."

- The Gospel of Thomas, Saying 2

The one that seeks to know the truth will find it, but the truth challenges everything that we thought we knew, and for a time it can trouble us. Yet its obvious perfection quickly becomes apparent as we begin to experience the ways in which it exceeds our former expectations, and we are left in awe at the glory of God. More than that, we experience the ways in which entering into this truth enables us to recognise our innate power over all of creation. Then, knowing the glory of God and of our sublime unity with Him through the Spirit that is both Him and us, we enter into rest.

In the first chapter I explained that the word "rest" ("repose" in most translations) within certain Gnostic texts refers to the ultimate spiritual state that others call "salvation", "Christ consciousness", and "nirvana", among other terms, and that I likewise use the word "rest" to describe the ultimate spiritual state because I can conceive of no other word that so perfectly expresses the experience of having attained it.

Yet rest is something that I have not yet elaborated upon, for I could not do so until I had first conveyed all other understandings.

I have previously made reference to the well known Hindu mystic, Ramana Maharshi. He made some statements that were quite controversial, because they seemed contrary to conventional spiritual wisdom (if spiritual wisdom can ever rightly be called "conventional"). One such statement involved the claim that meditation and other introspective practices that are considered mandatory by most are in fact strictly for novices. It was certainly a bold statement, and yet understanding why mystics have asserted such things is utterly essential to understanding what it means to enter into rest.

The understandings and the practices that I have recommended throughout this book make up the framework that I felt would most effectively achieve my end of leading you through remembrance. That framework is as a ladder that one may use to ascend to experiential unity with the Spirit, and each understanding and practice is as a step on that ladder. I could have built the ladder in many different ways, using different understandings and practices to form it—indeed, I scrapped two prior versions of this book because I deemed the ladders that I had built within them to be insufficient. Once you have ascended the steps of such a ladder, it is no longer of any use to you, but because it is still essential to those that would follow you, the one that has ascended must still emphasise the importance of each step upon that ladder to others.

If, having read this book, you do not then dedicate yourself to experientially confirming all that I have said, then all that you will have gained is insight concerning how I understand reality; you will know what I claim to know, but the only question that matters is, what do *you* know? I have no interest in encouraging souls to merely accept that reality is the way that I claim it to be; I want them to find out for themselves. I would rather that one soul put into practice all that I have recommended and come to different conclusions by doing so than that a thousand souls take everything that I have written to be true without having experientially verified any of it. I have found that—as was the case with me—souls abide with these understandings for a time until, at a certain point, something "clicks" within them, and at once they see the obviousness of the truth in a moment of gnosis.

You never needed to know or do anything, but you need to know and do so much in order to recognise that. You never needed to be liberated, because you were never truly bound, yet you need to free yourself from so much in order to know that. All that you need you already have, and any attempt to find something outside of yourself can only ever serve to distract you from that fact, and any answer that you might receive is necessarily going to be inferior to the mystery—the silence—that pervades in its absence. To know these things through a direct experience of the Spirit and to let go of everything beyond the Eternal Moment is to enter into rest.

"Rest" is such a perfect word to describe the ultimate spiritual state because in that state you carry the peace of deep sleep with you even while active in the world, and that world and all of its phenomenon, as with all phenomenon, is as a dreamlike reality—there, but distant and distinctly unreal. God and His Spirit are the truest realities, and it is impossible to ever lose sight of that. Whatever phenomenon rises and falls before you is immediately perceived in light of God's presence.

Although I cannot assume what the spiritual status of any contemporary mystic or spiritual teacher is, it has often been remarked that many of them speak incredibly slowly, often to the extent that some souls find them frustrating to listen to. I would suggest that the sublime peacefulness of rest is the reason why; when you are obliged to interact with another soul from the place of rest, you must first remember what it is like to be a soul still enamoured with the world, and having recalled that, you must then decide how best to articulate yourself to that soul in particular, taking into account the details of their egoic identity. Yet all the while your greatest joy is to remain silent within that rest. This reality is illustrated very well throughout the synoptic gospels where Yeshua is portrayed as having very little patience even with his own disciples, once calling Peter "a hindrance" and repeatedly and openly wondering how long God would insist that he remain in their company. But despite how negatively Yeshua may have experienced his ministry, he nonetheless persisted, and he persisted because of the great love that he had for God, and for those souls that were ready to receive his teachings, souls that he recognised as Children of God, even before they recognised themselves as such.

I will continue to elaborate upon experiential spirituality for as long as God requires it of me, but while I hope that my insights will prove useful to you, I am not called to form any kind of collective, and I have absolutely no interest in becoming anyone's guru. You should not depend upon me or upon any other soul—trust only in God. If you were to meet me, I would not elaborate upon mysticism at all unless asked to do so; I am more concerned with investigating aethereal phenomenon, looking for cryptids, delving into the mysteries of the past, and expressing experiences and thoughts through prose and poetry, for this is also my function in this world. On some days I am full of energy and enthusiasm for the activities ahead of me, while on others I experience the same fog of emotional and mental phenomenon that every soul sometimes does. But whatever I am doing and whatever phenomenon arises before me, I am always conscious of being the transcendent life experiencing life.

Every event prior to my entrance into rest are as memories of distant battles that, like a dream, threaten to slip from my mind even as I recall them, and I have absolutely no desire to retain those memories in any case. The past and everyone and everything within it are gone, and the future and everyone and everything within it do not yet exist. Those souls within the past belong there, just as those souls within the future belong there, but I am only ever here. After all of the grandiose subject matter that I have elaborated upon within this book and despite all of the understanding and authority that is mine as the Spirit, as I sit here now, I am concerned only with the mild hunger that I feel having delayed eating lunch in order to write this final section, I am concerned only with the barking of my neighbour's dog as it runs around its garden, I am concerned only with the sound of the children that are playing in a park nearby, and I am concerned only with the silence that permeates the space between us, a silence within which God is known to me. This perfect moment is our All.

Printed in Great Britain
by Amazon